LOVE

STRONG

AS

DEATH

LOVE
STRONG
AS
DEATH

by
RONALD WALLS

GRACEWING

 ST. BEDE'S PUBLICATIONS

Published in 2000 jointly by

Gracewing
2 Southern Avenue
Leominster
Herefordshire
HR6 0QF

St. Bede's Publications
271 N. Main St.
Petersham,
MA 01366-0545
USA

UK ISBN 0 085244 515 6
US ISBN 1-879007-41-X

LIBRARY OF CONGRESS CATALOGING-IN-PUBLICATION DATA

Walls, Ronald.
     Love strong as death / by Ronald Walls.
        p.   cm.
     ISBN 1-879007-41-X (paper)
     1. Walls, Ronald. 2. Catholic converts--Scotland
     Biography.
     I. Title.
     BX4668.W32A3 1999
     248.2'42'092--dc21
     [B]   99-26704
                                         CIP

Front cover: Fr. Ronald Walls by Vic Ayres, Buckie, Scotland

Typesetting by St. Bede's Publications
Printed in England by
Redwood Books,
Trowbridge, Wiltshire BA14 8RN

Foreword

To all who read it, this autobiography of Father Ronnie Walls will stand out as a sign of contradiction to the mood of the age. In an era of doubt, this is a story of faith, in an era of flux this is a story of commitment. Most of all it is a very moving and inspiring story of love.

Father Ronnie's fascinating description of his extended family's lifestyle and genuine religious attachment to the beliefs and practices of the Church of Scotland is the prelude.

There's something intensely moving about the kilted youngster making his own way in the world, full of enterprise and good will, eager to encounter fellow pilgrims, motivated by a deep awareness of God in his life.

These pages offer a valuable insight into many "nooks and crannies" of Scottish life during the 20th century, from the middle-class respectability of Edinburgh's suburbs to the idyll of Highland rural life in Logie Easter, from the friendly banter of the Glasgow tram to the evocative calm of Nunraw Abbey. Fr. Ronnie's writing skill is such that the reader will soon feel quite at home in these and in many other locations, and will follow with increasing interest the boy becoming a man, finding happiness in an exemplary marriage to Helen, his soul-mate, and settling down to parish ministry.

Outwardly, the young minister had it all, but inside the burning desire for truth would not be extinguished. The pursuit of truth meant running the risk of losing everything.

The crucial moment for me comes when Ronnie finds, in his own words: "the substance of the faith, not so much in the texts of confessions of faith, nor even in the words of scripture, as in the living voice of the teaching ministry in the Church." From that moment on he realised that, "the authority and unity of the word of truth required authority and unity in the Church."

In many ways the title of this book sums up everything. Love, to Ronnie Walls, is indeed as strong as death, perhaps even stronger.

His life has been blessed with many loves: the love of his good parents; the unifying and strengthening love of his late wife Helen; the strong paternal love he felt for his sons, evidenced very movingly in the account of the death of young Nicolas.

Then there was his pastor's love for his people, a genuine and deep love for the Church of Scotland in which he was raised and in which he still counts many friends and a love for the Catholic Church to which he "came home" at the beckoning of his greatest love, his Lord and Master, Jesus Christ.

As with all the main changes of direction in his life, the decision to become a Catholic priest was forged in suffering. The pain and loss experienced at Helen's death by this most devoted of husbands, was transformed into a realisation that he was now free to serve God with all his attention, time and energy.

The parable of the vine and the branches springs to mind.

God has asked much of Ronnie Walls, over the last half century, for he is a branch that bears good fruit.

He has been pruned "*ut fructum plus afferas:* to make you bear more fruit."

I have no hesitation in declaring that this inspirational, funny, fascinating and moving book is one of the best of fruits produced in recent years.

+Thomas J Cardinal Winning
Archbishop of Glasgow
President, Bishop's Conference of Scotland

Prologue

A flight of steps leads up out of the Waverly Station in Edinburgh onto Market Street. Having reached the top I drew breath then rounded the corner into the Aladdin's Cave that is Cockburn Street. Higher up on the other side, opposite the restaurant *La Rusticana*, I spotted an old friend whom I had not seen for fourteen years.

"Providential!" he called out, crossing the street. "Only the other day I was wishing we could meet, for there's something I want to ask you."

"And what's that, Charlie?" I asked.

"If you found yourself today as you were in 1948– a parish minister dissatisfied with the Church of Scotland and attracted to Rome—would you do the same now as you did then?"

"I would, certainly."

"Then you should write a sequel to the book you wrote after your conversion and explain why you still feel the same. So many people have got the idea that the whole scene has changed. You hear Catholics themselves saying that since Vatican II the differences between the Reformed Church and the Roman Catholic Church have been ironed out, so that there is no real need for anyone to move from one to the other, as you did."

"The main question, Charlie, is still the same: how do we identify the one Church founded by our Lord? I still answer the question as I did in 1948, using the same criteria."

"Well it's time you got down to writing about it, and bring your autobiography, *The One True Kirk*, up-to-date."

We parted; I went on my way up to the High Street where I sat down in a coffee shop and began to consider the direction my revised autobiography should follow. I would have to demonstrate that the events of my life since 1948 had not weakened but rather strengthened the belief to which my experience as a parish minister had led me, and which the Second Vatican Council had so clearly expressed in the document *Lumen Gentium*, that "The one mediator, Christ, established and ever sustains here on earth his holy Church, the community of faith, hope, and charity, as a visible organization through which he communicates truth and grace to all men…" and that "This Church, constituted and organized as a society in the present world, subsists in the Catholic church, which is governed by the successors of Peter and the bishops in communion with him." I would have to describe how life in the Catholic Church since my conversion in 1948 had convinced me that the Church and the faith it professes remain the same as they have always been, although it is true that since Vatican II opinions and practices have emerged within the Catholic Church which have no justification.

As I thought things over that day I realized that the work would be arduous especially as I would have to adopt a more personal tone than in my original book, for I wanted to develop the theme of marriage and show how my experience of marriage has molded my views about the appropriateness of celibacy for the priesthood. The writing of a revised and completed autobiography would have to wait until I was given a lighter assignment than that of parish priest in the busy parish of St Joseph's in Aberdeen. However, a train of thought had already started up when I left the coffee shop and continued my journey up the High Street, along George IV Bridge, and down the steep incline of Victoria Street that leads into the Grassmarket.

Victoria Street had always been one of my favorite haunts. The buildings, described by Stevenson as "smoky beehives, ten stories high" rose above the street where on the north side a mysterious gallery-like pavement led to closes and stairways. This part of Edinburgh comes back to me still as the topographical and architectural setting of dreams. Today the street has become very up-market, with a high-class French restaurant, a superb cheese shop, and several art and antique shops; but the chief delight of my youth was still in place: a specialist shop that displays ropes, balls of string, brushes and sycamore wood molds for the shaping of slabs of shortbread. For me this window display was an object of contemplation.

At the west end of the Grassmarket, on my way to the Sacred Heart Church in Lauriston Street, as I climbed up the Vennel past the back entrance to George Heriot's, my old school, the memory of these haunts of my boyhood and youth was well and truly aroused and my thoughts turned to the early years, wherein lay the germ of all the thought and action that was to follow.

Now, in the freedom of semi-retirement, I pick up my story and begin again at the beginning.

1

I awoke at 4:30, and from that hour until my mother called me I lay in a troubled daydream, rehearsing a thousand times all that might happen when I entered the school gate for the first time. An unknown, frightening world was creeping closer, minute by minute. At 8 o'clock I forced half a morning roll down my dry throat and swallowed a cup of tea. I put on my new school-bag, and then, to record the occasion, my father took a photograph. I set off down the steep hill to the village.

We were pioneers of Edinburgh suburbia and lived in a bungalow at the top of a hill in Corstorphine on the west side of the city. As I descended Clermiston Hill I could see every shadow in the quarry on the Pentland Hills across the wide valley, so clear was the late summer air. At the foot of the hill the lady in the sweet-shop conducted me across the main Edinburgh-Glasgow road. Having crossed this Rubicon, I continued along the pavement but soon had to halt. My meager breakfast began to show unwillingness to remain where it ought, and so, leaning weakly against a lamp-standard, I offered up into the gutter my first sacrifice on the altar of education.

At length, I reached the school in the heart of the old village. It had been designed to resemble a Gothic church but succeeded in looking like a prison. The high stone wall which enclosed the playground was interrupted by a spiked railing, in the center of which was a massive gate. The top of the wall was fortified by broken bottles embedded in cement. Had I been capable of mature reflection I might have asked whether the purpose of this fortification was to keep the scholars in or to keep intruders out. As the gate was open during school hours it could not have been the former reason, and it could not have been for the latter because the blessings of education are intangible, incapable of being stolen by the vulgar or undeserving. I am writing of the days long before even primary school became stuffed with expensive electronic equipment.

It was not the building alone, symbol of a grim concept of school, that frightened me. Coming down from the bourgeois isolation of incipient suburbia, I faced a gang of raucous children whom I had never seen before and who seemed to be perfectly at home in the place and with one another. I felt like a bee that has strayed to the landing board of a strange hive. I hadn't the right smell. In an instant the hostile league had surrounded me. "What's yer name?" shouted one, while another grabbed my cap and made off with it. Halfheartedly I gave chase. The cap was kicked through a puddle and thrown over the wall into a builder's yard. The hoots of applause which greeted this accomplishment became sweet laughter in contrast with the electric school bell which at this moment screamed into life, like a circular saw on a piece of loose tin.

By the time I had found my way round to the builder's yard and retrieved my cap, all was deathly silence in the playground. The lines of children had marched inside; I was lost and I was late. At last the janitor found me and delivered me to the proper classroom. "Well, where did you come from?" asked the infant-mistress. "Here is a boy who doesn't know that school begins at nine o'clock." A first and enduring impression had been made, that school is a place where you are for ever about to be on the mat for some crime wittingly or unwittingly committed. This apprehensiveness of authority has lasted all my life.

In the playground there was a primitive drinking well—a brass button set in the wall surmounted by a short iron pipe, below which hung, on hefty chains, two iron cups. When a cup was pressed to the brass button water flowed. During the morning break I saw a boy about to drink from the right-hand cup. Immediately a managing little girl shouted at him: "That's the fever-cup!" After that I never risked drinking; but nonetheless I made the well's acquaintance during the lunch break. The morning skirmish had been spontaneous, unofficial, extra-liturgical, one might say, but now with other newcomers I received public initiation, which consisted in being hauled as near as possible to the well and having water sloshed over me—from the fever-cup no doubt. In spite of a little physical discomfort there was the satisfaction of feeling somehow incorporated. The stranger-bee had taken on the smell of the hive and been accepted.

In the early afternoon I made my way out of the old village and reported at a baker's shop where the young woman assistant conducted me over the main road. There were no lollipop men in those days. Anxious parents had to make their own arrangements. It was sunny and I climbed happily home up the steep hill. "Well, what did you get today?" asked my mother. "Oh, nothing."

Few people today remember the Edinburgh trams; I dimly recall that in the early fifties the rails were still been lifted in some places and replaced with tarmac; but when I first went to school the trams were the lifeblood of city transport. By tram you could travel from Corstorphine on the west as far as the fishing villages on the Forth estuary, well to the east of the city center.

We used to make that long, dreary journey about twice a year. On and on we rattled and bumped, past Murrayfield, on to Princes Street, to alight at the GPO and enter a more primitive tram which took us on through Portobello and finally out as far as Port Seton. On the straight stretches the tram developed a sickening swing; in the town it was for ever stopping abruptly to take on passengers; when it filled up I was prodded to get up and give my seat to grown-ups.

The object of this exercise was to visit my maternal great-grandmother in Port Seton. Her little house stood gable end to the main street, according to the traditional plan in most of the fishing villages. Beyond the street, down a slight slope was the harbor. I was never allowed to cross the street and romp in the direction of the sea, lest I should "fa' in the herbour and get droont." Drowning was a powerful image in this community. The harsh North Sea and the rocky coast had claimed many men over the centuries. In our family, most generations had lost at least one man at sea.

It seemed always to be twilight in that house. My great-grandmother sat bolt upright in a high wooden chair beside a window with heavy lace curtains. Her white hair was tightly drawn back from a center parting, and her black dress creaked when she moved. The room was crowded when we visited, but I never saw any men there. The dominant characters were the matriarchal trinity: great-grandmother, grandmother and mother. It is perhaps inevitable that society should be matriarchal when men are away from home for most of the week, and the mother is in charge. In such a society—I am sure not just in the family I knew—a stern atmosphere prevails; a regiment of women does not necessarily generate the warm glow of mother-love.

The spirituality of these communities—certainly of my mother's family—matched this gray mood—human counterpart of the cold haar which rolls in over the land from the North Sea. It would be wrong to affirm that Calvinism was the cause of this mood and atmosphere, but it is true that popular Calvinism encouraged the fatalistic and superstitious character of the religious attitude one finds in this part of Scotland. A rationalistic, popularized version of the notion of predestination had induced a very gloomy outlook on life—and on eternal life. Submission to the will of God was a grim business; we must accept God's will silently lest a worse fate befall us; the will of God seemed to be concerned only with disaster and gloom. My great-grandmother's religion may have had a stronger dash of these elements than was common, for she came from Helmsdale on the northeast coast and had been brought up in the Free Church, later known as the "Wee Free" Church, who held more strictly than mainstream Presbyterians to the doctrines of seventeenth-century Calvinism. Such a brand of Calvinism had been little mollified by the hymn-singing evangelical fervor that invaded Scotland from England in the nineteenth-century.

These tiring journeys and dismal visits ceased when I was about ten years old. I presume that it must had been that "it was the Lord's good pleasure" to call the old lady "to higher service," but I never heard a word about her having died. Death was not a subject for conversation—at least not before the children.

This matrix of religious experience was not the only influence upon my young mind. From the predestinarian mist of the North Sea my mother had been partially rescued by my father, whose background was quite different. My paternal grandfather had been born in the Orkney Islands. At the age of about seven his father, who was a joiner, had come down to Edinburgh. My grandfather learned the carpenter's trade and later took up scientific instrument-making. From an obituary published in 1936 in *The Optician* I learned that he had constructed, from German specifications, the first x-ray apparatus to appear in Scotland and had supplied this equipment to Professor Dawson Turner at the Royal College of Surgeons in Edinburgh. The obituary also states that he made the first cinemato-graphic apparatus to appear in Scotland, and showed moving pictures before anything from America had yet appeared. A few years ago my brother visited a maritime museum in Stockholm and in the wheel-house of Nansen's ship the *Fram* saw a barometer bearing a brass plaque on which was inscribed, "Made by T.J. Walls & Son, Edinburgh." Later, with my father as partner, he founded an optician's business in Edinburgh. My grandfather's younger brother became an engineer and inventor. He worked for Coates of Paisley and spent some time in their mills in Milan. He was a wonderful storyteller who never allowed pettifogging accuracy to spoil a good yarn, and he spoke four languages. My Orkney background was anything but parochial.

After my parents' death I used often to visit my paternal grandparents. It was unusual to find my grandfather without an atlas or a copy of the Geographical Magazine in front of him. I think there was still a stirring of the old Viking blood in him. In his library he cherished a fine collection of Norse Sagas, and used to boast that he was descended from Leif Eriksen—Leif the Lucky—who had discovered America in about 1000 AD. I have sometimes wondered, considering the good fortune that always accompanies me on journeys, if I have not received this man's guardian angel as an heirloom.

Not until much later in life did I appreciate that the ambiance of my grandfather's home was that of sane Christian humanism; nor until my formal theological education was finished did I grasp the complexity of the scene within the Presbyterian Church in Scotland. Where and how did my paternal grandfather fit into the complex ecclesiastical picture? His formal Church background, as I now understand, was different from that of my maternal grandmother's folk; he had been formed as much by humanist intellectual forces as by dogmatic Calvinism.

Since 1560 much had happened in Scotland to alter the classic syndrome of Calvinism. The spirit of revolution which had made the break with the medieval magisterium of the Catholic Church possible, not only set up a new magisterium but had, in theory at least, let in the principle of revolt against that magisterium. Since the end of the seventeenth century, the history of the Reformed Church in Scotland is one of secessions and, even more confusing, reunions which sometimes left very small splinter-groups who refused to go along with a reunion. To his admirable *A Church History of Scotland* Professor J.H.S. Burleigh has appended a genealogical tree setting out the ramifications of Church division and reunion since 1690, which looks very like the diagrammatic map of the London Underground.

The underlying disruptive issue from the start was that of the relation between Church and State. This was what precipitated the Covenanting troubles. There were those who believed in a theocratic state: "A state Church in a covenanted State." Today only a tiny remnant remain representing this view. In the eighteenth century came the first secession by those who objected to lay patronage—the right of lairds to appoint ministers. This problem led to two later secessions, the more important being that of 1843, known as "The Disruption," when the Free Church came into existence. Theoretically the Free Church held exactly the same beliefs and acknowledged the same form of Church government as did the Established Church, but in the course of time, partly because it was strong in the remoter parts of the country, the Free Church held more doggedly to the letter of the Westminster Confession of Faith, while the Established Church—affectionately known as the "Auld Kirk," was strongly influenced by the Enlightenment. The ministers of the "Auld Kirk," usually well-educated and far from puritanical—it is said that while the General Assembly was in session some of them once attended a performance by Mrs Siddons in St Cecelia's Hall—were contemptuously referred to by the Free Church as "Moderates."

The first secession, today represented by the diminutive Original Secession Church, exerted more influence than is realized, for in this Church the principle of revolt became quite a habit. After 1733 further splitting occurred within this secession Church over minor points, usually related to civic-Church relations. In general a liberal evangelical theology coupled with a democratic notion of the Church developed, manifesting itself in individualism and a kind of Congregationalism. This spirit lived on and by 1847 was clearly evident when several small sects, all outside the Established Church and the Free Church, united to form the United Presbyterian Church. A prominent feature of this Church was the way in which they regarded and treated their ministers. The management and discipline of the local congregation lay in the hands of the elders, who formed the Kirk Session, and to a considerable extent of a board of managers, presided over by an elected layman called the Preces. There were even occasions when the minister was required to leave the room while matters concerning him were discussed. The minister was very much an employee of the congregation–so different from the minister in an Auld Kirk parish, especially if that were in the Borders, where the minister enjoyed an authority such as no Pope ever did. Decades later, after the United Presbyterian Church had been formally reunited with the Established Church, former United Presbyterian congregations were allowed to maintain their old constitutions.

In 1900 the Free Church and the United Presbyterian Church united to form the United Free Church, but there were those in the Free Church, especially in the Highlands and Islands, who could not stomach the liberalism of the United Presbyterians, and so they stayed out of the union to form what we now popularly call the "Wee Frees."

The purpose of this little digression into Church history is to identify the theological genes which I must have inherited through my paternal grandfather. He was attached to a formerly United Presbyterian congregation in Edinburgh. Although we never spoke explicitly about religion, I think that I sensed in him a spirit of quiet, humane spirituality, the product of his liberal evangelical background allied to literary and scientific instincts. I recall only one remark he ever made that was directly on a religious topic. I had made some comment about the Reformation. He said–and he had the Reformed Church in mind–"The Church is as much in need of reformation today as it ever was in the Middle Ages."

His wife, my grandmother, was a remarkable woman. She was small and neat, with beautiful green eyes. Very quick in her movements, she never rose from a chair but jumped up from it; her repartee was even quicker. Her grandmother, she told me, was French and had come with her grandfather, who was an Ayrshire Kennedy, to Ireland, where her father was born. She was born about the time her father came back to Scotland. They were Episcopalians. After my grandfather's death I used to visit her often. We played a card game called Bezique, which I have never come across since and which, for all I know may be of French provenance. At the end of each game we had to add up the score, and my grandmother would add up a long column of figures in a split second. When she learned that I had decided to enter the ministry she said: "Forgive an old woman for giving advice, but always preach about the love of God."

She was still alive when I was a minister in Logie Easter and at the time when our third child was expected she would ring up my wife and say, "Helen, are you still all in one piece?" If the answer was "Yes," she would hang up abruptly. In due course the answer became "No," and she insisted on making the long journey to see her youngest grandson. The train pulled into Nigg Station, Mr. Ross the Stationmaster was at the ready with his set of mobile steps, for there was no proper platform, but she opened the carriage door and before my sister could restrain her had jumped three feet to the ground and was heading towards me. On arriving at the manse she said, "Where's this bairn?" She took him in her arms and said, "Now I can die happy!" That night we found her lying on the floor outside her bedroom. She died next day.

Although the North Sea fishing village religion of my maternal ancestry persisted well on into my life, showing itself in occasional bouts of gloom and depression, the optimistic and creative spiritual urge that came from my father's side dominated. Early memories survive with me of our flat in the north side of Edinburgh, where I remember seeing a magical box of theatrical costumes and properties—colored jackets, cocked hats and cutlasses. My father had a very fine tenor voice and was a member of an operatic society that performed Gilbert and Sullivan operas. At that young age I was never taken to see a performance, but I do remember clearly going to a huge stadium to watch the fabulous Cossack Circus. When in the mid-1920s we went to live in Corstorphine the theater played an important part in our live. We were taken very solemnly in a high class Daimler taxi to the pantomime every Christmas, and on several occasions my parents went off to the theater. I remember the excitement on the evening that they went to the King's Theater to see "The Ghost Train," which was the new theatrical hit of the day. On one occasion, when my parents were going out in the evening to some function or other, my mother was wearing a dress that was very low cut at the back, and I remember feeling very distressed about this. I suspected too that my mother herself was not comfortable in it. My mother was perfect in her care of us, but it is strange that I have no vivid memories of her as I have of my father. In some ways she was a sad person.

Our house, designed by my father, was a bungalow on the brow of Clermiston Hill. Facing south with a view out to the Pentland Hills, the main entrance was at the center of a verandah on the south side. The rooms were on right and left of this door but in two blocks separated by a long oak-paneled hall, fitted along the entire north side with a bookcase. In those days Edinburgh was littered with second-hand book shops, and my father was for ever picking books up on his way from Forrest Road to the Waverley Station, which long before Beeching, was linked by a spur-line to Corstorphine. Our library was large and its contents were a good indicator of my father's mental make-up. There were the works of Scott and Dickens and Thackery and, perhaps less expected, the complete works of Smollet. There was a wide selection of poetry, including a scholarly edition of the poems of Burns. I spotted also works by Carlyle and Ruskin and H.G. Wells; and there were collections of essays and short works by people like Quiller-Couch and Eric Linklater. The only philosophical or theological writings I found were contained in a series of old fashioned brown volumes bearing the title, "International University Library." In this I found extracts from Fénelon, some of which I read at the age of fourteen. I even had a go at Carlyle.

There were Bibles, too, in the library, and my father once told me that he had read the Bible from cover to cover. One of the Bibles was entitled, "The Bible designed to be read as Literature." How anything can be read except as literature is a question one might well ask, but the implication of the title was quite clear: the Bible was presented, not as the word of God, but as the product of human genius, to be read without any presupposition that it is divine revelation. This probably was my father's viewpoint. He most certainly believed in God, took the teaching of the Sermon on the Mount, which he interpreted literally, very seriously and was resolutely anti-materialist, but he disliked theological dogmatism. He was essentially a humanist, but a pious humanist. He often quoted the text: "Man does not live by bread alone," failing, however, to continue, "but by every word that proceeds from the mouth of God." He loved sayings of our Lord such as, "Consider the lilies, how they grow" and St Paul's "Whatsoever things are true, whatsoever things are pure, whatsoever things are lovely,...think on these things." For him, however, the romantic poets were as much channels of revelation as was holy scripture. He would contemplate the superb sunsets which we could so comfortably view from our home on the extreme west of Edinburgh, and would speak of "something much more deeply inter-fused," and reminisce about the walking-tours of his youth.

The Romance of camping was in his blood, and he passed it on to me. All through one summer we had a huge bell-tent in the garden where my father and I slept on chaff palliasses. In 1934, the year before my father died, the family went on a camping tour in the Highlands. One evening near Moy and Tomatin we were on the lookout for a place to camp. There was a wood on the right of the main road, with a rough cart track running down towards the river Findhorn. In the hollow behind the wood was a house, which we approached by the main drive on the near side of the wood. It turned out to be the manse of Moy and Tomatin, and the minister showed us a suitable place on the cart track, where we could pitch our tent. After we had settled down the minister sent his son, a boy of exactly my own age, to show us where to get milk. The boy and I went off along the railway track to the farm. He told me that his name was Alastair–Alastair MacLean– later to become the author of *The Guns of Navaronne*.

Which of our parents supervised our prayers I cannot remember, probably because they were at one in their views. We always said a blessing before meals, very often: "Bless this food and make us good, for Jesus sake, Amen." My night prayers, always said after getting into bed, included a list of petitions: "Bless mummy and daddy and so on…" but formal expression of devotion was contained in the regular prayer:

> Jesus, tender Shepherd, hear me;
> Bless thy little lamb tonight;
> Through the darkness be thou near me;
> Keep me safe till morning light.

Alongside all of the philosophical and literary influences exerted mainly by my Father, the foundation of my parents' religion was expressed in this very simple child's prayer: it was a personal devotion to Jesus, the God-man. Even in early adolescence I remember that I still said this prayer, and found great comfort in it, especially through the long dark nights of those emotionally and physically difficult years when, after my father's death, I found myself lacking direct communication with any adult. Many years later this childlike spring of devotion resurged and broadened its stream in the devotion to the Sacred Heart of Jesus. It was from my parents that I had learned the basic principle of religious education: only through prayer does faith grow.

At home–I am writing of the period between 1925 and 1935–as well as celebrating the New Year, which was still *de rigeur*, we celebrated Christmas too, and that was not quite so usual then, at least not in the full-blooded and zestful way that my father did. We had an elaborately decorated Christmas Tree, my mother baked a rich Christmas cake, thirty circular slabs of shortbread and thirty black buns—mostly for "first footing"—as well as countless mince pies. The Christmas dinner could not have been more elaborate. What is even more memorable, however, is the intense excitement, especially on Christmas Eve, when we hung up stockings and awaited the mysterious advent of Santa Claus. My father had a great gift for selecting and giving presents. On one occasion, having no transport of his own, he borrowed a hearse from a friend who had a funeral undertaker's business near him, and in the space normally occupied by a coffin he brought back home our presents.

There were always two Christmas parties: one for family and friends and one for a crowd of children from the slums, whom my father contacted through a friend who ran a Gospel Mission in the Grassmarket. Both parties were sumptuous, and there was always a performance by a conjurer. I have spoken of my father's liberal theological outlook and hinted at his romantic mode of interpreting the teaching of the Sermon on the Mount. It would be more accurate perhaps to use the term "open-minded," for not all liberal theologians are as open-minded as he was. In fact some liberals are the most intolerant people one could find. My father's mind was open not just in a humanist direction but into another spiritual dimension as well. He would not allow us to speak of "Father Christmas." It was Santa Claus who brought joy to children at Christmas time. When I reached the age at which the mystery of Santa Claus begins to evaporate, he said to me: "You know it is your mummy and daddy that really put the presents in your stocking and round the Tree, but it's not just them. There was this saint long ago who showed great kindness to children in distress and it is his spirit living on that moves parents to give gifts to their children at Christmas time. So it really is Santa Claus who comes. Now don't say anything yet to your brother and sister."

Years later, after becoming a Catholic and being often penniless at Christmas time, I made a practice of attending Mass on the feast of St Nicholas on December 6th to pray that we would be able to give our children a happy Christmas. St Nicholas never let me down. The odd thing is that I learned this devotion from no Catholic source, but from my liberal Protestant father.

God could be worshipped in fields and in forests, on hillsides and in valleys or on the seashore—that I learned from my father—but I learned also, by example, that it was good to worship him in church. When we first went to live in Corstorphine my father would take me by tram on Sunday morning into the west end of Princes Street from which point we walked via Castle Terrace and Lauriston Street to the United Free Church in Lauriston Place, where my father had been brought up, and where I had been baptized by a minister who rejoiced in the euphonic name of Fergus Ferguson. The carillon of St Cuthbert's Parish Church faded out as we passed, announcing that the hour of eleven had come. We were always late and had to walk fast. When we arrived at the church we waited at the gallery door, watching through the peephole until the minister finished the "long prayer" with which the service began. This prayer over, we crept stealthily into our accustomed pew. I noticed that during the prayers, whereas all of the others bowed their heads and closed their eyes, my father looked up at the ceiling and kept his eyes open.

In 1929, the year when the United Free Church and the Established Church united, these Sunday morning journeys ceased, for we began to attend church in Corstorphine not, as might have been expected, with the former United Free Congregation, but at the Old Parish Church. This action more than any other demonstrated my father's open-mindedness, for long after the union people would travel miles across the city to find a congregation that upheld their former tradition.

Through this move, providence introduced me to another theological current within the Church of Scotland.

In this old parish church of Corstorphine I began, all unwittingly, to be molded by the High Church tradition that had been alive since 1560, but was reinforced and modified by the Oxford Tractarian Movement of the nineteenth century. The Scots version of this Movement had been led by scholarly men such as Wotherspoon, Kirkpatrick, Cooper and Milligan, whose interest lay not in liturgical paraphernalia–rubrics, vestments, candles–but in the doctrine of the Church, of the sacraments, and of the ordained ministry. Unfortunately, within a few decades this Movement lost its theological robustness and became dissipated into aestheticism and pseudo-Catholic nostalgia. At a fairly young age–I still had a soprano voice–I encountered this aesthetic type of High Churchism when I was sent by our school music master to sing in the Moray Aisle of the High Kirk of St Giles where, on Wednesday afternoons, there was celebrated something akin to Anglican Evensong. To my horror I was dressed in a purple cassock, surplice, and white frilly collar. Worse was to follow: we had to chant peculiar psalms I had never heard before, and to recite the Creed, also unfamiliar to me. The words "Virgin Mary" and "Holy Catholic Church" choked me and set my heart racing. I bolted out of the Church as soon as I could and never returned. I asked my mother if St Giles were a Catholic Church. She said, "No, but it is very ritualistic." To us ritualism, although undefined, was a strange and horrible thing like black magic.

The atmosphere in our parish church was very different from that. Our minister, the Rev. Oswald B. Milligan, as I now know, having read his excellent little book on the Sacraments, was most certainly theologically a High Churchman, but his Churchmanship expressed itself in solid Presbyterian garb and Scots culture. Above all the parish was well organized, with emphasis on pastoral care and systematic teaching. My father once said of Dr Milligan, "He has no small talk, but there is something very impressive about the man."

On Sunday mornings in Corstorphine in the 1920s a wakening bell pealed out at 10:15 from the parish church tower. The tones swelled up the hill to us, solemn and sweet, so different from the school bell. The young people were expected to assemble at 10:30 to attend the Sunday School, well organized in primary, junior and senior classes. The seniors met in the church and were taught by an assistant minister or theological student. At Christmas most children and young people took part in Nativity plays and carol singing. After seventy years I remember clearly the excitement and awe with which I bowed down and presented frankincense at the Crib in the Church Hall at Corstorphine.

At 11:30 the main diet of worship was heralded by a second tolling of the ancient bell. When quiet descended the organ played softly, and at 11:30 the beadle—a grave and substantial figure attired in a black gown with red facings—appeared from the tiny door in the chancel and carried in the Bible, which he placed on the lectern in the pulpit. He returned to the vestry and made a second entry, bearing a slender mace and leading in the minister. The pulpit was on the south wall of the nave and well down towards the west end of the fourteenth-century building. This little procession passed close by us, for our pew was in the old choir stalls along the south side. When the minister was in the pulpit we had to turn our eyes sharp left to see him. At his elbow on the wall was a large, very old hour glass, but to my disappointment it was never used. He never preached for an hour. After the sermon the collection was taken, and I never ceased to note with interest how an elder reached up to the pulpit to enable the minister put in his collection with the rest of us. The beadle appeared again and led the minister to the communion table in the chancel at the east end where he waited for the elders to bring up the collection. This was laid upon the table and the minister prayed, giving thanks and offering us all to God. Without knowing it at the time,

I was being introduced to the *Missa sicca*. Dr Milligan was a genuine High Churchman.

I never attended a Communion Service in this parish. There was no room for children at these celebrations. I do remember very clearly, however, my sister's baptism. The font was at the west end of the nave, under the little barrel vaulted gallery, where members of the family had been installed, so that we could see all that was going on. The minister sprinkled water liberally over the child's head, invoking the name of the Trinity. He then said that the child had been received into the Holy Catholic Church. This surprised me a bit, but I new that this was not a Catholic Church, and that Dr Milligan was to be trusted; so the word "Catholic" must, I thought, have another, and a perfectly respectable, meaning.

During the Easter holidays about three years later my mother took my brother and sister and me to stay with friends in London. I had been out sight-seeing with a boy of my own age and returned at lunch time to his father's office in the city. I was taken into the private office and sensed at once that something was wrong. "I want you to be prepared for rather a shock," he said, "your father is seriously ill." There was something artificial in his manner. I asked, "Is my father dying?" He answered: "I'm afraid you will not see your father again." "Was it an accident?" "Yes, he died instantaneously."

I suppose it was my Calvinist genes that came into play at this time. This calamity was the will of God, therefore there was nothing more to be said. Grief was mere complaint, and complaint was not so much rebellious as irrational. One must simply face the facts and look forward. The past was finished; I now had no father; the thing to do was to stop thinking about him and get on with the job in hand. The God I had come to know was not, however, the caricature of fatalism: he was love, and so if something was his will it must be a blessing in disguise. Nevertheless my immediate reaction was more Stoic than Christian, and I was impatient with my mother's terrible grief. She was completely struck down, and all the way home on that dreary train journey from Euston to Princes Street she could only mutter at intervals, "It's been to be."

The gloomiest moments were when people tried to offer the comforts of religion. Pious phrases were uttered in hysterical tones by my mother's family; the state of the departed was pictured in such a wispy way as to be frightening. There was something unreal about it all. I retreated into Stoic impassivity. My own solution was not one which could give permanent comfort and hope, for it was negative and theoretical. If this were God's will it must be good. But this attitude could not fill the dreadful emptiness which bereavement had brought, because in the religion which surrounded me, there was no satisfactory eschatology, no realistic image of the joys of the eternal kingdom of God, but only a tenuous notion of survival in a spooky kind of way.

After my father's death we stayed on for a year in our pleasant semi-country home in Corstorphine then, my mother finding this too expensive and too lonely, we moved into town to share a flat with her mother, whose tenement looked out at the back onto Samson's Ribs, the west flank of Arthur's Seat. Almost as soon as we had gone there my mother underwent surgery for gallstones; two years later one Sunday morning I was walking with her across the Meadows to Church when she began to speak incoherently, talking about the end of the world and the Day of Judgment. I got her home as best I could and called our doctor. Quite soon it was discovered that she was suffering from a brain tumor. She did not survive the operation. My brother and sister and I lived on in the flat with our grandmother and a very young aunt. Once again I retreated into myself to escape the gloom and hysteria that filled the air.

2

In spite of the shock of our mother's death, for me and I think for my brother and sister too the move from the fairly distant western suburbs into the center of town was not unpleasant. As a teenager I was happy to give up the joy of roaming the woods of Corstorphine Hill for the excitement of city pavements and lights. For several years I had already attended school in town. My social and other activities centered in school, and that was where my friends were.

George Heriot's School stands on the crest of the ridge above the Grassmarket, overlooked by the Half-moon Battery at Edinburgh Castle. It is a fine seventeenth-century quadrangular building with broad square towers at each corner, decorated in a slightly florid style with turrets and sculptured window pediments. A statue of the founder, Jinglin' Geordie, goldsmith and banker to James VI, looks down on the inner quadrangle from its niche below the clock tower. Cut into the pavement flags round the sides of the quadrangle are numbers, representing the foundationers, the hundred orphans of Edinburgh burgesses for whose education the school was originally endowed. The school, although no longer residential, provides free education and stipends for such pupils. At least it still did in my schooldays. For others the fees were remarkably small, so well endowed was the Heriot Trust.

Within this Scots Renaissance building I received part of my primary and all of my secondary education. In the nineteenth century Heriot's had been in the vanguard of the movement to liberate the teaching of science from the grammar school model of language teaching. From an early age we were introduced to scientific method. We began not with books but at the bench, carrying out and recording experiments, from which we deduced principles and derived definitions. Although there was a hint that brains were most usefully employed in the study of mathematics and science, languages were by no means neglected, but were taught in a thoroughly modern way. Grammar was still regarded as absolutely essential, but we had also to learn from day one to speak and write the language we were learning. At the age of twelve I was taught to write "free compositions" in German, that is to put down on paper in German simple thoughts that had not first been articulated in English. As a matter of course the prospectus contained French and German and also, unusually in those days, Spanish, taught then by a very scholarly lady. Few pupils learned Latin, but those who did received the very best teaching. It was also possible, after school hours, to learn Russian, taught by the elderly history master. The English department too was first-rate. I owe a tremendous debt to every department in that school.

It was, however, in the German class, under the tutelage of Mr Jo Halliday, that the most important element in the foundation of my cultural and spiritual growth was laid. Not only did we learn the language thoroughly, but this master discussed the substance of the texts with us, especially in the sixth year, when we used to read texts aloud without translating into English, except when we came upon a sentence we did not understand. Through the language and the books we read he introduced us not just to German literature, but to a wider European civilization.

On one occasion he stretched our minds in a theological direction. The short story we were reading told of a farmer who would let no one ride one of his horses, because it had been lent to the parish priest in order to take Holy Communion to a dying person. The class were mystified by this tale and so our master explained to us the Catholic doctrine of Transubstantiation. He did this carefully and with much gravity, objectively and without comment. Looking back I know now that his explanation was perfectly accurate. Few schoolboys are blessed with such humane pedagogy.

Culture flourished in the school. Music classes continued right through the curriculum; many boys studied art; and there was a school orchestra and dramatic society, as well as freelance musical and dramatic activity. Decades after my school days, when reading the biography of the South Tyrolean Jesuit Anton Sepp, I was struck by the similarity between the style of my schooling at Heriot's with the educational system built up by the Jesuits in the late seventeenth and early eighteenth century. The same spirit of that brand of Renaissance humanism had taken hold in Scotland too—a bit later perhaps.

The most formalized of our extra-curricular cultural enterprises was the "Lit," which met weekly in the O.P.L.R.—Old Physics Lecture Room—an amphitheater with a 45 degree slope in the auditorium. In the afternoon during school the secretary toured all the classrooms with a notice that was read out by the teacher in charge: "There will be a meeting of the Literary and Dramatic Society tonight at 7 o'clock in the O.P.L.R. The main business of the meeting will be a debate…" Sometimes the master would add a word, encouraging us to attend: "It is most important that you take part in these debates; in later life you will find it a great handicap if you have not learned to speak in public."

One of the advantages I gained by coming to live in town was that I could attend the "Lit" more easily. Not until I was in third year in the secondary school did I venture to attend. When I did, I was astonished at the eloquence and apparent knowledge of many of my schoolmates. Throughout several meetings I sat trembling on the brink of contributing to the debate, and when one evening I took courage and rose to my feet, very little sound came from my mouth. Slowly confidence developed and the "Lit" became one of my main interests.

Politics figured prominently in our agenda. In our ranks there were full-blown Tories, Marxists and even Anarchists. Others were more detached and cynical who, after a holiday in Europe, would speak on foreign affairs with an intellectual superiority based upon their first-hand experience of what they had seen for themselves. What enthusiasm and confidence was displayed at the "Lit"! It may have been after having presided at one of our meetings that our wise history master–the one who taught Russian–announced gently in class: "Please realize, that by the time you have reached VI Senior, you will have dipped only the tip of your toe into the ocean of knowledge."

Religion was discussed too, although usually as part of a political topic: Marx's opium of the people and so on. On one occasion when religion was being discussed I ventured the opinion that a Buddhist could be as much "Christian" as a Christian, if he acted according to a Christian ethic. My closest friend, who was a member of the Plymouth Brethren, jumped to his feet, shouting, "On a point of information, Mr Chairman, that view is contradicted by the Bible." The Chairman ruled him out of order, saying that everyone was entitled to his opinion about that.

After our "Lit" meetings a cluster of us would hang about at the main school gate, still arguing, the Royal Infirmary clock glaring down upon us like an artificial moon. The cluster would break up, some going east, some west. At the top of the Middle Meadow Walk a small nucleus of five or six would turn south and continue their walk across the Meadows via the Jawbone Walk. Outside each boy's house we would stop and argue a bit more. About an hour after leaving the school my Plymouth Brethren friend and I had arrived at the top of Marchmont Road. We walked on as far as the gate into the Blackford Pond, when the final Scots convoy began. We would "chum" each other several times almost the whole way back and fore between Arthur's Seat and the Blackford Hill until at last we struck a compromise at Lauder Road and parted.

On one such evening I reached a milestone on my intellectual and theological journey. My friend vehemently insisted that Christianity is not a matter of opinion because its truth is revealed in the Bible. You can search as much as you like for Truth, but in the end it has to be shown us, and it has been in the scriptures. I began to agree with him, and after I left school my education became almost exclusively the attempt to discover what exactly revelation is and what the relation is between reason and faith.

Our gregarious and social and to some extent, spiritual needs were provided not just by school organizations, but also by the Scottish Schoolboys' Club which operated in all of the Grammar Schools in Edinburgh and Glasgow. The main activities of this club were Sunday discussion groups throughout the year and a mammoth Easter camp, housed in bell tents within huge marquees. This was described as the thermos system—very necessary at that time of year in Scotland. If you were a real "he-man" you had a "total," that is a total immersion, in the river before breakfast; and if the ice had to be broken first, so much greater the merit acquired. During one very cold Easter I remember having to do this.

The Heriot's branch of this club held its own summer camp, run along the same lines. The most popular game played at these summer camps was Volleyball, and my introduction to this game was at Leaderfoot in 1932, quite a bit earlier than the game is commonly thought to have appeared in this country. Another of our games was podex, a cross between cricket and rounders, the bat being a small and light version of a baseball bat, and the ball a hard tennis ball. I have never seen this game played anywhere else. At the summer camps we observed the same macho conventions in respect of the morning "total," as we did at Easter, but as a rule the water was a bit warmer, and in the afternoons we would enjoy swimming in the deeper pools of the Tweed or the Leader. On one blazing hot summer at Leaderfoot—perhaps the most delightful of our campsites—a crowd of us were in the pool above the weir. It was regarded as "sissy" to wear bathing trunks. That afternoon one of the younger boys spotted three women walking on a path we had not noticed on the other side of the river. "There's ladies on the other side" he shouted. A veteran, standing only knee deep in the water responded: "If they're ladies they won't look, and if they're not ladies it doesn't matter."

At Easter camp we had discussion groups every morning. These resembled our Sunday meetings and the biblical background would often be the Sermon on the Mount. Almost anything might be talked about, but we tended to come back to discussing sayings like, "Turn the other cheek," and whether a Christian ought to take part in war. At night after the singsong we had a pep-talk from one of the leaders. Again the theme would normally be an aspect of Christian ethics. There was no official line, each leader giving us whatever "message" he thought fit. Occasionally a theological notion would flicker across the screen, as when once a visiting Anglican clergyman—to us a fairly exotic creature—stated that he believed all people would get to heaven, although not all theologians agreed with him.

In spite of doctrinal vagueness, however, these camp discussion groups did make us feel that it was normal to talk about serious things. We took this in our stride along with the "total," the games, the singsongs and the friendship. Most important of all was our learning that "it is good and pleasant for brethren to live together in unity." Healthy friendship was indeed engendered at these camps, and we felt we ought to carry this "spirit of Easter camp" back into everyday life. The motto of the Club was *teneo et teneor*—"I hold and am held."

It was through the Schoolboys' Club that I had my first holiday abroad. At the age of fifteen I went with a party of thirteen Scots schoolboys and students to an international camp at Ferch near Berlin. We embarked at Hull, and the first twenty-four hours' sailing was spent uneventfully in a state of pensive, semi-seasickness. Then as we entered the estuary of the Elbe the sea became calm, we saw lights on the shore, and we perked up, beginning to feel the exhilaration of entering a foreign country. We began to sing—Scots songs, nonsense songs and even hymns. The leader of our party was an accomplished musician and others were competent—all but one—who was tone-deaf, but humble enough to keep silent and mime the words. We rehearsed our repertoire as we sailed up the Elbe, and this proved useful, for at a reception in the *Rathaus* in Berlin we were asked to sing on the German equivalent of the British "In Town Tonight." Our kilts frequently dragged us into the public eye.

Next morning we disembarked and made for the railway station. As we walked through the streets, the first thing that struck us was the ubiquitous smell of cigar smoke; and we roared with laughter on seeing workmen digging up the street while smoking cigars. In an open air restaurant in Berlin our hilarity was again aroused when an enormous tureen containing soup and meat balls was placed before our leader. To our vulgar schoolboy eyes the receptacle was just too much like a chamber pot. Our mirth turned to consternation when a similar vessel was placed in front of each one of us. We had thought that the first tureen was intended for several people.

In Berlin we joined up with other national groups and sailed down the river by paddle-steamer to Ferch, where we were to stay for a week in the *Luther Rasthaus*. The pattern of activity was not unlike that of our camps at home, but the discussions were based much more directly upon Scripture. We were astonished at the detailed knowledge which the Germans in particular had of the Bible. They documented their statements, giving chapter and verse. We got the impression, too, that there was a greater deposit of cultural capital on the Continent than we possessed at home. Dolmetsch had recently revived the recorder, and in the evenings some of the Germans would play trios by Bach on these instruments. One night there was a power failure, but the musicians continued unperturbed to play from memory or by ear until candles were brought and the score was picked up again. Compared with all of this our "Old MacDonald had a Farm" or even "The Road to the Isles" sounded a bit rough and ready.

On the last night of this youth conference an enormous "fire of friendship" was kindled. The romantic symbolism of this was taken very seriously, especially by the Teutonic contingents. We all rushed about getting signatures written on the peeled bark of the batons we had cut from birch trees and decorated with black and red cord.

Throughout the time of the conference the eye of Big Brother had been upon us. Every morning there was a ceremonial unfurling of the Nazi flag, attended by the Germans and observed by all. Every night the official party representative—a bulky older man in a brown shirt, and who was seen one day at lunch drinking a quarter liter of vinegar—phoned Berlin from the telephone kiosk.

When the camp was over the Scots contingent set off on a tour. In Leipzig we visited the *Thomas Kirche* where Bach had been organist; in Eisenach we investigated the Wartburg and saw the ink stains on the wall where the Devil had ducked just in time; in Mainz we got a terrible harangue from the warden of the youth hostel on account of our noisy merriment after ten o'clock. It was in Mainz too that we were entertained by a family. After making sure that doors were closed and that we could not be overheard, the father of the family told us a little of the problems facing Christians in Germany on account of the totalitarian regime. From Mainz we sailed down the Rhine to arrive in Kaub in the evening, from where next day some of us swam out to Pfalz Castle on the island. The water in those days was clean, but the current so unexpectedly strong, that we were almost swept past the south end of the island. At Kaub we saw a labor camp and admired the brawny, suntanned guard at the gate, with a spade instead of a rifle in his hand. "He could give you a nasty clout on the head with that," one of us remarked.

The German holiday was over all too soon. In Hanover a youthful guide, proud of his ability to speak English, proudly pointed out the "beautiful backside of the

Rathaus." We moved on to Hamburg and back home from Hull. As a souvenir of the holiday and a mark of gratitude we presented the leader of our party with an object he had admired in a shop in Frankfurt–a small wooden statue of the Madonna, carved by Lang of Oberammergau.

Living now in town our family gravitated back to the church where both of my parents' families had always worshipped. I still knew nothing of the historical background to the differing traditions of this congregation and that of the old parish congregation in Corstorphine, but I was aware of a difference in atmosphere and ethos. In Corstorphine we knew none of the congregation, but worshipped happily in the parish church, unconcerned by our anonymity, but in town in this congregation which in the nineteenth century had belonged to the United Presbyterian Church we knew everyone, more or less, and they all knew us. The congregation was a self-contained affiliation of families, and at worship there was a corporate self-consciousness. The design of the building itself encouraged this sense: there was a central pulpit at the summit of a high flight of steps, and the auditorium, for it was basically an auditorium, surrounded this pulpit at two levels. Flanking the pulpit and behind it were the organ pipes–someone once said to me, "I see that in your church you worship the Lord God, the organ." Beneath the pulpit was the Communion Table with seats for the minister and elders, and in front of that an enclosure for the choir with the organ console in the center. The ground floor comprised three blocks of pews, the side blocks being separated from the center by aisles. The book boards on the ground floor were equipped on the under side with little metal rings into which were placed the diminutive individual glass cups after Communion had been received. Conscientious objectors to the individual cup sat in the gallery where the common cup was distributed. Communion was celebrated quarterly.

For me at the age of fifteen, the centrality of the sermon was acceptable and reasonable. We were seeking for truth—that was religion—and so the center of worship was the preaching of the word. In the old parish church at Corstorphine, although the prayer of offering after the collection was a prominent feature of the service, and one that caught my imagination at an early age, there too the sermon was given a central place. Religion was all about the word of God. From the age of fifteen I attended church willingly twice every Sunday, motivated by the desire to find the Truth. Gradually I formulated the notion that the function of a minister of the Church of Scotland was to study the Scriptures prayerfully and, week by week, to articulate his enlightenment to a congregation. I began to think that my function in life might well be the ministry of the word.

I confirmed this tentative inclination by taking an active part in the life of the congregation, in particular by helping to teach in the primary Sunday School. At the morning service there was a children's address before the main sermon. After this the children left the church and proceeded to the hall underneath. We sang hymns like:

> *For the beauty of the earth,*
> *For the beauty of the skies,*
> *For the love which from our birth,*
> *Over and around us lies,*
> *Christ our Lord to thee we raise,*
> *This our sacrifice of praise.*

After the hymn would come prayer and then a story, told by the superintendent teacher, for example the story of our Lord giving sight to blind Bartimaeus; then we separated into classes according to age, when the children would, in this case, be shown books in Braille and pictures of work among the blind in the mission field. At the end there would be intercessions corresponding to the topic of that Sunday. The program was well thought out and the teachers had to attend a weekly preparation session.

From an early age I had assumed that I would follow my father's profession and become an optician. My father had hopes that I might become an ophthalmic surgeon. When I first had an inkling that this might not be so, I spoke to my mother about it. I told her that I thought I should enter the ministry. She didn't look too happy, scowled a little and said, "I think that may be a passing notion; I don't think you could stick out the long course of study." Her lack of enthusiasm did not put me off, and in any case she died not long after, but there was another thing that worried me. I wondered if it was right that the ministry should be a profession, that a man should be paid for preaching the gospel. In those days one of the groups who used to speak at the foot of the Mound–Edinburgh's Hyde Park Corner–were called "The Tramp Preacher." They were quite educated people and talked a lot of sense. Was this not the method that Christians should use to spread the gospel? Then I thought, after all they do take up a collection after they have spoken, for they have to eat. I discussed the question with the lawyer who, after my mother's death, looked after our family affairs. He was a devout Episcopalian whose custom, however, was to attend Christmas Midnight Mass at the Jesuit Church in Lauriston Street. "The Jesuits," he told me, "are very evangelical." His advice to me was that although St Paul had earned his living by tent-making, he had affirmed also that those who preach the gospel may live by so doing. Both Old and New Testaments accepted the principle that ministers of the Church may be supported by the faithful.

These peripheral problems solved, I now had simply to make up my mind whether or not I had a genuine "call" to the ministry. The summer I left school, more or less on my seventeenth birthday, I attended a schoolboys' camp in Perthshire at the confluence of the Bruar and the Garry rivers, with Beinn a'Ghlo to the east and Schiehallion to the west. It was a perfect summer, and the camp a great success, but in spite of the distraction of many interesting activities, my mind never let go the preoccupation: did I have a "call" to the ministry?

One evening as the air chilled and the sky was turning to turquoise, I slipped from the field and picked my way along the river, over jagged ribs of rock, up to the salmon-leap on the Bruar. I entered the pine enclosed gorge and found a foothold in the blaeberries high above a deep pool. A solitary rowan tree peered out at the waterfall from a precarious ledge below. My mind was straining to break through into some supra-mundane experience. I was searching for that "something much more deeply interfused," of which my father used to speak, and for guidance too about the life's work that lay before me. I had withdrawn from human contact to be alone, conscious only of myself and the vast stuff of the universe around me. I was hoping for a mystical revelation.

The torrent of foaming water thundered into the black pool beneath me; my senses seemed to be sucked out into that inchoate, spooky vacuum; my desire was to come upon a clear vision, upon some rock of firm repose; but my experience was fast developing into a sense of weird disintegration.

It was darkening now, and with the grayness the uncomfortable sense of losing identity become more acute. I scrambled back to the road and reached the bridge over the river. Someone went by on a bicycle which squeaked. I leaned over the parapet, watching the water rushing beneath. I thought: Where is the road to knowledge of God? For some reason, at that moment, in imagination I pictured the Crucifixion. I thought: Here is the focus for all religious impulse; all other mystical excursions end in panic fear.

I followed the solid flint road back to camp. It was comforting to get back to the lamps, the faces, the wise-cracking and leg-pulling, to people—and to the nightly cup of hot cocoa. The image of God was in man; the revelation of God, too, was in a Man.

When camp was over I decided to make a retreat, but without any itch for religious experience. I set off walking with an enormous rucksack over the hills in blazing sunshine. Sometimes I walked alone and would sit down, leaning on the rucksack in the afternoon, munching bread and cheese and chocolate, watching the limpid hill-burns patter over pebbles. Sometimes I would find companions with whom I walked for several miles. In the evenings there was always cheerful company to be found in the youth hostel, where we cooked our meals on the stove and chatted into the night.

On the first day I walked twenty-four miles over three ranges from Kirkmichael to Glen Clova; then on over the shoulder of Lochnagar down into Deeside at Ballater; then to the clachan at Inverey where I stayed with a legendary old lady called Maggie Grewar, who was reputed to have had conversation with Queen Victoria. Next day came the climax. A climber with a car took me as far as Derry Lodge, from which point we began our climb to the summit of Cairn a Mhaim, from which height we looked down two thousand feet to the Corrour bothy in Glen Dee. Here we parted company: he returned to Inverey and I began the slow descent to the narrow, gloomy tunnel that has Braeriach on one side and Ben Macdui on the other. By the time I reached the valley my knees no longer formed part of my nervous system. I trudged on north up to the Pools of Dee, startled frequently by the abrupt croak of ptarmigan, came through the narrow gap at the summit, and proceeded down the Lairig Ghru towards the ancient forest of Rothiemurchus, where sparse clusters of giant pines stood in memory of past forest grandeur. Loch an Eilean with its ruined keep shimmered calm and bewitching in the evening glow. Nearer Aviemore the air was redolent of the resinous incense of felled timber.

It was a busy hostel at Aviemore. On that evening there was a Lancashire family touring Scotland in a rickety car, a bright friendly red-headed girl who had just begun to work for the Unionist party in Edinburgh, a hefty kilted agricultural student from Aberdeen, who had been sleeping under the shelter stone in the hills and collecting maggots from hill sheep—he showed them to me in a tin box. "And what do you propose to do now, lad?" asked the couthy Lancashire father, as we ate our supper. Before I had time to think, I replied, "In October I am beginning an Arts degree in Edinburgh, in preparation for the ministry of the Church of Scotland."

3

During my secondary schooldays, the return home from holiday in the autumn had always been colored by a mood of expectancy. With the crisp smell of falling leaves in your nostrils you prowled the streets, ferreting out old friends, not seen for some weeks, smearing rugger boots with dubbin, and wondering which team you would be in this season. There were about twenty teams at Heriot's in those days, and as you climbed nearer to VI Senior you hoped to get into the seconds or even the firsts. Great prestige was attached to this achievement, for not a few Scots internationalists had been there before you. Even in the classroom there was excitement—new books, new timetables, sometimes new masters. This was the most promising and creative time of the year. In 1937, the year I left school, for me this expectation of creative expansion was heightened as October came nearer. Some old acquaintances began to fade out of the scene, but a few remained, and there were fresh contacts as well as the reunion with a wider circle drawn from the boys from other schools, met at Easter camps and on the playing fields. In addition there was the stimulus of entering the world of adult study, a world, too, where girls were beginning to appear—for many of us a new experience in those days when co-education was not yet in vogue.

Through self-will aggravated by personal conflict with one master, and perhaps due also to some lack of over-all supervision, about half-way through secondary school I had been allowed to drop chemistry and study zoology and botany instead. This seemed to be in order, but unfortunately it blocked the way to a science or medical course. In any case my chief interest was in language, but what I did not realize at the time was that one had to have two modern languages in order to follow an honors course. I had only one language. A further complication, which came to light too late, was that English was ruled out because I had no Latin. This left me with no choice but to enroll for the philosophy course, which I was indeed very happy to do.

In our physics classes at school we had already had a glimpse of the frontier between physics and metaphysics. Our questioning had once prompted the master to remark, "Well now, here we seem to be entering the domain of philosophy." For me the theory of education had roused my interest while still at school. The problem of providing the right curriculum was one that touched all of us. True to the Scots tradition, our study menu contained a fairly wide variety of subjects, unlike the English system which, so I was told, concentrated more on specialization. My inclination was always to be critical of the status quo, and I questioned whether the Scots system were the better. I came to the conclusion that it was, and with hindsight I see its value. It may not equip a person with the expertise that is found to be required at some point, but it does enable a person to take an interest in many things and, if he is wise, to know how to ask questions of those who are expert. I think it also helps develop the art of seeing things from many angles, and of course it can make conversation easier. But it does have its drawbacks. Most people do have to develop towards expertise in something or other. I had a fear that I might become a Jack of all trades and master of none, and presented—at least to myself—the hypothesis that in the final school year the pupil should be directed to throw all his mental energies into one subject, pursuing a kind of mini-Ph.D. course. I thought that such a procedure would give the pupil confidence as he faced university. What I did not realize at the time was that the standard we had to reach in every subject was already very high and demanded all our strength. I smile when I hear the suggestions made today by politicians and others about the number of hours pupils ought to spend on homework. In the 1930s we were all doing about four hours per night. If there was a weakness in the Scots system it was that by the time we reached the university at the age of seventeen we were a bit exhausted and also unused to the style of working that had now to be adopted.

At Edinburgh in those days one was permitted to join the philosophy class only in one's second year. This meant that the honors philosophy course lasted five years. In one's first year one studied the "outside" subjects, in my case English literature, German and natural philosophy, which at school we had called physics. For me as for all who came from Heriot's the natural philosophy class taught us nothing we had not already learned at school. I was able to concentrate on the German class where we learned about the Deism of the Enlightenment through reading Lessing, and about the Romantic movement as we read Goethe and Schiller. As at school care was taken to encourage fluency in the spoken tongue. We used Dr. Marie Barker's *A Handbook of German Intonation*, the first such book to be produced and published in 1925. This book uses what is called "Graphical Representation," which resembles plainchant notation. I owe a great debt to this book and to Dr. Barker. I keep the book still to hand.

The English literature class was presided over by Dover Wilson who had the gift of insinuating seminal ideas into our heads. By accident at this time I came across Francis Thompson's essay on Shelley, which seemed to me the most wonderful thing I had ever read. One of the tutors asked us to write an essay on the idea of progress. Looking back I see that the work I put into that exercise was the start of enduring reflection on the Christian doctrines of sanctification and eschatology.

In the Dialectic Society, which I joined in my first year, I found continuity with the activity of the school "Lit." The atmosphere was, as one would expect, much more professional than in school, although the topics were often similar. Not only were some of the older students both eloquent and well-informed, but we had the benefit from time to time of the company of guests. I remember well a visit by John R. Allan. The subject I forget, but not his *bon mot:* "You see, a'body in Aiberdeen has an auntie in the country."

It was in the Dialectic Society that I first encountered serious Atheism, and realized the urgency of providing sound arguments for the existence of God, or at least for the invalidity of arguments that deny his existence. In my first year at the university I began to think hard about the relationship between reason and faith, and I have never stopped working at this task. I now discovered that the expertise I desired to acquire was the ability to solve this problem. As it happened I had blocked for myself the way to follow purely scientific or literary inquiries; but surely the enterprise upon which I now embarked was more than worthy of the undivided attention of the human intellect.

In May 1938 just before the end of my first year at Edinburgh University my eye was caught by the word *GRATIS* on a poster in the entrance to the Old Quad. The poster contained an invitation to English-speaking students to be guests in families in several central European countries. All they had to do was to speak English with the children of these families. I applied at once, stating a preference for Hungary, mainly because two of my friends with an older student had gone there during the previous summer, and their report had aroused my interest. The agency did not reply, and so I wrote again. This time I received a reply almost at once from a Hungarian family saying "Come on July 1, but already in June if possible." That meant that I had four days left to get to the east side of Hungary by July 1. I had a friend in a travel agency who the same day wired a booking to his London office. That night I took the coach to London, picked up my tickets, and in the evening caught the Harwich boat-train. The return journey from London to Budapest—with student concessions—cost me £5.19s.

At Harwich the wind was screaming in the loading cranes, and seamen were lashing down everything that could possibly move. A ship had just docked, arriving from the continent sixteen hours behind schedule. One of the crew was placidly eating bacon and eggs in the saloon. I told myself that seasickness was psychologically induced, went below and got into an upper bunk in a six-berth cabin, hoping to fall asleep before we left the quay.

I did fall asleep quickly, having been already twenty-four hours on the journey, but about two hours later I awoke, dimly aware of a bumping sound. Something was being thrown from one side of the ship to the other. I found myself on the floor, clutching the sides of the hand basin. After the first bout I climbed back into my bunk, but was down again almost at once, and remained there all night, shivering on the floor, too weak to climb up again, spattered over by the spilling contents of the now choked basin, and calculating how soon I could hope to die of pneumonia.

With morning came a calmer sea, and we were in Hook of Holland. I walked unsteadily to the train, and eventually reached Cologne where I boarded the Istanbul Express, a luxury train with carriages made entirely of steel and leather. We sped down the Rhineland, stopping at Frankfurt where a jolly group of Austrian youth, returning from a holiday sponsored by the new post-Anschluss government, joined the train. Night covered the landscape as we moved into Bavaria and I slept soundly, undisturbed even by the frontier control at Passau who, while I slept, removed the passport from my sporran and stamped it. In the early morning the train stopped at a signal; I awoke and opened a window. We were in hilly country and the air was laden with the scent of new-mown hay. In a field near the line a farmer was working, adorned in a green, conical hat with an enormous plume like a giant shaving brush, and wearing leather shorts and white ankle-less stockings.

We arrived in Vienna early in the morning. On the train I had met a young Dutchman who was visiting Vienna on business. He knew his way around and took me to a restaurant where on his recommendation, I ate a traditional Viennese breakfast—crisp, crusty, white rolls and butter and *zwei Eier im Glass,* that is two eggs in a glass and coffee. The eggs were soft-boiled and one mixed in with them pieces of roll and some butter, just as I had done as a child in Scotland. After breakfast I took a stroll on the Kärntner-Ring and bought a copy of Goethe's *Faust* bound in pretty pale blue leather. The bus for Budapest left at noon. It was an enormous red and white bus. Never have I known such furious driving. When a peasant cart appeared far ahead, the driver pressed down the horn and drove straight on without slackening speed. The rickety cart would be dragged from the road into the ditch by a terrified horse, while the Hungarian shook his fist and shouted imprecations at the Austrian driver. At Györ we paused. I bought Hungarian currency—in those days the pengö—and in the open air restaurant ate a roll with a slice of *szalámi,* costing the quivalent of one shilling (5p. today), which I thought excessive, but was told that *szalámi* is very concentrated food, made from among other things, donkey flesh. I enjoyed it.

In Budapest I sought out a pension where my friends had stayed during the previous summer. The woman who opened the door was taken aback at the sight of the kilted youth. She asked who had recommended this pension to me, and when I named my friends all was well—they must have made a good impression. To make up for her hesitation on receiving me, the lady sat beside me at supper and chatted kindly. In those days German was the second language in Hungary. The food, which my hostess said was typically Hungarian, was very good, and to me not at all exotic. The *gulyás,* apart from the tomato content, was basically stewed hough, and the *hús leves* (beef soup) was also quite familiar to me. After spending one night in this most agreeable pension I set off by train to travel eastwards across the celebrated great plain, the *Alföld.* The journey was slow and we sat on hard wooden seats. Most of my fellow passengers began to eat bread and very fat bacon as soon as we started, and they kept on munching as long as their journey lasted. The heat was dreadful. At every station passengers jumped out to fill water bottles. In the little townships I saw many horses, some with hides of unusual color, with leafy branches on their backs to protect them from the sun. There were different sorts of carriages, but those that interested me most were the peasant farm carts with sides sloping outwards from a fairly narrow center floor, their joints fastened not with nails but with cord. On the bumpy roads this allowed flexibility and prevented breaking. I observed another feature which seemed almost oriental in its subtlety—men carrying huge sacks of grain which were only partially filled, allowing the bearer to let one half drop over his back while the other half hung down across his chest. The weight was perfectly distributed and he had no difficulty holding onto the load. I was entering a new world.

I had become so absorbed in the journey that I had almost forgotten I was going somewhere. Late in the afternoon the train reached my destination, Püspökladány about forty miles short of the Romanian frontier. What sort of people would my hosts turn out to be? No sooner had I jumped down onto the ground, dragging my rucksack after me, than I saw approaching me—I was easily identified by my kilt—the most beautiful girl I had ever seen. She was small and neat with light brown hair and brown eyes—about seventeen, I guessed—and her name was Sylvia. For two and a half months her image was to be the constant accompaniment to my every experience.

All my life I had had almost no contact with girls. My own sister was eleven years younger than I so that there had not been even indirect friendships through her. Apart from the three years in the local infant school I had never enjoyed the benefits or distractions of girls in the classroom. Heriot's was, I suppose, trying to move into the approaching age of enlightenment by having a Christmas Prefects' Dance. The organization of these events was most correct. One presented a name to the headmaster who then sent a formal invitation to the lady named. As I produced no name, the headmaster asked me if I hadn't a sister or cousin or someone who would like to come; I said that I hadn't. He would probably have thought it indecent to ask if I had a girlfriend. I hadn't that either, and I had no idea how to dance. So I just missed out on the occasion. Not all pupils were as backward as I was; the dance was enjoyed by many, and next day there was quite a bit of coy murmuring in the corridors.

There was my cousin, however, perhaps two years my senior. As young children we met occasionally, but she went off to live in London and I saw her only very infrequently. One summer—I must have been about six or seven—she came to spend a holiday with us in Gullane on the coast. We were both quite innocent as far as physical sexual development was concerned, but I remember still the indescribable pleasure I felt in her presence. I had at that time very strong attachments to school friends, but this attachment to my girl cousin was quite different.

In a holiday context too, a little later, but still I think in pre-adolescence, I met a young woman—in her twenties I judge—who helped take care of and amuse the young, and who, for me was an icon to be worshipped. Here again I was unaware of any connection between infatuation at the perception of a woman's personality and the awakening of physical sexual development. The latter kind of development seemed to run its own course, operating in the world of fantasy and dreams.

During my first year at university, that is immediately before my Hungarian jaunt, I did have a more genuinely adolescent encounter with a real woman. She was a little older than I, and our acquaintance came through the Church and a shared interest in music. At that time I was fanatically interested in music and sang in the Reid Choir, conducted by Sir Donald Tovey. The calf-love experience I had at this time with this lady was wrapped around in the ecstasy of Haydn's *Creation*, for this was the piece performed by the choir in that year. To speak of this encounter as a love affair would be totally misleading to a reader today. It was intense; we spent a lot of time together;

we went for long walks together; but still the attachment, though tender, produced no physical resonance. This was the stage in emotional sexual development I had reached when on July 1, 1938 I jumped down onto the non-platform of the station at Püspökladány in eastern Hungary. When I returned to Scotland at the end of September the strong emotional attachment I had known during the previous year had lost its grip.

Sylvia introduced me to her father, a bulk, gruff man who spoke neither English nor German. I learned later that he was the factor of a large estate on the Alföld, where they lived, and himself owned a small property in the north on the Czechoslovakian border. We climbed up behind a coachman in braided uniform, and drove along earth roads across land as level as a bowling green, stretching as far as the eye could see. This was the great plain which for centuries had made Hungary such a desirable prize for invaders. It produced pasture, which supported sheep and cattle, wheat and Indian corn. There were clusters of acacia trees near small villages, where flocks of geese cackled brashly across our path, and ragged barefoot children peeped out at us shyly. After a short journey we arrived at the farmhouse–the mansion was some distance away in a copse, gaunt and looking desolate. The owner was an absentee landlord, living in Paris on the rents from the estate. The farmhouse was a long, low building of one story. Sylvia's mother was dead, but I was welcomed by her grandmother, a warm-hearted and thoroughly Hungarian old lady who, like her son, spoke only Hungarian. It was Friday, and in a corner of the sitting room a red lamp burned before a statue of the Sacred Heart. I noticed that this lamp was lit every Friday.

Soon after my arrival we sat down to supper–it was almost nine o'clock, the normal time for this copious meal. A whole roasted piglet lay on the table. When it became necessary to lift up the bone in order to remove the last flake of flesh, one looked at Granny and said, *"Szabad?"* which means, "Is it permitted?" The answer was always "*Szabad.*" Whereupon one picked up the bone in one's fingers and chewed. The piglet with plenty of vegetables had been preceded by the celebrated beef soup and always ended with a dish of the fruit that was in season. At that time it was red currants, which we ate twice a day until replaced by the next crop, which was, I think, peaches or apricots. Not only was the fruit repeated, but so was the piglet. He appeared twice a day—2:30 p.m. and 8:30 p.m.—until not a scrap remained. Pork was popular as were chicken and turkey, but there was also plenty of meat, usually hough (shin). For drink there was red wine diluted with an equal volume of water and the same volume of soda water. This was known as a *Spritzer*. These two meals were identical in content and were in fact the only meals. I don't know what the others ate, if anything, in the morning, but in deference to my being British I was given hot chocolate and fried bread—which they took to be toast. I soon persuaded them to give me tea and normal bread.

Most of the rooms in this long, one-story house led into one another, which made life complicated at times. The bathroom/lavatory luckily was not part of this strange corridor plan, but it did possess features that were unnerving. There was a fairly normal lavatory bowl and seat, but I had to accommodate to the equipment. Some years later I was amused to learn from *The Specialist*—the book that describes the work of Lem Putt the American privy builder—that early twentieth-century rural America must have enjoyed the same advanced civilization as I found in the 1930s on the Hungarian plain. Lem Putt asked his clients if, in their privy, they wanted cobs or Sears Roebuck's catalog. In this Hungarian bathroom I found just that—dried corn cobs in a box and a catalog hanging from a nail—but no toilet paper.

This estate farmhouse—the *Gatáj pusta*—on the great plain was where I and the family stayed for most of the time between July 1 and the middle of September, but only a few days after my arrival we all went off to spend almost a month in the family's own little property on the

Czechoslovakian frontier–a place called Balassagyarmat. We traveled by train and I saw how the landscape changed, becoming more hilly and wooded as we moved north. To me the most striking feature was the way the shallow valleys were scored across with long lines of closely planted poplars. As we moved northward, villages became more frequent. Much of the land here had been divided up into small holdings, unlike the eastern plain where there were huge estates, and where there was an atmosphere of eighteenth-century feudalism. On one trip in the carriage across the estate in the south, I had seen Sylvia's father take the whip to a young boy asleep on the grass when he was supposed to be herding sheep. In the north there was an atmosphere of a more cheerful and thriving peasant economy. Life was still hard. All week the reapers would sleep out in the fields, coming home, singing, on Saturday evenings. On Sunday afternoons and evenings a Gypsy band would appear, and there would be dancing in the streets and in the farmyards–the vigorous, restrained two stroke knee jerk of the Csárdás, which in this foreign ambiance I was able to learn.

Besides the coachman and three servants our company comprised Granny, the father, Sylvia and her slightly younger brother, Puci, Marthi, a school friend of Sylvia's from the Sacred Heart Convent in Budapest, and a Swiss French tutor. This man was several years older than I, and was treated more as an employee than as an *au pair*. When we visited restaurants, as we did after an outing to the hot springs in the east, he would be entrusted with adding up the bill and seeing to practical matters. Our common language was German, but when the Swiss was not present–and even when he was–I was expected to speak only English. Sometimes father would appear when we were together, and suspecting that one of his children was speaking German, would shout, *"Nem néumetül,"* that is, "Not German." When playing cards–the most popular game was *Stöck,* resembling the Bezique I used to play with my grandmother–we would fall into a strange polyglot language, but the only phrase I now recall is *három trèfle* (three of clubs). I found almost no opportunity to learn Hungarian. The young people preferred to speak German among themselves. Sylvia told me that their mother tongue was very difficult and that her grandmother frequently had to correct them.

Most of our time was spent out of doors. Never in my life had I enjoyed such continuous spells of really hot weather, interrupted only by the very occasional and exciting thunderstorm. We played tennis, swam and went for long picnic excursions in straw-lined farm carts. On these occasions we took bread and chickens and fruit. In the evening the chickens would be roasted over a fire by the cook. No excursion, however extended, was allowed to disrupt the normal eating schedule. Sometimes a Gypsy band appeared from nowhere, quite happy to play for ages for only a few pence. During this holiday I was introduced to a custom of which I had never heard, that of celebrating the Name Day, that is the feast day of the saint whose name one had received at baptism. The household had retired for the night, it was already quite dark and I had just fallen asleep, only to be wakened by the sound of violins, violas and the *cimbalom*. In the garden a Gypsy band was serenading under Marthi's window, for it was July 29, the feast of St Martha. I could see them because the trees were festooned with Chinese lanterns. Here we were living in the afterglow of the Austro-Hungarian empire.

On Sundays the carriage transported us all to Mass. There was a Reformed Church in the region, but I was not permitted to attend. The first Sunday at Mass—it was the first time in my life—I felt a bit nervous. I stood up and sat down when the others did, but I would not, could not, kneel, for the sedate habit of sitting firmly upon man's chief end during worship was too deeply ingrained. Nonetheless, I was educated enough to know that the Catholics paid special reverence in Church at the moment when the words of Consecration were recited, and I had no qualms about respecting this moment, which was easily identified by the accompanying bell ringing, when I bowed my head reverently. After a few weeks I became quite familiar with the pattern of the Mass and ceased to feel things strange.

While still in the north, one Sunday we went to Mass in a neighboring village. Hitherto although the liturgy had never appeared undignified, the priest had been portly, a bit angry looking and gabbled somewhat. Here, however, in this nearby village I was struck by the ascetic demeanor and vigorous preaching of the young priest who was the celebrant. As well as this, on entering the church a few minutes early, I had heard a group of women fervently murmuring prayers in unison. Their devotion—I now know that they must have been praying the Rosary—was clearly most sincere, and I thought, "They are quite unself-conscious and have deep faith." Back home in Scotland I found myself saying, "You know, Catholicism isn't all mumbo-jumbo," and shooting the personal experience line that had been such a winner at the school "Lit," "in Hungary I have seen intense faith and piety both in people and in priests. It varies from place to place."

The last four weeks of the holiday were spent back in the eastern plain. It was there that I saw the hand of St Stephen exposed for veneration, for it was his ninth centenary. At Mass the priest preached an impassioned, patriotic sermon. At the beginning of this Mass a woman went forward and knelt before the priest in the center of the church. I asked what was happening. "She is a Protestant," I was told, "and is being received into the Catholic Church." How strange!

Now and again I had to report to the police. On the first visit I was asked, "What is your religion?" I replied, "Christian." This did not satisfy them, but I obstinately refused to give an answer that committed me to a denomination. The officials who were very polite, whispered together, about to write down something. I overheard the word "Anglican" and as this disturbed me greatly, I invoked the name of Calvin. "Ah," said the officer in charge, "Knoxist!" He seemed very happy with this, so I let the matter rest.

Throughout the whole summer I had been quite close to Sylvia, the first time I had ever had such an experience. I think I was in love in a more serious way than ever before. I never knew what she thought or felt about me. Once when I tried to put my arm round her shoulders she gave me a very decisive brush off, and once when on my drinking *per tu*, that is formally beginning to use the familiar second person pronoun form of address with Marthi, I kissed Marthi on the cheeks, Sylvia was very angry and told me that this was most improper. On the whole Sylvia and I were very friendly, but although my attachment was strong, reaching the lower slopes of a kind of worship, still there was no convergence of sentiment and physical resonance.

Sylvia and I sometimes discussed religion. I must have raised the question of priestly celibacy, wanting to make a case for my own belief that I could marry and be a minister of the Church. Perhaps I wondered if I could ever marry Sylvia. At the end of September the thought did cross my mind that I might find a way of staying in Europe and not returning to Scotland. Sylvia argued strongly that a priest had to spend so much time in prayer and caring for his entire congregation that he could not possibly have time or energy to care for a wife and family. I objected that such a man's experience might be very limited. "No," she said, "he must pray." I could not imagine what all this prayer, in a vacuum so to speak, would be like. She also told me that she could never marry a Protestant or a poor man. Was this to counter the fantasies that she sensed were buzzing round in my head? She was a normal and kindly girl, genuine in her religious faith. I don't think she was mercenary, perhaps just totally realistic. It was probably providential that in her I had encountered not just a beauty and attraction I had never known, but also this realism and adherence to prudent rules, which damped down my too uncharted romanticism.

At the end of the holidays the whole family came to Budapest; the youngsters went back to school, Puci to the Jesuits, Sylvia to the Sacred Heart nuns; grandmother, father and I stayed with relatives in Buda. I spent a week in Budapest when I visited the most important places. I went shopping in the open market, buying presents to take home. One day I was waiting for the tram to take me back across the river to Buda when a man started up a conversation with me. He had a sly face and I felt uncomfortable. He asked where I came from and so on and then said, "I could put you up for a few days if you like." I told him I was staying with friends. "Do you know why I would like you to come" he added. "I haven't the slightest idea" I replied. This was only partly true; I guessed that he must be in the prostitution business—I did know that there were such things as prostitutes—but I did not know, as with hindsight I now know, that his interest must have been in the homosexual department. For me this was still a closed book.

The week came to an end. Grandmother came with me to bid farewell to Sylvia. My mouth was a bit dry as we waited together in the convent parlor until Sylvia came in, accompanied by a demure nun. We talked for a while in English; then came a very formal parting. Sylvia now wore a school uniform, severe and elegant, but her bone structure, her hair, face and eyes, were outstandingly fine and gentle. She appeared to show no emotion; standing up, I at last said my formal Goodbye— *"Kezét csókolom"*—"I kiss your hand"—and I did. Granny burst into tears and begged me come again another year.

By this time Mr Chamberlain was in Munich and I was advised not to delay but to get home as quickly as possible. My ticket allowed me to take a detour through Styria and the Tyrol, but I considered altering this plan. A cheerful Austrian I met told me not to worry, for if war came it would only be a skirmish on the Polish or Czech frontier, and so I went ahead as I planned. I left Budapest on a late evening train for Vienna. Near Vienna the conductor asked me if I had somewhere to stay overnight. I said I hadn't and he explained that on account of the Nürnberg conference all hotels and pensions were full up. He told me that his wife always came to meet him when he went off duty and that I should wait for him on arrival at Vienna. I saw him confer with his wife on the platform, then he came to me and said that his wife would be very happy to give me lodging for the night. I went home with them and they gave me supper. Unknown to me his wife had roused their young daughter, transferred her to their own bedroom, and prepared her room for me. In the morning after breakfast he suddenly began to speak to me in quite good English. "I must learn English," he said, "in order to do my job well." Before I left–he took me to the train himself–I offered to recompense them for their hospitality, for I could see that they were far from well off. Again he conferred with his wife and then asked me if I could give them the equivalent of one shilling and sixpence to cover the cost of food. It saddens me to think that I will probably never see this man again. His name was Josef Prassl.

From early morning until after dark I traveled through some of the most beautiful scenery in the world. There is great and subtle beauty in the Scottish landscape, but I had never seen such massive peaks, like *Der Wilde Kaiser*, which I photographed from the moving train. In the compartment were a group of young Austrians, all exceedingly friendly and jovial, and one little boy, put on the train at Vienna by his mother who thought that, considering the international situation, he would be safer with his grandmother in Gratz. As we approached the junction where the others had agreed to see him onto the branch line to Gratz, the little fellow started to weep buckets. As I could not understand his Viennese *patois,* the others explained that his mother had forgotten to give him the few shillings he required for his ticket to Gratz. They were all going to contribute a few pence: could I help too? I had about thirty English shillings worth of

Austrian currency, which I no longer required, so I insisted that they take it and give it to the boy. At this time there was obviously not much money about among the ordinary Austrian people. The little boy's eyes dried quickly and he said something which made them all laugh. They translated: "Please thank the Chinese gentleman for the money." To him my kilt was an oriental dress.

Late in the evening, after dark, the mountain peaks were illuminated by the most spectacular blue sheet-lightning. In a tavern in Innsbruck I got something to eat and watched a group of four intellectual looking elderly men playing chess and drinking wine from a long-necked bottle. At about midnight I boarded a *Bummelzug* (one that stops at every station) for Friedrichshafen on Lake Constance. All night long I sat on a narrow, white-painted wooden bench. In Friedrichshafen I bought a pair of cherry-colored shoes and a Tyrolean hat, which claimed to be *"wasserabstossend und Luftdurchlässig"* (water-repellent and air-permeable). Both of these articles I cherished for years. From Friedrichshafen I traveled by a much faster train down through Bavaria until I reached Cologne. I was sitting, disconsolate and very tired, upon a large wicker basket in Cologne railway station, dreading the long sea voyage back to Harwich, when I spotted a young man and woman whom I recognized. They had graduated earlier that year from the German department. Very soon they had explained to me how to alter my route and come back by the much faster Ostende boat. Soon we were on the move and back in London the next afternoon. I spent a night with my uncle in London and traveled to Edinburgh next day by bus. I had one shilling in my pocket.

The family in Hungary had given me a bottle of Tokaj to take home to Scotland. With the help of my very old Plymouth Brother school friend, Stuart Harris, who later became Deputy City Architect in Edinburgh, and my friend of more recent vintage, Jim Whyte, later to become Principal of St Mary's Theological College in St Andrews, and whom I would sit next to on university benches for some years to come, I opened and we drained the bottle of Tokaj. The next week we began our second year, Stuart at the Art College, Jim and I at the university in the first ordinary philosophy class. My adult life had more or less begun.

4

Norman Kemp Smith was professor of logic and metaphysics, and lectured three times a week to the First Ordinary class. He was assisted by W.S. Sinclair, who gave a course in traditional formal logic, and by tutors–who came into action infrequently. I have a vague memory of one or two seminars, but the main duty of the tutor was to discuss the essay which one had to write once in a term. Looking back I see this as a serious weakness in the teaching method of the university at that time. From a friend who had studied at Oxford, I learned that there the custom was to write essays often–weekly I think–and to discuss the essay with the tutor each time. This system encouraged constant dialogue, which is the only efficient way to progress in philosophy; the system to which I was exposed was too desultory and discontinuous. The root problem was–as we are well aware today–funds. First class education required lots of cash. There was another snag which affected me: my tutor was a bit of a rebel–from Kemp Smith's point of view–a devotee of the Cambridge Analysts, a Logical Positivist. I became sufficiently influenced by this man to get into some confusion, and to express notions which were anything but agreeable to the professor.

Like Dover Wilson in the English literature department, Kemp Smith devoted the First Ordinary Course to whetting our appetites by introducing us to the basic classics–to the Socratic Dialogues of Plato, and to Descartes, Locke, Berkeley and Hume. I remember nothing of what he said about these philosophers, but do remember many of his anecdotal asides. He made quite a long digression one day into the subject of hypnosis and the way the sub-conscious mind works, citing examples of calculating genius. In conclusion he gave some advice, to which I have paid serious attention ever since. He said: "When you are writing an essay, as soon as possible study the relevant material thoroughly, then leave it, and give your subconscious a chance." Mentioning Behaviorism, he offered as an example the little girl who, when told to think before she spoke said, "How do I know what I think till I hear what I say?" On another occasion, making an aside on the subject of Solipsism, he told of a woman at an academic reception who, when introduced to a philosopher, inquired, "Which brand of philosophy do you adhere to?" "I'm a Solipsist" he replied. "Oh how wonderful, so am I; I can't understand why there aren't more of us."

These are only a few examples of the kind of thing that Kemp Smith would throw out for the edification and entertainment of his young students, but by means of these asides he did set us off on lines of philosophical exploration. Towards the end of the course he summed up his general philosophical viewpoint by expounding what he called the "Coherence Theory of Truth," which he preferred to the "Correspondence Theory of Truth." Memory is an unreliable instrument, especially when it spans fifty-eight years, but the interest which Kemp Smith's theory aroused in me was great and may have counterbalanced the caprice of memory. His theory went something like this: to establish a perfect correspondence between reality and our description of that reality is beyond human competence; a wiser goal is to enunciate a philosophy, a picture of reality, that is coherent, one that as a whole makes sense. At the time this line of argument appealed to me, although not until much later did I realize that it was its implications that were so important. The theory was one of the ways of expressing the idealist outlook which, through the nineteenth-century German philosophers, notably Hegel and Kant, had formed men like Kemp Smith. In discovering ultimate reality we are at the mercy of our perceptions; our minds construct reality for us, the thing itself remains a mystery. But philosophers like Kemp Smith did not despair, there was validity in the ideas the philosopher constructed, so long as they formed a coherent whole, and there did exist beyond our ideal constructs an objective reality, however elusive. Later, in the honors class, when Kemp Smith declared, "Objects are real, but I know them in and through my sense perceptions," Jim Whyte commented to me afterwards, "It's rather like wearing knickerbockers, you're in and through them."

For me and for Jim Whyte, who was my close accomplice throughout the philosophy course, Kemp Smith's theological alignment was his most interesting feature. One of our older colleagues had described Kemp Smith as "a pious agnostic." Piecing together what he taught in class, including his anecdotes, and remarks made in private as, for example, his telling me over lunch of a very fine sermon he had heard in a little village church in Bavaria, I would say that the stress should have been on "pious" rather than "agnostic." His agnosticism was the theological counterpart of his philosophical hesitation to profess a direct awareness of reality. His piety was an acknowledgment of God's existence, his agnosticism a sign of humility, a statement that the true God is the unknown God, too great for the mind to grasp. These perceptions are where mystical theology begins.

For the Christian this humility before the Mystery that is beyond our reach is fundamental. At the same time it is accepted as an axiom that real life lies in the knowledge of God. In St John's Gospel we find the plain statement: "And eternal life is this: to know you, the only true God, and Jesus Christ whom you have sent" (Jn 17:3). While humility and common sense lead to a kind of agnosticism, human nature cannot relinquish the desire to know God. To know God the Creator, to have at least an inkling of what is in his mind, is the key to the fullness of life. My basic interest in the relation between reasoning and faith was developing during the years under Kemp Smith's tutelage, and I was beginning to see dimly that reasoning and faith perform different functions, that there is a distinction although no contradiction between the knowledge that is open to natural reasoning and the knowledge that is given through revelation.

In one of his most important asides, Kemp Smith touched on the subject of revelation. He had mentioned the holy scriptures and the fact that Christians held these writings to be inspired and a source of infallible truth. The question he posed was this: does the Christian Church and what it teaches depend upon the scriptures or are the scriptures themselves a product of the Church's life and thinking? In retrospect I realize that he was much more aware than we were of the debate about scripture and tradition which went on between the Reformed and the Catholic Church. He did not elaborate on the problem, but remarked that it was not a version of the "chicken or egg first?" conundrum. The two notions, that of the authority of scripture and that of the authority of the Church's voice, were complementary. Neither could be sustained apart from the other. These remarks, although they left the question still unresolved, stuck in my mind, and set me off on the line of thought that in a few years would seriously affect the direction of my life.

In the summer vacation following this year of study I attended a Student Christian Movement conference at Swanwick in Derbyshire. From then on my extra-curricular activity became centered in the S.C.M. This proved to be a critical move, for not only did I, through the S.C.M. form contacts with Christians other than Presbyterians, but also met the girl I was to marry. S.C.M. was said by some to stand for "Society for Christian Marriage"—not a bad purpose.

The Swanwick conference was an elaborate affair. Lectures were given by high power theologians, and the seminars and discussion groups were led by people, many of whom later became distinguished Church leaders. In 1939 the chief lecturer was Prof. Reinhold Niebuhr, whose *An Interpretation of Christian Ethics* was widely acclaimed at the time. He was an impressive lecturer and we delighted to hear his paradoxical affirmations about "impossible possibilities"—or was it "possible impossibilities"?—rolled out in a rich American accent. He left the conference before it ended, and some wag composed this limerick:

> *At Swanwick when Niebuhr had quitted,*
> *A young fellow said, "Now I have hit it:*
> *Since I cannot do right, I must think out tonight,*
> *What sin to commit, and commit it."*

In the Bible study and other discussion groups, for the first time in my life I met and talked with well-informed Christians whose theological background was different from my own. There were Welsh Calvinistic Methodists—more akin to me than most—there were low Church Anglicans and Anglo-Catholics—a breed I had not heard of before—there were several Non-Conformist groups, including some who objected to infant baptism. Not only was there a wide spread on the theological spectrum, but all faculties were represented. In one of the seminars we discussed the necessity of baptism for salvation. One of the group, a Baptist who although in his early twenties had not yet been baptized, said as he left our session before the end, "I hope when we meet again tomorrow you will be able to let me know my fate." These discussions, although touching on subjects on which people were deeply divided, were always conducted in a spirit of charity and often with humor. Through this discussion about baptism I was introduced to the very important question of the relationship between the Mystical Body of Christ and the visibly identifiable Church that we see in this world, a question I did not fully clarify until reading *Lumen Gentium*. It was in this same seminar that I ventured to express the notion that differences in dogma and outward form of worship were compensated for by the providential equipment of a subjective filter which caused all who followed their consciences and worshipped God sincerely to profess essentially the same religion, and to be in effect members of the Body of Christ. A muscular Anglican Oxford don exclaimed, "You Scots are all incorrigible individualists; you ought to become hermits!" My notion, I know now, was inadequate, and yet I find it modified and complemented in *Lumen Gentium*.

Attendance at the Swanwick Conference in 1939 and at Subsequent S.C.M. meetings seriously influenced my attitude to worship, at least in its outward expressions. There was a chapel in the grounds at Swanwick where people would go, not only for public worship, but also at odd moments to pray privately. Although some of my compatriots would kneel at prayer, my feeling was still strongly in favor of prayer as a sedentary enterprise; kneeling was the first step on the slippery slope of idolatrous ritualism. However, one day at Swanwick I began to think that I was perhaps being a bit closed-minded on this issue; I took the plunge and dared for the first time in my life— apart from the press ganged incident in the Moray Aisle— to kneel in a place of public worship. What I offered to the Almighty then could scarcely be called "reasonable service"; my mind had gone blank as I tried to *feel* the presence of God; I sensed some detachment from my past habits, but also a residual sense of guilt, for I had at last, as it were, "bowed the knee in the house of Rimmon."

This first bowing of the knee proved to have no ill consequences. In fact I did experience a liberation, and began to explore and benefit from new forms of devotion In a dimly lit brick church in Birmingham I attended a retreat during a missionary conference, when a cadaverous Anglican clergyman, attired in a cassock, talked quietly to us as he sat in a chair before the altar in the center of the sanctuary. The Anglicans, I thought, use atmosphere so effectively. The same atmospheric effect I encountered on a later occasion at a Scottish Episcopal eucharist. The Scots Episcopalians were more High Church than their Anglican counterparts, and on this occasion had called off the incense, out of deference to the visiting Presbyterian contingent, but the celebrants wore vestments and moved about much in the same way as I had seen Catholic priests move in the sanctuary in Hungary. There was a difference, however, between this Scots Episcopal eucharist and the Masses I had attended in Hungary. Here there was a corporate self-consciousness, not unlike what I remembered from my childhood in the very self-contained Presbyterian congregation I attended with my father, but with the addition of an almost sensuous emotional quality, whereas at Mass in Hungary I had felt no atmosphere or sensuous appeal or corporate self-consciousness, although there had at times been a noticeable demonstration of fervor. The whole proceeding had been relaxed, matter of fact, almost taken for granted.

Another benefit I gained from membership in the Student Christian Movement was my introduction to Anglican authors like Hebert, Ramsay, and Dom Gregory Dix, and to prominent Non-Conformist theologians like Jenkins. With the help of such writers I came to realize the necessity of forming a clear idea of the nature of the Church, and of resolving the problem of the relationship between the Mystical Body of Christ and the visible sacramental Church. Not until I had studied Dogmatics and Church History and then experienced Church life in reality as a parish minister was I able to reach a satisfactory solution of these problems.

Meantime in parallel with my theological progress and fostered too by the S.C.M., my emotional life was developing. At Swanwick the Scots and Welsh contingents tended to gang up. In the Welsh group there were several very attractive young women, one of whom in particular made a strong impression on me. Besides being beautiful she showed great animation and theological perception in conversation and discussion, and she was, like myself, a musician. She introduced me to the *penillion,* a kind of improvised descant on a tune, which we occasionally sang together. We would also now and again find enough seclusion and privacy to have a *tête-à-tête.* Without any doubt when I was with her I felt very much in love, and a new dimension had been added to my Hungarian experience. As yet I was unaware of any sexual excitement, but there was bodily resonance of a sort, that moved both of us to embrace and to kiss. Here was a personal companionship that I had not enjoyed before. I hesitate to use the word "relationship" because today it is used so carelessly that it is misleading. It is an abstract noun and in itself tells very little of what is denoted. Today the young use the word to mean one very specific relationship. A young woman, seeking my advice in her troubles, recently told me that she was twenty-two before she had her first "relationship." For her the word "relationship" meant simply "copulationship." In my youth we could still say that we had a deep personal relationship, as I had at this time with the Welsh girl, without suggesting that physical consummation had been reached.

Jim Whyte had also attended the conference at Swanwick. When it ended we came home and spent a month in a cottage in a little glen at the foot of Soutra, a mile or two east of the A68. Ostensibly we were reading next year's texts, but we spent a lot of time wandering about and amusing ourselves, among other things by trying to make raspberry wine. We walked over to Humbie on Sundays to Church where we were befriended by Mr. Bain, the minister, and his wife, who used to send us home with a bag of home-made melting moments. The Bains also comforted us by letting us take baths.

After a week or two we became restless and decided to travel south and visit some of the friends we had made at Swanwick. We would accomplish this by hitch-hiking, at that time a fairly new style of travel. One of our older friends had refined the technique in America and had initiated us in the art. Step one: you turn and face the approaching car, smiling. Step two: as the car passes you wave your hand, pointing the fingers in the direction of travel—never use the thumb. Step three: as soon as the car is past and driver can see you in his mirror you begin to run after the car, for the driver is swithering, "Will I stop or will I not?" When the driver sees you in his mirror you make up his mind for him, and it is almost certain that he will stop. Jim Whyte and I became very proficient in this art. In those days the main arteries were like the quiet country roads of today. I doubt if our technique would be of any use now. The world has changed.

By the evening of the first day of our journey south we got a bit bogged down near Kirk Yetholm, but eventually we reached Northumberland and, exhausted, were on the look-out for a farm where we could buy milk. We found one in the fog near Northallerton. The milk revived us instantly and we walked on a bit further until we came to a country church. It was late and all was quiet. There was an open porch into the church and here we laid down ground-sheets and a blanket on the stone flags and fell sound asleep. I have never slept so well in all my life. Next morning we woke about six o'clock and moved out before anyone found us. Not long after a car stopped and the driver got out, already talkative and welcoming. "You're lucky," he said, "we usually take the road through the town, but today we decided to take the bypass." About an hour later he stopped, and his wife offered to share a picnic breakfast with us. Luckily we were able to contribute fresh tomatoes and some oatcakes. This delightful couple took us with them all the way to Welwyn Garden City. Leif Eriksen's luck was with me again.

After London our next stop was in Reading where we stayed with one of our Swanwick friends, took part in a Baptist prayer meeting, and spent a day visiting Oxford, still a quiet, sleepy university town. Finally we set off for Wales, my ultimate objective. Somewhere near Gloucester we got a lift by two men who were, we guessed, connected with the BBC. There was a bottle of brandy rolling about on the back seat of their powerful and up-market car, which they drove at high speed towards Chester. This suited us very well, and by early evening, having traveled the last lap into North Wales in a sumptuous taxi on its way to pick up a fare in Wales, we arrived at our destination—the home of the girl with whom I was now infatuated. On the afternoon of the day before we left North Wales we climbed a hill near the town. We sat down on the heather and Jim Whyte fell asleep—or perhaps only pretended to do so. I was filled with great excitement. What would we talk about now, what would we do? Although I was only just nineteen years of age the prospect of finding life-long companionship with a woman was becoming quite real, much more than a dream. Perhaps this was because, being an orphan, I was very much on my own and, indeed, my own master. In the past the direction of my life had twice been affected, changed I suspect, by sudden and apparently meaningless deaths. Now on this mountain in Wales I was about to encounter another change of direction, or more correctly change of the potential direction to which I was beginning to look forward—and to me at the time it looked like a calamity. She spoke first. "You know, I do like you very much, we are very much in tune, not just musically but in every way, but I must tell you now: I am engaged to be married to a theological student in Aberystwyth."

On returning home that day we learned that war had been declared. Next day Jim Whyte and I set off on our not too comfortable journey back to Scotland. A motherly woman who gave us a lift as far as Warrington was so concerned about our well-being, that it was with difficulty we dissuaded her from giving us money. Most of the way north and over the Shap we traveled on top of a heap of steel rods on the back of an enormous, very slow-moving lorry. Late at night we got back to our snug little cottage near Humbie, and within a few days were home in Edinburgh getting into gear for our inter-honors year in philosophy.

As far as academic subject matter is concerned, the inter-honors year is only a vague memory. There were some lectures on Spinoza, some on Leibnitz, whom the staff did not seem to take very seriously, and then at some point Kemp Smith held seminars on Kant. The central part of Kant's metaphysical classic, the *Analytic*, bewildered me, and I found Kemp Smith's commentary on this equally indigestible. I got side-tracked by becoming fascinated by a little-known work by a Scottish ultra-idealist philosopher called Ferrier, introduced to me by my Logical Positivist tutor. Prompted by my half-baked understanding of Logical Positivism I would ask questions in the seminar, to be answered by the professor's reiteration of what seemed to me to be a dogmatic statement of his "in and through sense perception" theory. Making this statement he would invariably strike a pencil rhythmically on the table, rotating it at the same time so that both ends received an equal thumping.

By now I was becoming philosophically frustrated. Kant in my view led down a cul-de-sac; there was something superficial and weak about the natural theology that underlay deism; Karl Barth appeared on the horizon and seemed to hold out some hope to one whose quest was for the knowledge of God. Impatient with philosophy and heartened by a superficial acquaintance with Karl Barth and others like him, I began to look forward to entering the theology faculty. As I now know, I was being lured by the phantom of fideism. The outcome of this was that by the middle of the following honors year I decided to forego the normal fourth year in philosophy, take the final exams and be done with it.

But this move into a fideist phase of thinking was not all that moved me to impatience with philosophy and to get on with things. In youth nothing is so distracting from the single-minded pursuit of wisdom as the pursuit of love. Not only had I, thanks to Kant, found myself in a philosophical cul-de-sac but, thanks to the incident on the Welsh mountain, my love life too had reached an impasse; but at the turn of this third year in the faculty of arts I was to experience the most critical encounter of my life. Before that consummation could be reached a short time of transition was still to come.

At the end of the winter term I went over to St Andrews to take part in an undergraduate celebration. In those days, as it still does, St Andrews attracted students from far and near, and my partner on this occasion was an

English girl whom I had already met at Swanwick. I had been quite friendly with her there, but felt none of the deep attraction I had felt for the Welsh girl. Nonetheless I found her attractive. She was a bit more sophisticated than any of the girls I had hitherto met, and she dressed well–for those days almost seductively. In the course of that evening, walking on the sands and then accompanying her home to her room, for the first time in my life I felt serious physical excitement in the presence of a living woman.

The young–and perhaps not so young–of today may find it hard to understand what I say about our reaction to this situation. Many if not most of our generation, brought up in a Christian environment, accepted quite simply that impurity of any kind is sinful. It was not that we had received a great deal of indoctrination on the subject, but more that we had not been exposed to propaganda against purity, as are the young of today; the natural law, written in our hearts as St Paul puts it, had been left uncorrupted by false doctrine. In particular we knew that fornication proper was gravely sinful, and we connected intercourse directly with procreation. Love between a man and a woman could be seen as something sublime in its own right, but the urge towards physical union was clearly tied up primarily with the continuation of our species. The notion that this natural primary purpose could be disconnected from intercourse to allow a man and a woman to get on with enjoying their love, unhindered by the burden of children, had not yet taken hold, at least not in the normal Christian circles in which we moved. The way I thought then was entirely the product of my Presbyterian up-bringing and had no reference at all to Catholic moral teaching, about which I as yet knew virtually nothing.

And so, on that night when we became distinctly aware of the urge of the flesh and of its potential pleasure, we called a halt and said goodbye. And it was goodbye, for there had been no deep attachment such as I had experienced earlier with others. It was the end also of the penultimate stage in my emotional development. I had mounted a plateau.

Almost at once when I returned to what remained of that term and to the Christmas vacation I found that I had attained a kind of emotional neutrality. It was at this time too that Jim Whyte and I and some others discussed the notion of clerical celibacy, no doubt because we were beginning to take account of the existence of the Catholic Church. We knew also of one or two of our own ministers who were unmarried. One such, whom I admired greatly and who gave me a great deal of spiritual help, was Roy Hogg. Although we were all convinced Presbyterians, the notion of celibacy was not abhorrent to us. I think that the general view was that there was no real issue: each man must follow his own temperament. On the whole, however, we tended to think that experience of marriage and family life was valuable to a minister. My own view at the time was much in line with this, but I remember saying that I felt no inclination to either state, either as a future minister or as a layman: I could imagine being perfectly happy either married or single, and I believe that I had reached this emotional balance because I was now able to imagine what marriage could mean.

St Paul, exhorting the Thessalonians to be watchful in preparation for the coming of the Lord, wrote, "It is when people are saying, 'How quiet and peaceful it is' that the worst suddenly happens." For me at this point in my life, when all seemed quiet and emotionally settled something suddenly happened, but it could not be described as "the worst." It was the best that has ever happened to me, although it was pregnant with much suffering as well as with indescribable joy. No sooner had the spring term begun than after a debate in the Men's Union I was introduced by a theological student to Helen MacLeod, and the three of us went off for a meal in the Chinese restaurant in Chambers Street. Helen had spent some time at university, but returned home to Applecross where her father was parish minister to help with two little

Austrian Jewish refugees; now she was back in Edinburgh to pursue a course in Domestic Science at Atholl Crescent. On this our first meeting I felt an electric shock run immediately through my whole system. Her personality struck me violently before I had even taken in what she looked like. Her over-riding quality was the sheer transparency of her character, and she was robustly beautiful with a beauty that flowed from bone structure and carriage supported by the neatly muscular figure of a gymnast. The easy mobility of her body was seen too in her face, and her eyes, vividly blue, sparkled with an expression that was gently kind and always on the brink of laughter. The plateau of neutrality which I believed I had now reached in my emotional life was not destroyed by this unexpected encounter, but became the starting point for the life that now opened out before me. As the following years were to prove it was a life devoted above all to the building up and perfecting of marriage.

After our first meeting early in 1940 we met each other at every possible opportunity. On most evenings I would cycle across town and we would sit and talk or else walk around the town, often through the Dean village. Not long after we had met we were crossing the Dean Bridge late at night; clouds were rolling across the sky letting through the very occasional shaft of moonlight; I don't know whether it was the mood of the sky or a subconscious surfacing of the sad elements in my past life, but I found myself telling Helen that if she shared life with me I might bring her a lot of unhappiness. This may have been a genuine premonition, or perhaps was just a rational guess, for all of our lives are bound to contain sadness as well as happiness. Her response to my expression of romantic *angst* was to embrace me with great warmth.

My preoccupation with this serious affair of the heart joined forces with my impatience with Kantian philosophy, indeed with all philosophy, and confirmed my decision to forego the final year in philosophy and begin theological studies in autumn 1941. In one sense I was right:

the deism of the natural theologians whom I was beginning to read was unsatisfying, and Karl Barth's emphasis on the primacy of faith in the revealed word of God was inspiring. As yet I had not reached a final resolution of the relationship between knowledge of God through reason and knowledge through faith, but I now found satisfaction in a type of fideism—that there is a direct knowledge of God imparted by himself, and that salvation lies in this knowledge. Besides this the prospect of getting down to theology and taking up active work in a parish as soon as possible was linked for me with the prospect of marrying Helen. For the time being, however, during what was left of my philosophy course I suffered from serious distraction. I did get my degree but paid for the distraction and the forfeiting of the final year by having to settle for a poor grade.

That was fifty-six years ago; looking back I have no regrets, for I have been able to continue the pursuit of wisdom all my life, while the concentrated pursuit of love during the final year of our courtship taught us both what could not have been learned in academia, and which is better learned early on in life. We learned above all that the two ends of marriage are inextricably bound together. For the first time I discovered intense joy in a woman's presence converging with powerful physical desire. Union of the persons became identical with union in the physical sense, as when we say, "she hid the love letter upon her person." At the same time we were well aware that complete union of persons was potentially procreative. The only satisfactory conclusion to such love as we felt was marriage in which the partners were committed to all the responsibilities which marital union demanded. The notion of consummating love while excluding the possibility of procreation appeared to us as irrational. Contraception was not widespread then as it is now, but we had heard of it, and saw it as a preposterous flying in the face of the contingencies set by nature. Moral behavior is rational behavior, that is acting in conformity with the way things are. They are as they are because God created them so, and to respect the order of nature is to submit to the will of God. Our abhorrence of contraception, of the severance of the unitive from the procreative end of marriage derived not from knowledge of Catholic moral teaching, of which we were still ignorant, nor yet from positive teaching in the Reformed tradition, but from a strong sense of its irrationality. Many today would think this a very simplistic notion of natural law, but it was a notion that we could never eradicate from our consciousness—from our conscience. St Paul was right when he said that the law is written in the hearts of all men and women. All people possess a fundamental instinct for the law; this is not the same as the instinct that directs primitive urges, but is a deeper kind of instinct, an intuition of the order of things, pointing to the One who orders. Fallen as we are, there are times when superficial instincts war with the deeper sense of natural law, and it is to cope with this contingency that we have to rely on the use of practical reason, that is on conscience. Helen and I were fortunate in that we had never been subjected to the anaesthesis of conscience by false teaching.

Like all people we faced temptation. The solution was either to rationalize our way out of the demands of natural law and make some compromise, as is so commonly accepted nowadays, or to get married. Fortunately my parents had left sufficient funds to allow us to survive for about four years, and so we decided to marry at the end of my arts course and before I entered the Divinity Faculty.

During the period of courtship and waiting we learned a very great deal. In particular we learned of the depth and intensity of the passion that can find satisfaction only in the fullness of marriage. While convinced of the primacy in the natural order of procreation, we became ever more acutely aware of the fact that there is a unique spiritual quality about the personal union that is in marriage. This union begins even before consummation and as the experience of later life proves, extends on far beyond the time when procreation or even intercourse is relevant. Although consummation was yet to come, perhaps because of that, we were learning of the depth and extent of giving ourselves to each other "without reservation," as the *Catholic Rite of Marriage* now expresses it.

It so happened that at this time I read Helen Waddell's version of the life of Abelard. I was startled at the similarity between our love and that of Heloise and Abelard. We could both identify with the almost idolatrous mutual offering of these two. The author puts these words into Abelard's mouth—"and having thee having nothing else besides"—which is precisely the kind of statement we should make to God alone. I felt a kind of jealousy of God, fearing that he might be liable to demand the diversion of my total attention away from Helen. One of my friends, perceptively no doubt but also perhaps with a shade of presumption, hinted to me that our love was a bit obsessional, especially as my intention was to serve in a dedicated ministry. Like Job I stood by my affirmation of innocence from any fault in this respect, for I was convinced that genuine marriage must contain this idolatrous flavor, for it is a form of worship—at least it had to be the veneration of an icon of the creative love of God.

In spite of my conviction that in our attitude to marriage we were on the right lines, I became uneasy, but was unable to formulate my problem intellectually. My friend's remark may have set off in my mind a subliminal assessment of the problems that work in the ministry could put in the way of marriage as I conceived it; the episode ended not in any rational deduction, but in a momentary and rather frightening fantasy, which I immediately and successfully suppressed, so that the memory of it returned only very much later in life. It was while reading the story of Heloise and Abelard that the thought struck me: "The only way out of my problem would be if Helen were to die." The thought was so horrific that it jolted me back to reality. We were both sure of one thing: whatever problems might arise our vocation was marriage.

5

In summer 1940 Helen and I attended an S.C.M. conference in Durham. The year before at Swanwick I had met a girl with whom I had become enamored, only to discover quite soon that she was already engaged to be married. Less than a year later I was living in a totally different emotional world, burning with love for a girl who responded completely to my passion, and who was both free and willing to marry me. Very soon after we first met we more or less assumed that we would get married; certainly after this conference, during which we had been thrown very close together, we no longer asked the question, "Shall we get married?" but "When will we get married?" We decided to marry in the following summer.

Very often throughout that year of our engagement we would meet at nine o'clock on Sunday mornings and attend the Communion Service that took place in the Memorial Chapel at St Cuthbert's at the west end of Prince's Street. Apart from the powerful part that must always be played by simple natural passions in drawing two young people together, there was no doubt that our love was fired also by the vital ingredient of our common faith and desire to serve the Church, to be active in the work of the Kingdom. This meeting on Sundays at St Cuthbert's was therefore of great importance. I had already been influenced as a youngster at Corstorphine Old Parish Church by the solid Presbyterian High Churchmanship of Dr. Oswald Milligan. This High Churchmanship was superbly represented by Dr. Kirkpatrick who conducted these Communion Services in St Cuthbert's. I think they were celebrated every Sunday. The Memorial Chapel in a kind of crypt was small and had a Communion Table which I think stood against the wall of the apse. Most significant, however, was the rite used by the minister—a little booklet entitled *É Theia Leitourgia*, which was based upon the second century liturgy of Hippolytus. These ancient texts supplied the impulse to the liturgical revival in the Church of Scotland which became embodied in the *Book of Common Order* of 1940. Helen and I were not aware of the origin of the text of this service, which we delighted to attend, but were carried away by its ring of biblical truth. These Communion Services, as I now know, were almost indistinguishable from the present Second Eucharistic Prayer of the Roman Mass, which likewise derives from Hippolytus.

Our encounter with the genuine High Church movement in the Church of Scotland, that found expression in these Sunday morning Communion Services at St Cuthbert's influenced our thinking in planning our wedding, which took place on July 17 in the Kirk of the Greyfriars, which stands in an ancient graveyard at the head of Candlemaker Row, separated by a high wall from my old school and only a few hundred yards distant from the Old Quad of the University. The sun was blazing over Edinburgh when at the gate of the Kirk I met my best man, Stuart Harris—whose Plymouth Brethren fundamentalism had jerked me, while still a schoolboy, away from liberal Protestantism to an appreciation of the concept of revelation. In a mood of unusual tranquillity, both clad in kilts, we walked into the church, took our place and awaited the arrival of the bride. The marriage service was conducted by the Reverend James Stewart, minister of North Morningside Church. He was once described by a colleague as "the last of the Mohicans," by which he meant the last of the great evangelical preachers in the Church of Scotland. At our wedding he was assisted by one of our friends, Crawford Miller, who had very recently been ordained, and was the quintessence of High Churchmanship. His function on this occasion was to preside at a Communion Service which was dovetailed onto the marriage service. It did not strike either of us at the time that this was an innovation. Our dear friend the Reverend Roy Hogg told me at the reception that he had brought an

English friend with him who wanted to know what a typical Scots Presbyterian wedding was like. "I didn't expect," the Englishman said, "the typical Presbyterian wedding to be a Nuptial Mass."

As we moved out into the sunlight Helen asked me, "Have I married a cripple?" "I hope not," I replied. "Then what is wrong with your feet?" I listened to my tread; sure enough, one foot sounded clearly on the flagstones, the other was silent. The day before I had bought new shoes, but they were not quite a pair: one had a leather sole and the other was of rubber. With this imbalanced gait I began my married life.

Helen's bridesmaids were her sister Christine MacLeod, her cousin Catherine Maciver, and my ten-year old sister, Margaret. Stuart Harris, the best man, made a delightful speech, toasting the bridesmaids. With his accustomed literary resourcefulness Stuart applied to them the words of Sappho: "The fairest apples, gleaming from the topmost branch, which the gatherers forgot—forgot?— nay, they could not reach them." Some years later he reached one of them and married Catherine. Thus Stuart, as well as being my oldest friend, became my cousin by marriage, so that his children and mine are second cousins. (I write this recollection of that wonderful day in July 1940 three days after attending Stuart's funeral. I had better get a move on.)

The first few days of our honeymoon were spent in Oban where Crawford Miller was minister of St Columba's. He had found a place for us in a guest house, which turned out to be a guest house with a difference, in that the residents deviated a little from normality. It was a kind of nursing home. We were assigned to a table where one lady insisted on pushing her chair back about two feet, only to be repeatedly pushed in again by an attendant. We soon moved on and made a tour of some of Helen's West Highland relations. The most memorable part of our honeymoon was that spent in Fort William where Helen's uncle Isaac Maciver, a lapsed Free Presbyterian, was doctor.

He was doctor to and a great friend of Monsignor MacMaster, whose housekeeper Miss Johnstone entertained us royally, introducing us to the use of carragheen which she had sent from her home on the Island of Barra. The Catholic Church stood exactly opposite the Maciver's house. For the first time in this country I met Catholicism, and was fortunate to do so in Lochaber where Catholics and Protestants live together in perfect harmony. Many people in Great Britain think of Catholicism as a foreign importation, but in parts of the Highlands and Islands of Scotland one becomes aware of the universality of the Catholic Church and its historical continuity back through the Middle Ages and beyond.

We had found a flat in Saxe-Coburg Place, a half-completed rectangle of terraced houses designed by the artist Raeburn. At the bottom of the garden ran a loop of the Water of Leith. We were on the top flat, with an open view westwards to Corstorphine Hill. On the east side of our sitting-room, a window overlooked the rectangular garden, which had locked gates. This view, framed in the perfectly proportioned window with its original small panes and astricles, was comfortably controlled and urbane. The contrast between the open view to sunsets on the west and the limited, framed view on the east reminded me of lectures in the German class on the distinction between the Romantic and the Classical outlook on life.

On first calling at this house we discovered that it was the family home of Ronnie Selby Wright, the Radio Padre and minister of the Canongate Kirk, whom we both knew quite well. You cannot go far in Scotland–if you are a Scot–without meeting someone with whom you have some sort of connection. Like many terraced houses in the New Town, which in times past housed a single family, this house was now let out in flats and rooms. Recently I read a novel by Alice Thomas Ellis, the setting of which is a roomery in faded Chelsea. I thought I recognized the people of Saxe-Coburg Place in her characters. I remember a diminutive, elderly spinster who inhabited a room beneath us. She came up, in a cheerful mood one day to "borrow" sugar, sat on a flimsy occasional table which collapsed under her, and then walked out into the linen cupboard. There were also dark sides to life in that part of the New Town. In the basement lived a widow with her son who was a street orderly or "scaffie" in the normal politically incorrect language of those days. He used to ask me if I could give him a pair of old strides, that is trousers, hence he was known as "Strides." But poor "Strides" was a little off-beat and sadly ended up with his head in the gas oven.

Outside in the Square one could see interesting sights. There was one aristocratic young gentleman whom I observed running round the Square shouting vigorously, but almost inaudibly because, out of consideration for others whom he did not want to disturb, he held a handkerchief stuffed into his mouth. He was indeed a gentleman, and he wrote erudite letters to *The Scotsman*. An old lady who lived in a nursing home used to be locked into the garden on sunny days. She would speak to all who passed by, giving them notes to be delivered to relations and lawyers requesting that she be taken home. She always bid people farewell in the same way: "Shadows of the evening flit across the sky." Her nickname was "Shadows of the evening." Another feature of the Square was a hostel for girls who had got into trouble. Two very dear old ladies, whom we got to know later when we returned to this Square, named this hostel, "The Home for Tiresome Girls." All in all the Square was a wonderful place in which to live.

For a wedding present our best man, Stuart Harris, had decorated our flat. The bedroom walls were painted with thick white emulsion into which he had inscribed, using his finger, a repeating design composed of our intertwined initials. Jim White had asked what we would like and remembering the beautiful little Madonna we had given our leader at the end of our visit to Germany, I suggested that he give us something like that. He could not find anything suitable in Edinburgh, but happening to be in London that summer got what he wanted in a shop beside Westminster Cathedral. When we opened the crate we were surprised to find an eighteen inch bronze Immaculata, one foot firmly clamped upon the serpent's head. We placed the statue on the sideboard, and at Christmas set up a crib in front of it, illumined with two small candles.

At the beginning of October the new session began and I entered the Faculty of Divinity. Every morning I climbed up the steep ascent of Church Lane towards Princes Street and then up the Mound to New College, where the enormous statue of John Knox stands guard, his outstretched hand pointing in admonition at each generation of students as they pass through the gate.

At nine o'clock we had lectures in early Church history, and I made the acquaintance of St Ignatius of Antioch, St Polycarp and St Clement. I learned about St Cyprian and his dispute over the efficacy of heretical baptism, and how Stephen, Bishop of Rome, settled the matter. I learned about Docetism and various forms of Gnosticism; of the Montanists, the Donatists and the Arians. The plot thickened; we learned of the struggles which ended in the sad Monophysite schism, and of the intrigues and terminological quibbles attending the rise of Caesaro-papism and the Byzantine Empire. To me this was a completely new world and I began to see my own little pocket of Presbyterian Christianity in perspective. The notion dawned that the Church was a mighty river, flowing uninterrupted down the ages, carrying upon its stream the healing water of life irrigating the waste lands of the whole world.

To my astonishment and sorrow I discovered that not all my fellow students shared my enjoyment of these lectures, delivered by Professor Burleigh. Walking down the Mound one afternoon a classmate remarked that these lectures supplied us with no sermon material. On another occasion the professor commented, in private, that ninety per cent of the students were not really interested in truth, but only in learning a trade—how to produce two sermons per Sunday for the rest of their lives. Even allowing for a little cynical exaggeration by this professor, it was true that many students considered this delving into long past Church history a waste of time for a minister of the gospel today. All that they wanted to do—and it was a laudable object—was to provide Sunday by Sunday an edifying discourse based on a scriptural text.

By the end of the year we had arrived at the fifth century—the Council of Chalcedon. Professor Burleigh considered that by that time all that was worth knowing about Church history had already happened. From then on there was just a reshuffling of the same old issues. Thus he was in no hurry to cover the ground. It was more important, in his view, to study doctrinal development down to Chalcedon thoroughly, for that was Church history. One day he concluded his lecture with a casual aside, uttered as he left the lectern: "St Augustine," he said, "accepted Scripture as the Word of God because the Church told him it was the Word of God. Work that out for yourselves."

Our chief task in this class was to write a long essay on any topic we chose suggested by our reading of Augustine's *Confessions*. Having impatiently ditched philosophy for the study of theology, I now found my old preoccupation with the relation between reason and faith again taking center stage. Near the beginning of his book Augustine writes:

> Grant me, Lord, to know and understand which is first, to call on thee or to praise thee? And, again, to know thee or to call on thee? For who can call on thee, not knowing thee? For he that knoweth thee not, may call on thee as other than thou art, Or, is it rather, that we call on thee that we may know thee? But how shall they call on him in whom they have not believed, or how shall they believe without a preacher.

This was the text of my essay and the question encapsulated became my main theological interest.

The question was treated systematically in the first year Divinity class conducted by Professor John Baillie, author of *Our Knowledge of God*. His course was a kind of philosophy of religion, during which he expounded the history of theology, instructing us on the classic solutions to theological problems. We learned about the great medieval synthesis of faith and science–the baptism of Aristotle by Aquinas–of St Bonaventure, in whom the Stoic and Platonist stream of thought erupted in the Middle Ages, of St Anselm, whose *Monologion* and *Proslogion* became my favorite texts. It seemed to me that Anselm's *Fides quaerens intellectum* was the best possible slogan for a theologian. Faith was God-given and primary, but man had to think about his faith and try to understand it. Man did not climb up from reason to faith as the natural theologians like Paley suggested, but, having faith tried to explain why and how he possessed it, and to refute the arguments of unbelievers, especially when they denied the existence of God.

At this stage in my theological growth I was still a bit muddled, and there was a large element of unsound fideism in my theory. There was a debate in the Divinity Faculty at Glasgow to which Edinburgh students were invited. The motion–which I had provided–was "That natural theology precludes faith." I thought that I was being very clever when I affirmed: "All arguments in the end rely upon a *reductio ad absurdum* of the contrary proposition"–a notion I had picked up from a very erudite lecturer in the ancient philosophy class–"and so, to prove that God exists, as natural theology maintains we can, we would have to say, 'Suppose that God does not exist,' which is a supposition that a believer may not make. Therefore natural theology precludes faith."

My stance was not, however, undiluted fideism, and I repudiated also the sentimentalist school of Schleiermacher; in my view we did not have a direct mystical experience of God, but had to rely on his revelation for real knowledge of him and his will. Reason operated in the systematizing of the knowledge faith supplied; but reason—natural consciousness—operated also independently of faith and demonstrated that God is. In fact it is, I believed, in response to this rational metaphysical intuition that we are morally obliged to decide to call upon him or not to call upon him, that is to make an act of faith—to begin to pray. And our fundamental prayer is: "Lord, show me your face." While still at New College I did arrive at a notion of the capacity of reason to prove the existence of God that was very much in line with St Thomas's Five Ways. God's existence was deduced from knowledge of the things that are seen. I think I had put my own slant on it, however. What impressed my mind most was not simply that there is a Prime Mover, but that he must be also the Prime Mind. Creating, initiating motion, seemed to me to imply that the Mover grasped intellectually all that is. My own experience of contingent being was basically my sense of very limited intellect, and the certainty that I never could, nor could any created being, understand all. But there must be, so I thought, an intelligence that knows no bafflement, that is at rest in perfect knowledge. If I am not the perfect intelligence—and I know that I am not—then God is.

In the first year of the course we began study of the Scriptures. As one would expect in a theological college within the Reformed tradition this study was central and foundational; and it was guided by first class scholars—as were the studies I have already mentioned. In those days New College professors were theological and scholarly heavy-weights. New Testament studies began with the presentation of the Synoptic Problem and a sentence by sentence examination of the Gospel according to Mark, presided over by Professor Curtis—a bit dull and long-winded, but very thorough. In the second year we took St Paul's Letter to the Galatians to pieces, directed by Professor W.T. Manson. More important even than the detail of his teaching was his insistence that scripture scholarship must proceed from the standpoint of faith.

From that standpoint he maintained that the New Testament writings possessed a unity, the key to which was the apostolic preaching (*kerygma*). While using every insight that textual criticism could provide, Professor Manson totally rejected the approach of most nineteenth-century biblical scholars. For him liberal theological humanism in scripture study was already outmoded. Bultmann's star was only beginning to ascend, but I think that Professor Manson tried to inoculate us against that Gnostic poison too, but as is proved by statements made today by reformed Churchmen in Scotland, he was not wholly successful.

My understanding and appreciation of the Old Testament I owe to two men of outstanding scholarship and teaching expertise—Professor Norman Porteous and Professor Oliver Rankin. As with the New Testament teachers, these men combined top-class critical scholarship with a genuine commitment to traditional Christian Faith—to the ancient Creeds of the Church. In the Old Testament classes we were pointed to the beginnings of revelation in the religion of a primitive people whose worship, in spite of human limitations stood, in marked contrast to the pagan cults around them. Their religion may have been primitive in some respects, but it was genuine in essence. "Listen, Israel: Yahweh our God is one Yahweh. You shall love Yahweh your God with all your heart, with all your soul, with all your strength." Even before this formulation in the Deuteronomic recension of the Law, the seed of true religion was present in Abraham's hunch that God was above and beyond all that is on the earth and in the heavens. Spurred on by the sense of God's transcendence, Abraham left the sophisticated but earth-bound Sumerian civilization behind him, and set out on a pilgrimage which we now continue some four millennia later. Like a city dweller returning to visit the earth, the water, the grass and cattle of his ancestral croft, so we returned to the world of the Old Testament to breathe the air of the promises made to Abraham and to his descendants forever.

When we came to read the Hebrew texts of the historical books, Professor Rankin's lectures became entertaining as well as instructive. He was an anthropologist as well as a biblical theologian, and drawing on his experience as a country parish minister he could relate ancient Canaanite practices to some of the ongoings still to be found in rural Scotland. Through his interpretation every narrative in the Old Testament became like a scene from a contemporary play. I will never forget the words with which he introduced the narrative of David's designating Solomon as his heir. "David was in bed; he was old, and he was cold, and he was doddery..." Professor Rankin proceeded to explain how Nathan and Bathsheba manipulated the situation, not neglecting to tell us that it was an accepted practice to put an attractive virgin into bed to help keep up a doddery old man's blood pressure. In this case it was Abishag of Shunem who provided the necessary medication, but to no effect. Clearly it was time that something be done about the succession.

Professor Rankin's anthropological approach to the Old Testament, his ability to depict the human dimension in the word of God, made some students doubt his orthodoxy. There is a hint of this in a verse of a College song which ran:

> 'Tis Rankin's delight to reveal Moses' plight
> For he'd no copyright on his stories, he thinks.
> It really was shabby to crib Hammurabi,
> and copy from old Babylonian ginks.

Another light which this professor threw on the Old Testament was his demonstration that the priestly caste in Israel, by their constant upholding of the ancient traditions and their care of the Temple worship, were as important as the prophets in molding the spirituality of the people. Such enlightenment was significant in a Presbyterian theological College, where the tendency had been to stress the figure of the prophet, who in the eyes of many was seen as the prototype of the New Testament presbyter. Off the record, as it were, that is apart from the formal content of his lectures, Professor Rankin would encourage us to avoid–when we took up our work in parishes–becoming enslaved by the fashion of the age. We, like the priests of the Old Testament, stood within the flow of a timeless faith and of a liturgy which possessed a timeless quality. We ought to try to assimilate our prayers and sermons to the spirit of that tradition. He advised us never to be long-winded in public prayer: a short prayer of adoration and then of penitence, ending with a collect was quite enough to start with. Intercessions should be composed of a few direct petitions ending with the Lord's Prayer. On at least one occasion he conducted a retreat for his class, when he celebrated Holy Communion. This was conducted in the High Church tradition, as he used the same models as I had been accustomed to on Sunday mornings in St Cuthbert's. On these occasions he attired himself in a cassock with a row of small buttons down the front. I admired this teacher so much that when I was ordained I had a similar cassock made for myself by a Catholic tailor in Chambers Street, who probably sewed on each button to the accompaniment of a Hail Mary. My friends called this vestment the "popey cassock." It cost £9.

The study of medieval Church history came in the second year and was direct by Professor Hugh Watt. His style was quite different from that of Professor Burleigh. We took a great leap from the world of Chalcedon and *The City of God* across the Dark Ages, regaining ecclesiastical consciousness in the early Middle Ages amid the lurid lights and horrific shapes of corruption in the Church, but looking expectantly towards the dawn of the Renaissance and evangelical enlightenment. It was good old-fashioned stuff, very scholarly in its way, but with no confusion or hesitation. All was black and white. I have forgotten much of the content of the lectures, but in my memory the picture of Zwingli eating sausages in the middle of Lent in defiance of the Church will never be erased. It was as though the professor were himself relishing these sausages in front of our eyes. And there was the magnificent declamation: "Hordes of cardinals traversed Europe, their retinues full of women disguised as page-boys." In a modern context this would no doubt have to be amended to run: "...their retinues full of page-boys disguised as women."

Towards the end of this year Professor Watt became Moderator of the General Assembly of the Church of Scotland, which prevented him completing the session. Professor Burleigh stood in and gave us a few seminars on Luther, to whom on one occasion he referred as "Adolf Luther." For my part I took a dislike to Luther on account of his attitude to the Peasants' War. Calvin, on the other hand, seemed to me to be a very great theologian and a very sane man. My view of this period became colored, however, by my chance purchase on a second-hand bookstall of a copy of the *Catechism of the Council of Trent*. This book became regular reading when eventually I settled in a parish.

The pattern of our college day was this: lectures ran from nine until one. At 10:45 we assembled for prayers in the Martin Hall overlooking Princes Street and the Forth. There would be a scripture reading, a prayer and a hymn. We took it in turns to lead this public worship. At one o'clock we had dinner. It was said that long ago a student had died of malnutrition, and so an endowment had been made to enable all students to have a substantial meal at very low cost. Certainly we got an excellent three-course meal. Grace after the meal was always sung; and if it had been particularly heavy—soup, steak pie and rice pudding—the precentor would most likely choose the doxology which ended:

> *And all that in me is*
> *be stirred up his holy name*
> *to magnify and bless.*

After dinner someone would play the common room piano, and we would lounge about there for a while, and then go off to study in the library or at home.

There was a theological society and a missionary society, the activities of which were an over-spill from our formal academic work. There was a musical society too where we sang not only liturgical music but many lighter works as well. One of our number, Walter Ferrier, who later became a highly respectable parish minister in North Berwick, was a gifted pianist, who could turn his talent towards Vaudeville. A group of us, under his tutelage, used to put on shows for old folks' clubs. Life at New College was far from dull.

The musical society was directed by Professor G.T. Thomson, the most colorful character on the staff. Legend had it that when a young minister he had gone to a fancy dress ball dressed as an Arab Sheik. He had served as an Arabic interpreter—so it was said—with Bedouin in the First World War—about whom he told several earthy stories. It was alleged also that as a young minister he used to parade up and down in his manse garden, dressed in a kilt, playing the bagpipes, a practice to which the local Wee Frees objected. This was ironic, for he of all the professors at New College was the closest to the Wee Frees in doctrine. He was probably the last genuine Calvinist in the Church of Scotland, and to him I owe a very great debt.

He was professor of Dogmatic Theology, and it was not until well on in our course that we became subjected to his influence. He re-introduced us to the perennial question of the relation between reason and faith, and discussed the distinction between philosophy and theological science. He talked about the truth that is accessible to natural reason, which he contrasted with the truth that is revealed by God's word and then systematized by theological science. Someone in the class asked him if, when he made this distinction, he was speaking as a philosopher or as a theologian. He adjusted his monocle, paused for a moment and replied: "I am speaking as a human being." We didn't quite know what to make of that. I think it was his way of saying, that truth from both sources is required if the soul of man is to be satisfied, and that there can be no contradiction between the truths of reason and those that are revealed. The students were required to write a long essay on a subject connected with these lectures. I chose as title for mine, *Fides Quarens Intellectum*. Karl Barth had written a short work on Anselm, using the same title. To help me with my exercise I translated Barth's little book but when the essay was completed I lost the manuscript of my translation. It never occurred to me that a publisher might be interested in it.

When he got down to the study of specific topics his method was to follow the text of a German dogmatic treatise, comment upon it after each section and initiate discussion. On the subject of unbelief and judgment a student lamented over the hard line of Calvinist orthodoxy. "Surely we cannot believe that if a person rejects the Gospel he will be condemned for ever." The professor's response was immediate and very clear: "A Kirk without a Hell isn't worth a damn!" On another occasion a student, defending his position, unwisely claimed a too close familiarity with the Holy Spirit. "I am quite sure that what I say is true, professor, the Holy Spirit convinces me." "The Holy Spirit!" exclaimed Professor Thomson, "That's a bird you want to watch!"

To the Dogmatics class I owe my discovery of the *Westminster Confession*. Having been brought up in the more liberal Reformed tradition, as a child I had never had to learn the *Shorter Catechism,* which derived from this Confession, and so had never been exposed to pure Calvinism. As the session drew to a close we discussed how much of this classic Calvinist document was still acceptable to the Church of Scotland. In the end arguments turned on the denotation of the phrase, "the fundamental doctrines of the Christian faith contained in the said Confession," which phrase is to be found in the formula, according to which all ministers and elders of the Church of Scotland, at their ordination, profess their belief in the fundamentals of the Christian faith, while being allowed "liberty of opinion on such points of doctrine as do not enter into the substance of the faith." Most, if not all of us assumed that some of the doctrines enunciated in this Confession were not of the substance of the faith, but the professor disagreed: "the substance of the faith contained in the said Confession" meant that this Confession of faith was the substance of the faith. In other words the phrase "liberty of opinion on such points of doctrine as do not enter into the substance of the faith" referred only to doctrines that did not appear in the Confession. The exemption did not touch any doctrine that was formulated in the Confession. Argument continued in class but no satisfactory conclusion was reached. Next day the professor entered and began at once: "Gentlemen, I owe you an apology. I've looked up the whole thing carefully. You're right: since 1892 you can believe any damned thing you like."

This conclusion was one that I could not accept. I was sure that one could discover a core of doctrine that was assured. Moreover, I thought that I was on the right trail, which had earlier been sign-posted in discussions we had in the Divinity class with Professor John Baillie. Baillie had once remarked that if anyone ever thought of writing a Ph.D. thesis, a suitable subject would be "The difference between the mode of operation of the Holy Spirit in the Old Testament and in the New." He knew of nothing that had been written on that subject. The brightest member of our class—it was Jim Whyte—observed that he found in the library two books of essays by Dr. Wotherspoon and others entitled *The Pentecostal Gift* and *What Happened at Pentecost*. I immediately took these books from the library and learned from them something that profoundly affected my thoughts on the nature of the Church and set me off on a line of inquiry which promised as well to lead to a resolution of the problem of finding out what was the solid core of Christian belief. Assurance of faith, I began to see, was inextricably linked with the Church as the vehicle of the Holy Spirit who, as "the spirit of unity is in naething contrareous to himself." These two books were the product of the theological High Church movement in the Old Church of Scotland before the union of 1929, a movement that derived from the Oxford Movement.

The theologians and parish ministers who followed this school of thought had come to believe that the Holy Spirit no longer operated in a sporadic way as in the Old Testament—not unlike the way he operates with the modern charismatics—when the Spirit of Yahweh would "clothe himself" temporarily in the flesh of the prophet or champion, utter oracles or perform mighty deeds, and then depart. The Holy Spirit now operated through a permanent dwelling in the whole Body of Christ, the Church. The Holy Spirit was Christ working all the time through the Mystical Body. His power was really present in the physical sacramental media, and his voice was to be heard in the contemporary preaching of the gospel by human voices.

At the close of my theological course I had come to look for the authentic word of God, for the "substance of the faith" not so much in the texts of confessions of faith, nor even in the text of scripture, as in the living voice of the teaching ministry in the Church. Assurance of faith, I was now convinced, could not be separated from reliance upon the Church. The authority and unity of the word of truth required authority and unity in the Church. I found too, that this notion was expressed in the formula used at the ordination of ministers and elders. Doctrinal reformulation, it was affirmed, must be in agreement with the Word of God, that is the scriptures, "of which agreement the Church itself shall be sole judge." The Church of Scotland, it seemed, acknowledged a real, contemporary magisterium.

And so I finished the theological course of studies at New College in a spirit of optimism. By ordination I believed I would come to see clearly the outline of the apostolic *kerygma* and receive the strength effectively to preach this Gospel and administer the dominical sacraments of Baptism and Holy Communion. First I would have to spend a year as a Probationer, before becoming eligible for ordination. Early in 1945 I was licensed to preach the Gospel by the Presbytery of Edinburgh at St Giles's–in the same Moray Aisle from which I had fled in terror fifteen years earlier.

6

During the three and a half years I spent in New College—I had tucked in an extra semester on account of my entering the College innocent of the Greek language—it was not only my intellectual grasp of the Faith that grew; our marriage also developed. Tangible proof of this was the birth in June at the beginning of the first summer vacation of our son Nicolas. We called him Nicolas chiefly because at the time I was impressed by the writings of Nicolas Berdyaev and had just discovered Nicolas of Cusa. His entry into this world was attended—as was his leaving it twenty-two years later—by sore trial and pain. Helen endured thirty-two hours labor, during which time she was left on her own by the three sisters, ex-hospital matrons, who ran the little nursing home which our doctor had recommended. In those days husbands were not expected, probably not permitted, to be around at the time of their wife's confinement. On the evening before the birth, having been dismissed after spending an hour with Helen, I decided to go to the King's Theatre where there was a performance of *The Magic Flute*. This was the first time I had ever seen and heard that opera. I was delighted, especially by the Papageno/Pagagena theme. My next visit to the nursing home allowed me to extend the joyful mood of this theme into real life for, following an anterior-occipital presentation, Nicolas had at last been born. I was allowed to hold him whereupon I felt an overwhelming sense of responsibility, and recalled—I hope without presumption—our Lord's words, "for their sakes I sanctify myself." I greeted the child's arrival with the song I had heard, sung by Papageno the night before:

> *'Tis love they say, love only,*
> *that makes the world go round...*

Most people have the tune in their heads, so there is no need to print the score here.

Within a few weeks we were receiving in our mail literature advertising contraceptives. We found these leaflets distasteful and threw them into the bucket. It had never occurred to us that the frustration of the natural biological end of marital intercourse could be anything other than a kind of anticipated abortion. In the months that followed until the conception of our second child, David, who was born fully three years later, we often found it hard to remain true to what seemed to us the clear demands of natural law for, considering the very painful labor Helen endured before the first birth, we were sure that we ought not to have another child just yet. David's birth was very different. For a start he was born in much pleasanter surroundings, in the Chalmers Street Hospital. When he was put into my arms the nurse looked astonished.

"You know how to hold him!" she exclaimed.

"Well he is the second," I answered.

"You both look so young."

This same little nurse, Helen told me next day, was a Catholic, and she told Helen she had lit a candle for David in the Sacred Heart Church, which was very near.

Looking back I can see that the periodic abstinence which true marriage requires is as important in the creating of a perfect union as is the blessing of physical ecstasy.

Since schooldays my chief recreation had been singing. During my student days I sang occasionally as a professional, my principal achievement being to sing the tenor solos in a performance of Handel's *Messiah* in the Usher Hall; but I much preferred to sing as part of an ensemble. While still at school I had joined the Reid Choir, conducted by Sir Donald Tovey, when I entered a world of indescribable beauty with the performance of Haydn's *Creation*. Towards the end of my time at New College I joined the Edinburgh University Musical Society. In that year they prepared and performed Mozart's *Requiem*. I think that this was an even deeper musical experience for me than the Haydn. Perhaps not, for I think that Haydn is probably greater than Mozart; but at that particular point in my life Mozart's work spoke to me musically and also theologically. With the music I imbibed the spirit of the liturgy for which it had been composed. It erased from my soul the gloomy images of death and the hazy hereafter of my childhood, and replaced these with a sense of the continuity of life after death and our real communication with the departed.

At that time there was in this Musical Society a student destined for the ministry also, but a bit younger than me, Ian Pitt Watson, who was a very competent musician. He got together seven others in the Society, who were particularly keen, and could really sing, and formed what at first we called "The Wee Choir." We sang for our own pleasure, but also went here and there singing often to raise money for charity or simply to sing in some church or other. We decided to compete in the Edinburgh Music Festival and this obliged us to find a name. The name we hit on was: The Edinburgh University Singers, and this choir, I believe, is still in existence, although in number it much exceeds the original octet of "The Wee Choir." At that festival we competed in the Madrigal Section, in which we took first place, singing *Sweet Honey-sucking Bees.* On one or two occasions we were accompanied by Thea Musgrave, then a student at Edinburgh, now a distinguished composer and pianist. A great sorrow for me when the time came to leave Edinburgh and move into the work of the ministry was having to break away from this quite serious musical enterprise. There was a good Choral Union in Tain which I joined a year or two later, and on two successive years I sang tenor and baritone duets with Charlie Green, the chemist in Tain, at the Dingwall music festival, but all of this was very much a side-line.

After being licensed Probationer in the spring of 1945 I engaged in pulpit supply work every Sunday. I enjoyed doing this, and through meeting different types of congregations and kirk-sessions, and as a result of traveling to many places, my knowledge of Scotland increased. If I arrived in a town like Hawick or Cupar on Saturday evening, I would spend at least an hour exploring it thoroughly. In August I was asked by my brother-in-law Roddie Smith to become *locum tenens* in his parish of Urray and Gilchrist, which is centered on Muir of Ord. Roddie had been an army chaplain but at this time was convalescing in Inverness after surgery. A *locum tenens*, if he is still a probationer, has no responsibility within the disciplinary structure of the Church. Presidency of the kirk-session falls to the interim moderator—usually a neighboring minister—who also conducts baptisms, weddings, and the Holy Communion services, which take place infrequently— in the Highlands usually twice a year. The probationer conducts all other services of public worship including funerals, and visits people in their homes—especially the sick and house-bound. This part of the work I did on foot and on a bicycle, which I bought from Logan the blacksmith. In Muir of Ord there was quite a lot of work to be done, but I still had time to continue to study and mull over what I had learned in the long period of training. There was a pleasant garden at the manse in Muir of Ord, and the children thrived.

A year from the date of my licensing I would become eligible for a parish of my own, and so after Christmas that year I began to look around. Sometimes a vacancy would appear in *The Scotsman*, and if it were in the country—for we did not want to live in a city—I would apply for it. Sometimes my application was acknowledged; in only three cases was I invited to come and preach—in Friockheim, Methil, and Golspie. None of the vacancy committees of these parishes made me sole nominee or put me on a short leet. I began to wonder for how long this haphazard preaching competition would go on.

As in life, certainly in my life, the course of events is often determined by what seems chance encounter. There was an old retired minister in the parish at Muir of Ord, Mr Cameron. He was in Dingwall one market-day and met a farmer from Easter Ross, who told him that one of the applicants they had chosen to preach for their vacant charge, had pulled out at the last minute. "I've got the very man for you," said Mr Cameron; and that was how, ten days later, I came to preach for the parish of Logie Easter. On the appointed day I preached there at the morning and evening services. On the way home Mr Cameron, who had accompanied me, told me that the vacancy committee had decided there and then to ask me to be sole nominee, although they still had a candidate to hear, and that I would shortly be getting a formal request to go up again and preach as sole nominee.

And so it worked out very smoothly; after preaching again I received a Call from the parish, that is a document containing signatures of parishioners, in this case more or less everybody in the parish. A minister may not be ordained unless he receives such a Call from the people. The names were divided into two groups: members and adherents. Members are those who receive Holy Communion, adherents are those who attend but do not receive this sacrament. In the Highlands there were in those days many people who would not dare to receive Communion until they had one foot in the grave. With age, apparently, one ceased to be sinful.

On a perfect evening–6 April 1946–the Presbytery of Tain met in the Church of Logie Easter to ordain me a fully-fledged minister of the Gospel, and to induct me into the care of this parish. The coronation of the British monarch excites a Highland parish less than does the ordination and induction of a minister–at least it was so in those days. The church was packed. On this occasion it was the "down church" that was in use, for the parish had two church buildings: the "down church" had belonged until 1929 to the United Free Church, and stood on the main road opposite the War Memorial; the "up church," which stood on a hill in the center of the graveyard, had been the old Parish Church. After the union of 1929 the united congregation used the better equipped "down church" in the winter and the "up church" in the summer. Only such an arrangement could satisfy the two allegedly united groups within the parish. For the ordination service the ministers of the Presbytery—about twelve in number—sat in the little enclosure beneath the central pulpit. The Moderator of the Presbytery conducted the service, while another minister—the most recently ordained—preached the sermon, which he addressed partly to the ordinand and partly to the congregation. After having been questioned and approved I was ordained with prayer and laying on of the hands of the Presbytery, and inducted to the charge. The interim moderator, that is the minister who had presided over the kirk-session and been in charge of the parish during the vacancy, took the chair for the social evening which followed. This took place in the church—for the hall was far too small—and began with laudatory speeches all round, which gave the impression that the kingdom had come. New ministers tend to be hailed as a kind of Messiah. I had to make a speech and said something rather clumsily about feeling that my commitment to this parish was a kind of marriage bond.

There were two old ministers there who regaled us for hours with humorous anecdotes and reminiscences. The evening was beginning to take on the mood of a sober ceilidh. The choir sang intermittently to maintain a religious tone. The precentor, with eyes closed, sang *There were ninety and nine...*, and a sweet girl of sixteen sang soulfully, *O the years in sin I've wasted.* At the end, when it fell to me to take over the presidential chair, the choir sang, *Lead kindly light, amid the encircling gloom.*

When it was all over we went home to the manse with a few friends and relatives who had come for the occasion. A few minutes later the noisy bell clanged, and there, smiling at the door was the beadle, John Urquhart. He was a man of about sixty, tall, lean, black-haired still, with sallow skin and a drooping black mustache—Hungarian looking.

"Good evening, Mr Walls," he began. "The wife thought that with guests you wouldn't be offended at her giving you a fowl."

With this he handed over a very plump fowl, dressed ready for the oven. "And there's a few eggs too, they're handy." Then he made off with the remark that should I ever need anything at all he would be "near hand." Very soon I learned that a beadle, especially if like John Urquhart he were a hangover from the Auld Kirk days, is unreservedly the "minister's man." In his eyes the minister can do no wrong and possesses an infallibility and authority on a par with scripture. The parish was composed mainly of a few large farms on the fertile coastal plain of Easter Ross, but the fertile fringe was not very broad, and not far from the sea the land began to rise westwards to merge into a mountainous wilderness the breadth of Scotland. In the shelving rougher west side of the parish were a few little crofts, including Brennachie, the home of Alec Ross, one of the elders.

In the center of the parish, on the dividing line between the rich farms and the croft-land was a dome shaped gravel and sand hillock. The old church–not an impressive building–stood in the graveyard half-way up this slope; a little higher the manse garden was encircled by the outer defense of an overgrown holly and hawthorn hedge, behind which, encircling the brow of the hill, rose up a giant crown of magnificent beech and Spanish chestnut–fully two hundred years old. Islanded in a wide lawn within, and having pride of place on the crown of the hill stood the manse, a perfect example of eighteenth-century Scottish architecture, a delightful feature of which was the cross-gable in the center of the facade above the front door. The perfectly proportioned stable and barn were continuous with the gable end of the house, and had doors painted a deep earth-red color. The crow-stepped gables gave a flavor of antiquity, while the overall primrose-washed harling radiated joy.

On the evening after that of the ordination we explored the house and grounds, the children poking into every corner. At each door of the outbuildings Nicolas would ask, "Who lives in this house." Not only was the parish my first charge, but the manse was our first settled home, and we could have imagined none more beautiful or peaceful.

One evening about four weeks after my induction to the parish the front-door bell clanged loudly. I was using a large room in the back wing of the house as a study, and I hesitated a moment before going down the long passage to the door. I was happy in the prospect of parish work, but the noisy summons shook my confidence a little. Would I have to deal with some awkward disciplinary problem or was one of my cherished ideas about to be challenged?

I was put at ease: there stood a tidy, pleasant man, smiling shyly. He came in walking nervously and sat down on the chair nearest the sitting-room door.

"Well," I said, "how can I help you?"

"We have a little girl, Sir, and wondered if you could baptize her first week. We should have had her done during the vacancy, but we wanted to have our own minister do it when he came."

"That is a pleasant job for me," I said.

What should I say now? It was wrong, I knew, to administer baptism before knowing something about the belief and practice of the parents. I was a newcomer and therefore ought to learn something about this family. He repeated his question, "Do you think Saturday first week would be suitable?" which showed me that my first problem would be to persuade him to come to public worship on a Sunday for the baptism. The rule, as clearly stated in Cox's *Practice and Procedure* was that baptism must be celebrated at public worship. This rule had been honored in its neglect, especially in the Highlands; I meant to enforce it, but to do so as gently as possible. Would I have the determination and the tact to accomplish my aim? I hurriedly remarked that it would be best if the ceremony were carried out in church, and then before he had time to respond, said I would be back directly with a little pamphlet I had about baptism, which I was sure he and his wife would like to read. On returning to the sitting-room I said, "I hope you find time to read this soon, and I'll come to visit you on Friday evening to make arrangements."

He seemed pleased and rose to go after giving me directions how to find his house, but without telling me his name. I didn't ask, for it looked as if he expected me to know who he was. Ministers, I was soon to learn, are presumed to be omniscient. I soon found out who he was; the modern Internet is but a poor copy of the jungle telegraph that existed in Easter Ross long ago. Next morning Meg came to help in the house. Her first words were, "I hear that Donald Robertson wants to have the wee girl baptized first week." She told us not only his name but all about his interesting genealogy. His father, who was the beadle of the "down church," was the son of a girl who had been a laundry maid in Tarbet House, where at the end of the nineteenth century many very distinguished persons had been guests.

On Friday evening I sped off on my bicycle to visit Donald and his wife. A rabbit darted across the drive and bolted into the enormous orange and white rhododendron at the end of the lawn. The cycle shook violently on the rough manse road, for I had pumped too much air into the tires. On the main road the machine settled down and I was soon within a mile of the Robertson's home. I walked the last stretch because the track was primitive.

All the way I was wondering how I could persuade them to come to church on Sunday for the baptism. It was indeed the law of the Church, but how could I insist on a law that had been so long flouted? The previous minister had not insisted, nor did all of my colleagues insist. Why should a new minister take a stand on this issue? I felt that I would have to rely on persuasion, and much would depend on my handling of this first case. An old minister had once said to me, "Make any changes you intend to make at once–they'll never let you make them later."

A bit tense with all my argumentative rehearsal, I arrived at the Robertson's cottage and was offered the best chair in the room. The baby was asleep in a basket and Mrs Robertson came out of the little cupboard-like scullery where she had been washing up after the evening meal. A heavy green runner was draped over the table; everything in that house was in perfect order. The conversation rambled pleasantly on about the baby, the relatives, the district, the people, and about our impressions of our new home. After quite some time we arrived at the subject of the baptism.

First of all I read the scripture passages appointed to be read at a baptism, then the comments from the *Book of Common Order.* Donald was worried about when and how to answer the questions and when to hold the baby. These matters were easily dealt with, but were still keeping us at a distance from more awkward things.

My first real difficulty was this: the Church of Scotland demands that at least one parent be baptized and profess the Christian religion, but there is no creed or confession to which assent may be demanded. A set of questions is suggested, and I was free to use these or not as I wished, or I might compose a set myself. I thought this method too vague and had decided to use the Apostles' Creed as a baptismal profession of faith. I did not know what I would do if anyone refused assent to this, but with the Robertsons I had decided to take this course. In reading the Creed to them, however, I would change the word "Catholic" to "universal," because of the association of idolatry attached to the former word–of which my childhood memories reminded me; and I would present the Creed as though it were a sermon I was composing myself, not as a set formula. I had earlier learned from contacts in the West Highlands, that even the Lord's Prayer, because it is a set form, is often suspect in public worship. I hoped that by a sympathetic presentation of the Creed I would at the end elicit a spontaneous "I do" from Donald and his wife.

I now set about this part of my task, explaining that I was giving them a summary of the Christian Faith and that after I had read it out at the baptism would raise my eyes so that Donald knew when to affirm his consent with the words, "I do." Having thus got under way I led into a brief exposition of the doctrine of baptism.

"When we receive the gift of a child," I began as informally as I could, "we are filled with joy and gratitude, but also with apprehension; we think of the future and all its dangers for our new-born child; we want to give it security, knowing that it is not entirely in our power to do so; in particular we want to ensure that it will grow up able to resist all temptation to do evil and so be fit to enter the kingdom of heaven. In our helplessness we turn to the author of life and ask him to add to the gift of life the gift of grace. The sacrament of baptism is God's perfect answer to all our needs at this time. We can do little: God in response to the prayers of faith can do all. By sprinkling the child's head with water, in the name of the Blessed Trinity, the source of evil will be removed. You know how food is preserved by salt. The materials are at first good and fresh, but if left they corrupt, but salt blocks that potential corruption and they do not go bad. Our Lord said, 'Have salt in yourselves.' Baptism is a divine salting which preserves the infant's soul by destroying the hidden seeds of corruption. Here is another comparison: at baptism a divine seed is planted in the soul of the child. That seed is perfect and will grow into a mature plant, fit to grow also in the soil of paradise. But we must remember that just as no plant can grow without tending, so the child's soul must be given proper care. The Church, but the parents in particular, are the gardeners who keep the soil around the child well worked and free from weeds. From God alone comes the seed of divine life, but we have our part to play in producing the perfect plant."

I thought my comparison apt because Donald was gardener at Shandwick House. I had got into my stride and found it difficult to round off neatly. The fire round which we sat came to the rescue: a burning log tumbled out, and by the time it was replaced in the hearth the atmosphere had changed. It was Donald who revived the conversation.

"We were wondering if you could come on Wednesday." I plunged right in.

"Would you not like to come to the church for the baptism?" His reply was unexpected.

"My sister told us that the new minister wanted to do all the baptisms in church, but I think we would rather just have it at home. I'm too nervous."

How his sister knew this, I don't know. My mind was being read by the mysterious parish Internet; but I was pleased that the ground had already been broken.

"I know that sometimes it's a bit difficult," I said, "and I want to make things as convenient as possible. The trouble is that we are supposed to have baptisms in church unless illness or great distance makes that impossible. Unfortunately this rule has been neglected for a long time; but today there is more need than ever for it to be enforced, and this is why. There are many people who never go near the church but expect the minister to baptize their children. The minister goes to the house to do this. Now, if the minister could enforce the rule that they must come to church for the baptism that might cause them to take the matter more seriously, and perhaps even come regularly to worship. If I am to lead the way in this I will need the co-operation of good church-going people like yourselves. I cannot enforce a rule on defaulters if God-fearing people are exempted. If you were to set an example you would be doing the Church a great service and strengthen my hand in dealing with the slack members. This is your first baby and it is my first baptism. Shall we both begin in the right way? What do you think?"

Donald turned to his wife. "What do you think, Ellen?"

She replied: "You know, Mr Walls, my people are Free Church, and our ministers insist on baptizing babies at the morning service."

Here was help from a source I had not thought of—from the Wee Frees. "Yes," I replied quickly, as though I knew of this, which I didn't, "in the old days it was the rule and the Free Church have been more faithful to it; we have slipped a bit. What do you think then, will you come to church?"

"I don't think I would mind," she said, "it's just that Donald is so shy," and she looked across at him, with a hint of appeal in her eyes.

"I can assure you," I said, "there is no need to be shy. The congregation will be delighted to see a baptism, and in any case the child ought to be commended to their care too. The whole parish must set a good example to our children."

I could now see that Mrs Robertson was happy to have her baby baptized in Church, and Donald was about to acquiesce. Perhaps all my diplomatic effort had been needless; they might well have accepted from the start my insisting on the rule being followed. Now it did not matter; the end was achieved. Donald said that if it were for the good of the parish he would try to overcome his nervousness, and they would be at the morning service a week on Sunday with the baby.

As we had some tea and cakes I explained a few details of the order of service and then cycled home, elated. The horizon was purple-gray and there was clear light in the north-west. The rabbits were nibbling voraciously near the cover of the big rhododendron at the manse gate. I put away the bike and went in for the night, my first major mission in the parish accomplished.

7

Sunday morning in the Highlands of Scotland feels quite different from any other day—perhaps I ought to say that it felt so fifty years ago. So it certainly was when I was minister of Logie Easter. In town one might have attributed this numinous sensation to the absence of traffic and the quietness, but in the country it was never noisy and yet the difference was there. The air, the sunlight, everything seemed to have undergone a transfiguration. The minutes as they moved gently by seemed to whisper the ancient Hebrew *Kadosh, Kadosh, Kadosh.* The old-fashioned Scottish Presbyterian Sabbath was the sacramental presence of the Almighty, and although it had blemishes, in its dying out we have lost something precious.

On that particular Sunday morning, when the Robertson baby was to be baptized, with everyone else I sensed the sacred hush of the day. Outside, as I went about the few odd jobs that had to be done even on the Sabbath, I felt the exhilaration of the sheer natural beauty of the earth. I wondered if there might not be something natural and pre-Christian in the awe of the Highland Sabbath. A woman at Muir of Ord had once said to me that although they never went to church she always insisted that her children observe the Sabbath.

Today I was specially buoyed up for I was going to church not just in response to reverence for the Sabbath, not just to preach the Word of God and try to help the congregation raise up their minds and hearts to God, but to perform an action in which our Lord would become present and implant the life of his Spirit in a child; and it was to be the first time I had ever done this.

After breakfast I wrote out the Order of Service. First we would sing some verses from a psalm:

From infants' and from sucklings' mouths,
Thou hast ordained strength.

Then would follow a short prayer of adoration and confession of sins, and finally a prayer of supplication for grace. This was simply the standard order at the statutory morning service in the Church of Scotland.

The action began, introduced by the old German chorale:

Blessed Jesu, here we stand
Met to do as thou hast spoken
And this child at thy command,
here we bring to thee in token,
That to thee it now is given,
For of such shall be thy heaven.

The child's father would already be standing beside me behind the Communion table beneath the pulpit; at the third verse of the hymn the beadle would usher in the mother and baby and Godparents and lead them down to join the father at the font. After the hymn would come reading of scripture, which included the passage giving warrant for the sacrament, and finally, after the baptism, my affirmation: "This child is now received into membership of Christ's Church and is engaged to confess the faith of Christ crucified and to be his faithful soldier and servant unto her life's end." The mother and baby would retire to the vestry and the father return to his usual pew in the church, while the last verse of the hymn would be sung:

Write the name we now have given,
Write it in the book of heaven.

When I had climbed back up into the heights of the pulpit the beadle would shut the door of the pulpit firmly upon me—as he was accustomed to slam shut carriage doors at the railway station where he worked–and the service would proceed much as on other Sundays, but I hoped to use the occasion to impress upon people's minds the fact, that in church we not only listen to the Word, but carry out actions wherein our Lord truly becomes present, that something happens at Christian public worship.

My little private rehearsal was interrupted by Helen who brought in coffee and pointed out that time was running out. I drank the coffee quickly, put my notes inside the covers of the *Book of Common Order*, and made off across the lawn towards the gap in the hedge opposite the back-gate of the church. As I went through the gap a long branch caught my jacket, as it did every Sunday, and I resolved, as I did every Sunday, to start trimming the hedge next day.

Cars were parked in odd corners and people were walking in groups along the two roads leading to the church. Between the churchyard gate and the vestry door lurked Alex Skinner, one of the elders. He was of moderate height, fairly broad, with fair hair and tidy appearance. I had no wish to avoid him, but was not prepared for a long chat; but there he was, right in my path, on purpose I thought. He bade me an absent-minded "Good Morning" and pointed to a tombstone, saying nothing. After allowing me time to focus my mind on the tombstone he began to tell the tale of him whose mortal remains lay beneath. That was only the introduction: the kirk-session, he explained, were bound to keep the stone in repair out of a fund bequeathed for the purpose. The stone was beginning to sink, and the repairs would be costly. "They hadn't thought of that when they left the mortification," he said. I did not know what I was expected to do about this just then. Fortunately the session clerk arrived on the scene and the conversation about the tombstone was broken off. I disliked being distracted just before a service, but people did not seem to understand that. The elders would all come into the vestry before the morning service to say "Good Morning" and also to hang up their hats, a symbol, I think of possession. They were all, with me, ruling elders, and the vestry was really the kirk-session room. On Sunday morning they stayed only a moment, and then I was left in the charge of John Urquhart, the beadle, who summer and winter had my robes airing beside a paraffin stove. On Sundays he was dressed in black Tweed and wore a narrow white collar.

"Well, it's just a perfect day," he announced, pulling himself up straight and his waistcoat down firmly. "It couldn't be better; and you'll have a fine gathering the day. All her people are coming over from the Black Isle, and it's a long time since we had a baptism in the church."

"I hope they'll all come now, John," I said.

"And so they should, so they should, so they should," came his threefold Amen.

He went off to ring the bell, while I donned my cassock and Genevan gown and bands. I had noticed, when I first came, that John would look out along the road at about twelve noon, and if he saw no one he would give the bell a perfunctory ring. If he saw anyone still on their way he would wait until they were nearly in church before ringing. Remembering the well ordered bell-ringing of the parish of my youth, I decided to reform this custom. I had only to mention the matter to John and all was rectified forthwith, rigidly, for he was a clock-conscious servant of the Highland Railway. The Sunday following his reform I overheard him in altercation with Jockan the Miller, who had been accustomed to have his regular four-minute lateness covered up by the beadle's former laxity. On the Sunday of the baptism the bell began to sound at precisely seven minutes before noon; the precentor tip-toed into the vestry to get the list of hymns; at two minutes to twelve John returned, produced his grandfather's watch from his waistcoat pocket, concentrated on the dial, and having voiced what became a regular ritual phrase, "It's on the very meenite," solemnly carried in the Bible, returning to lead in the minister.

Mrs Robertson was approaching the vestry door as we left, and all was set for the baptism. The church was well filled—the downstairs area quite full, the galleries comfortably full. There must have been about a hundred and thirty people there from a parish that numbered 153 houses—the same number as the fish caught in the Lake of Tiberias after the Resurrection. At length we reached the point when Donald responded with a tremulous "I do," and the baby was baptized in the name of the Blessed Trinity. Now, having accomplished my first aim—to establish a precedent concerning the place of baptism and to impress upon people the importance of this sacrament—I had to preach an appropriate sermon. From the Old Testament I had read the passage about Moses raising up the brazen serpent, from the Gospel the passage telling of Nicodemus coming by night to interrogate the Lord about the meaning of "being born again," but the text I used—in the Church of Scotland it is customary to preach on a specific fairly short text—was, "They brought little children to Jesus that he should touch them." As I announced the text Miss Fleming, the very perjink, little, elderly organist slid down from her stool, moved to a seat on the front pew, adjusted her mauve stole, coughed delicately and raised her eyes to the pulpit, while Alex Skinner, under cover of blowing his nose, deftly introduced one or maybe two pandrops into his mouth, and likewise focused upon the minister, several feet above him. Now the sermon could begin in earnest.

"For all of us this sacrament was our gateway into new life. We were all born into a particular human family; by baptism we were born into the universal family of God, the household of faith.

"This receiving of a child into the household of faith should be symbolized by its baptism in the presence of the local congregation. I rejoice today that my first baptism as minister of this parish has been celebrated in the proper manner, and am deeply grateful to the parents of this child for their co-operation in my endeavor.

"How fortunate were the mothers of Salem, we might say, who presented their children to our Lord so that he might lay his hands upon them and bless them! Yes, but not more fortunate than we, for our Lord instituted this sacrament so that until the end of time he could continue to lay his hands upon children to bless them. The touch of baptism upon this child's head today was no less than the touch of Christ, implanting in the infant's soul the seed of eternal life."

The peroration over, I led the congregation in a prayer of consecration of ourselves to God, after which we sang from paraphrase 47:

> *When to the sacred font we came,*
> *Did not the rite proclaim*
> *That washed from sin and all its stain*
> *New creatures we became?*
> *With Christ the Lord we died to sin,*
> *With him to life we rise*
> *To life which now begun on earth*
> *Is perfect in the skies.*

I pronounced the benediction and descended the steps slowly, enjoying a sense of real accomplishment, believing that I had the backing of the congregation. I must have been smiling as I crossed over to the vestry door. I took off my gown, threw it onto a chair, and laid the black stole decorated with two golden crosses on the table, when someone knocked on the door. "Come in," I said, and the door opened very slowly.

A smooth, round, pink face, tufted with bristles on the cheek-bones appeared, and Alec Ross–Brennachie as he was known, from the name of his small-holding–stepped reverently into the room. He was not the session clerk, but was the most senior of the elders, a powerful character in his own right and a front for his wispy but domineering wife who, they said, made the shots while he fired them. His face wore its customary pale, sad, Christian smile, and he began, "I'm sorry if I am disturbing you." His eye rested momentarily on the unfamiliar golden crosses, and on the cassock and cincture which I had not yet removed. "Have you a minute perhaps?"

"Certainly!" I replied brightly, to disguise my rising apprehension.

"It's about the sermon," he explained, his voice dropping a fifth on the last word.

"You mean my sermon this morning?"

"Yes," said Brennachie, "about baptism. Are you taught in the divinity hall that infants should be baptized?"

"Oh yes," I replied, feeling on safe ground. "The Church of Scotland, has always held to infant baptism."

"Can you tell me of a case in the New Testament of an infant being baptized?"

"There's the centurion's household, you know. There must have been children there, I suppose."

"Mr Walls, we may not go on suppositions; we must have clear statements where the Word of God is concerned."

There was an awkward pause, then he continued, "Apart from the question of infants, Mr Walls, if anyone is baptized, did I understand you to mean that when water is poured onto that person's head they are born again?"

"Yes, I think that is a fair statement of what I meant. Of course it is the Holy Spirit who effects the new birth."

"Then why lay such stress upon outward baptism with water? A man can receive new birth at any time quite apart from baptism with water–before or after. 'The wind bloweth where it listeth'; baptism is only the outward sign of inner conversion. Today, Mr Walls, you made far too much of outward ceremony."

"Well, Mr Ross," I answered wearily, "it is not our place to judge what is important when we have our Lord's plain instructions: 'Go and baptize'."

"Are we commanded to baptize infants?" he returned to his first theme.

"You are quibbling now," I replied, "you know that the Church of Scotland has always maintained the tradition of infant baptism." I tried to assume a more light-hearted tone, but he would have none of it.

"Tradition has no place in the Gospel. The truth of the word alone matters," he answered abruptly.

"But why distinguish between infants and adults? Both are human beings; both have souls to save."

Brennachie seemed to think that I was being facetious and said, "This is a fruitless argument. I know that our Church does baptize children and perhaps no harm need come, provided we know what we are doing."

"Mr Ross," I said, "there is no doubt what we are doing in baptism. Today we sang—and the words are an accurate paraphrase of St Paul:

> *When to the sacred font we came*
> *Did not the rite proclaim*
> *That washed from sin and all its stain*
> *New creatures we became?*

"Is that not quite clear? We became new creatures at the font of baptism."

"The hymn does not mean that at all," he answered. "The rite only proclaims that we become new creatures, but it does not itself effect the new birth. To say that it does is just blind, Popish superstition."

"Then, Mr Ross," I said, "we interpret scripture differently."

"There is no such thing as interpreting the scriptures; the scriptures mean what they say."

"Do you not have to invoke the Holy Spirit to illuminate the scriptures for you?" I asked.

"Of course I do; but the Holy Spirit will never pervert the pure meaning of scripture as you have done today, Mr Walls."

"I too invoke the Holy Spirit when I read the Bible."

Momentarily he was at a loss, then the Christian smile, which had gradually become a bit jaundiced, returned in full sweetness. "This distresses me a great deal," he said in a paternal tone, "perhaps we had better leave the discussion for the time being. I will give the matter prayerful thought, and suggest that you do the same. The evangelical fire in your sermons when you first came here was so comforting; I hope that the Lord will preserve you from lapsing into nominal Christianity."

The phrase "nominal Christians," I was soon to discover, was one of his favorite expressions, frequently applied to those in the parish who before 1929 had been members of the Auld Kirk, the Established Church of Scotland. I was beginning to learn that in some parts of Scotland at least these historical divisions still meant a very great deal.

He took his hat from the peg and left. The other elders came in and hurried off with their hats. They must have been waiting in the church, embarrassed, for about twenty minutes. There was a note of nervousness in their Good-byes, as though they had more than an inkling of what had been going on, had almost expected it. When they had gone John, having locked up the main door, came in.

"You've been having a session meeting today?" he inquired.

"Not exactly, John; I was just discussing something with Brennachie."

"Huh," he spluttered, "excuse me for saying it, but the less you discuss with that one, the better."

I walked listlessly back to the manse, through the gap, across the lawn; the light was greyer now. I didn't much relish dinner; I wished there was no evening service; I hadn't the heart to preach again that day.

On Monday morning I began work on the overgrown hedge, and was compelled to think of Brennachie, because I had borrowed a hedge-clipping tool from him and was using it. The hedge clipper was not all that useful, and I had laid it aside when John appeared.

"Excuse me for telling you, Mr Walls, but you'll have to cut it right down to near the ground and then keep it low next year to let it fill out from below. You can't be too severe on it; it must be twenty years since anybody touched it."

I set about the task, following John's advice. Halfway through the first trunk, which was about six inches in diameter, the saw began sticking, so that by the time I got through I was breathless. I sat down and began to think. How was the dispute with Ross Brennachie to be settled? Did the scriptures answer clearly the questions he had raised about baptism? It was too naive to think that there could be no disagreement over the interpretation of scripture. His affirmation meant simply that he could not imagine that anyone would disagree with him. If my interpretation contradicted his, had I a more objective criterion than he or was my view merely subjective? How were rival interpretations to be judged? The possibility of dispute over the doctrine of baptism derived from the problem about the substance of the faith and about the Church itself being the sole arbiter of what doctrines are in conformity with the scriptures. The difference for me now was that the issue was no longer an academic issue, but a living issue for people. I was a minister of the Word, commissioned to feed hungry sheep; I was not just the chairman at a debate.

I reflected, too, that Ross was not alone in his views about baptism. Within the Church of Scotland some thought as I did, others as he did. The doctrine of baptism, I reflected, is fundamental. If there is disagreement on this doctrine there is bound to be disagreement on other things. The problem, which had excited us as students in the Dogmatics class, of finding out what is the substance of the faith, I had temporarily resolved by using the Apostles' Creed. But could I insist on profession even of this classic formula? The only rule of faith for the Church of Scotland was the Bible itself, and, as was now only too obvious to me, the Bible could be a bone of contention, and not an agent of unity. Authentic interpretation of the scriptures was necessary, but the individual's reliance upon the Holy Spirit was clearly not sufficient. How did the Holy Spirit operate in a more public or corporate way? I found myself recalling Professor Baillie's suggestion that a study ought to be made on the mode of operation of the Holy Spirit after Pentecost, in comparison with the mode of operation in the Old Testament.

The theological foundation, acquired after eight years of study, and which had allowed me to set about the work of the ministry with some zest, seemed now to have become very insecure. My hope, that by ordination and membership of the Presbyterate I would be enabled to tie up all the doctrinal loose ends left over at the end of the time of study, had not been realized. Instead I found that the problems raised in the classrooms were now doubly acute, because the truth is not an academic luxury to be discussed, but the spiritual bread which real people need to eat.

I worked for two hours on the hedge, cutting down about three yards of holly and hawthorn, and pulling the trunks towards the lawn. I had regained some of my confidence. I might not have a monopoly of the Spirit's enlightenment, but I had been given responsibility to teach in this parish, so that I was justified in relying on some grace to enable me honor this responsibility. If ordination meant anything it must mean that the minister has some special spiritual backing. St Paul had magnified his office and told the young Timothy to stir up the gift that was in him through the laying-on of hands. I would follow their example and trust my judgment—within reason. I still wanted to find out what could be accepted as the substance of the faith, and when sure of this I would courageously insist on its acceptance within my own parish at least.

I put away the tools, taking great care to oil Brennachie's clippers. As well as clippers he had lent me an old twelve-bore, double-barreled shot-gun, to which we owed many a tasty dinner.

8

That evening Helen and I went to visit the MacDiarmids in Alness. Duncan MacDiarmid—about twenty years my senior—was minister of Rosskene parish, not our immediate neighbor, but only about ten miles away. Duncan and his wife Bessie became our closest friends and remained so even after we became Catholics. On this occasion I learned from Duncan that the Synod was to meet on the following day. The notice of this meeting had been given before I came to the district, and by an oversight I had not been informed. Synods are courts of the Presbyterian Church intermediate between the presbyteries and the General Assembly. All members of presbyteries within the synodal region, that is the minister and one elder from each parish, are members of the synod. I do not know how things stand today, but at that time the synod was regarded as more of a decoration than a substantial agent in Church government.

"Is the synod meeting really important?" I asked Duncan.

"Not in the least," he answered, "but there won't be a circus up here for a long time, and you get your lunch for 1s.3d."

Still distressed by my inconclusive doctrinal argument with Ross Brennachie, I thought that the operation of the Synod might guide me in my search for a living voice in the Church that possessed an authority superior to that of individual conviction. It turned out that I had been taking the Synod too seriously.

On Tuesday morning I went down to the main road to wait for the bus, but was offered a lift by a young man driving a small van. There was already a passenger, who moved sullenly into the back and remained silent for the whole journey. It was a noisy van and the driver whispered,

"My mate doesn't hold much with padres—a Bolshie type—but never mind him; I'm an R.C. actually." The driver was friendly and our conversation quite serious—mainly about the countryside and the social set-up in the north of Scotland. I discovered that his job was to take film-shows round the hydro-electric schemes. We reached Dingwall in good time and the van swung into a side street, to halt at the bar entrance to the National Hotel. I found my way to the church a little way further down the same street.

At eleven o'clock the synod began with worship at which the retiring moderator preached. The business began with the election of a new moderator. This was a perfunctory affair because an order of seniority had always been followed. This done and the minutes of last meeting having been read and approved, Robert Begg, a minister from my presbytery, immediately rose and with open-voweled eloquence humbly suggested that in future the custom of electing the moderator by seniority be discontinued. He hoped that he would not be mis-understood. The man who had just been elected was a worthy man, as were all who had hitherto held the office, but he felt that it was a pity that younger men rarely had an opportunity to preside over the synod, as synods met so infrequently. The newly elected moderator nodded his white head affably; a dapper man pointed out that there was nothing to hinder Mr Begg nominating whomever he pleased; the clerk, sensing that we were about to spin off into endless free-wheeling discussion, jumped to his feet and remarked that this had all been well aired before and the general feeling was that things should be left as they were—custom could easily be departed from if anyone thought that advisable. There was a vague shuffling of feet in approval and the matter was dropped. We moved on to hear reports from several convenors of committees.

An ancient, wizard-like man in a black suit which had developed a greenish tinge reported on social and industrial problems affecting the Highland region. He asserted that the Church is not at liberty to disregard social and economic factors because these affect its life directly and indirectly. The Church must have something to say about these problems. He made a quick transition to his own special interest—bee in his bonnet—the mineral resources of the Highlands. His report developed into a geological lecture incorporating a half-page quotation from a scientific journal. Eventually the moderator, after whispered consultation with the clerk of synod, rang a bell and asked him to wind up quickly as there were several reports to be heard before one o'clock, at which hour, as we all knew from past experience, the good ladies would have a delectable lunch ready for us.

Next came a report which included reference to problems relating to baptism. My hope rose that I might learn something, but I was disappointed. Nothing I heard helped me with the kind of problem I had already encountered. The discussion was wound up by a bright-eyed, middle-aged Gael who, interspersing his speech with occasional amusing Gaelic asides, intelligible to less than half of our members, suggested that those who claimed to get better sermons on the radio than from us should be told to have their children baptized by the BBC—over the air.

The morning session ended and we adjourned to eat sausage rolls and sandwiches. The phrase "delectable meal" proved to have been optimistic. The geological cleric could find nowhere to sit and seemed unable to concentrate on eating. He moved around still trying to interest others in "dolerite, epidiorite, and hornblende schist." In his opinion the Church in the Highlands was not getting down to rock bottom.

The afternoon session was desultory, the main topic being the function of the synodal court itself. There was a small group of progressives who believed that the synod ought to lighten the work-load of the General Assembly by taking up issues which need not go to the final court of appeal. Mr Begg was prominent in advocacy of this idea, in support of which he made his second resonant speech of the day. In the end a committee was appointed to look into the matter and report to the next meeting of the synod, and Begg was unanimously nominated convenor.

Many ministers spoke to me afterwards and all welcomed me warmly. All asked how I was faring and wished me well. It had been a pleasant day and worth the 1s.3d which was all it cost me, for Duncan MacDiarmid drove me home, picking up his wife on the way, and they both came to supper with us.

Once the cold spell at the beginning of the month was past, the end of May brought in a surge of blossom and leafy beauty. As well as cutting down and trimming the wild hedge, I planned to plant a few trees in the late autumn. This place had already become a true home and we could not imagine ever wanting to move from it. Later that year I happened to meet Professor Thomson in Edinburgh. "Oh, you're up there!" he said, "Take my advice, never budge."

I had begun to make a routine visitation of the parish, especially of the sick. I did this sometimes on a bicycle and sometimes on foot. I preferred walking to cycling. To buy and run a car was out of the question. My stipend was £405 p.a., and the manse although rent-free, was expensive to run, and there was no allowance for telephone or other expenses.

Each house I went to had its own atmosphere–sometimes in the physical sense. There was Mrs MacKay who lived with three grown-up sons and one daughter in a tiny ivy-covered cottage. One forenoon I went to visit her. I paused for a moment in the kitchen while her daughter Betty, hand on the bedroom door, told me in a whisper that the doctor had been pleased with her mother yesterday, and had given her a bottle–"The very newest thing." I was inexperienced and still a bit nervous, but on entering the room immediately sensed serious illness–the atmosphere of death indeed. Mrs MacKay was ready to talk, and all the time Betty stood with her hands clasped, addressing me, "Sir," every time she opened her mouth. I was stifled by deference. I said that I hoped Mrs MacKay was getting better, feeling very uneasy as I spoke.

"Oh yes, Sir," she replied with fervor. "If it's the Lord's will I'll be in church to hear you by the summer Communion—surely by then—the doctor was much better pleased yesterday. He's a fine gentleman, Dr. MacKenzie—a skillful, good man. There's many a poor soul here knows that."

Betty went off to put on the "boys'" potatoes while Mrs MacKay praised the other fine gentlemen in the district. The elders were all on her list as were the older and more prosperous farmers. She had a great respect for gentility and office. Her deep lament, which she frequently repeated, was that she was unable to get to church.

"Yes," said Betty on her return to the room, "I never knew my mother a day out of church, and she often with a sore bad cold on her. People isn't like that nowadays."

I made what I thought was a suitable sound.

For ten minutes I had been on the look-out for my cue to introduce some spiritual ministration. During a lull in the conversation I opened my Bible and moved towards the window to catch the light, for the room was ill-lit. There was a pious hush and I began to read the twenty-third psalm, "The Lord is my shepherd..." I then prayed slowly and in measured tones, thanking God for life and all its blessings, asking for comfort in tribulation, and ending finally with petition for restoration of health, expressing our faith that whether in joy or sorrow, sickness or health, we were always in the Lord's safe keeping. I raised my hand and gave a blessing.

"It was very good of you to call, Sir," said the old lady. I'm sure you've plenty to do. Give our respects to Mrs Walls." As I left, Betty gave me some eggs in a paper bag—they kept hens.

I walked on to visit an old man who had recently taken ill. I had never met him, but Meg our daily help had told me all about him. He had never been known to attend church, and the cause of his recent collapse had undoubtedly been the cessation, through present poverty, of his formerly copious dram. His house—if it could still be called a house—was on the main road near the post-office. There had once been two rooms in this cottage, but the roof over one of them had fallen in. I could scarcely believe that anyone lived here, but this was Donald's mansion, and within I found Donald—a ghost. I pushed open the outer door, found myself beneath the rafters of what had been the living-room—the "ben" in Scots parlance—and knocked on the door of what had been the kitchen—the "but"—where Donald now lived.

"Who's that?" came the hoarse response.

"The minister," I shouted.

"Oh, well, come in," he replied, after a lengthy pause.

The door had to be pushed with some force, for it was warped. More like a house-breaker or fireman than a minister of religion I made my way into the room.

It was a bright room, having a large window in the south wall and a little window in the east gable. A low fire burned in the hearth and there was coal and kindling wood in a corner. A couple of pans lay by the fire. Donald was sitting bolt upright in bed when I made my entry, with one leg projecting from beneath the blanket and a skinny hand reaching for the floor, as if he were trying to get out of bed. His bed-wear consisted of a heavy flannel shirt, long woolen drawers, and grey socks.

"Can you find somewhere to sit?" he asked in a worried tone.

I found a stool and drew it over to his bedside.

"I'm fair stuck altogether in this bed; it's just the weakness, terrible weakness."

"I'm sorry to hear that," I sympathized, looking straight at his one eye, which was working overtime in an attempt to scrutinize the new minister.

He was reassured, and sank back, more relaxed, onto the pillow.

"I've no circulation now, either," he continued, "the district nurse put on the fire this morning. By, it was cold last night—frosty I think."

"It must be awkward for you if you can't rise," I said, "how do you get a bite to eat?"

"Oh, the bread and butter's here by the bed, and Hughie the Post comes in on his morning round and boils me an egg."

"That's not a lot to eat."

"It's as much as I ever did," he replied. "The doctor says that's the bother—malnutrition he calls it. But I'm not as bad as I was." With that he began to bend and stretch his arms.

"See!" he croaked, "I couldn't do that last week."

Donald was indeed suffering from malnutrition and general collapse, resulting from a life of heavy drinking. Hughie the Post had found him lying behind the door a fortnight before. The doctor had given him a tonic, the district nurse looked in every day, and the ever-obliging Hughie—who was an elder—did his bit too.

I asked Donald if there was anything I could do for him now. After a moment's hesitation and a second good look at me, he said that the nurse had left him two bottles of stout, which he was to have warmed and in small doses.

"Will I warm some for you now?" I asked.

"If you wouldn't mind."

While I was warming the stout I heard a chuckle from the bed, and thought he must be smacking his lips, but then he said, "I was just thinking it would be a right joke if Hughie the elder came in now and found the minister putting drink to me." Hughie was a strict tee-totaller.

The stout cheered Donald up, and he talked a bit, telling me how to keep hens profitably.

"Women is no use at hens—they're too alike, the same weaknesses. Hens has to be studied and need regularity. Never a hen of mine died in debt."

"I got a present of nine Rhode Island Reds from someone in Arabella," I replied, "so I'll heed what you say. It'll have to be my job then, not the wife's?"

"That's it; that's it!"

"Well, now," I continued, cheerfully, "I'm going to say a prayer for you."

I praised the Almighty and bluntly asked him to restore Donald's strength. No sooner had I said, "Amen" than Donald spoke up.

"I used to meet some very religious chaps in India—Indians of course, not British. They wouldn't eat meat or pigs or something—very strict."

"I'll leave these eggs for you, Donald," I said, "and I hope your religion won't prevent you eating them."

"There's not much my religion would stop me eating—or make me eat either," was his reply.

"Good-bye just now then—and see you get your strength up."

"Thank you, minister, thank you."

I left Donald in his solitary immobility, closing the two doors very carefully, lest I should bring the rest of the roof down on his head.

In the afternoon I set off for the opposite end of the parish, and after half an hour's walking reached the woodland path that led up to Miss Euphemia Grant's cottage. The door of this fairy-tale cottage was opened by the demure, middle-aged housekeeper, Miss Sarah Nicholson. She brought me ceremoniously into Miss Grant's parlor. It was very much a parlor—mahogany inlaid table, china cabinet, a severe chaise-lounge, three or four upright mahogany chairs, on the mantelpiece, china shepherds and shepherdesses and a French carriage clock.

The window was behind Miss Grant who had no interest in the prospect onto the neat and colorful garden, for she was blind. It would be truer to say that she no longer had need of the prospect, for this and many another scene was treasured and still enjoyed in her very exact memory. She was a happy woman, through whose unseeing eyes I learned much about the parish as it had been years ago, in the days when children walked miles to school, when all the crofts were cultivated, and when the parish supported three times as many people as it did now, when Miss Grant had beehives in front of the honeysuckle-covered wall, and drove a pony-cart to church on Sunday, when the minister farmed the glebe and himself moved around the parish in a pony-cart and not, as I did, on foot or on a bicycle.

Miss Grant's life had been centered on the Church, although she made no moan about how long it was since she had been able to attend. She could remember all of the ministers for seventy years back, and all about their families. I learned later that she was one of the few parishioners who before the 1929 union between the Auld Kirk and the United Free Church had belonged to the Auld Kirk, and this explained how her style of piety differed greatly from that of Ross Brennachie, with whom I had had such unhappy controversy. On one occasion Brennachie had said to me, "They are still holding us back." In this context "They" referred to the Auld Kirk remnant who, he believed, were only nominal Christians, lacking true evangelical fervor.

On my visits to Euphemia Grant I never felt nervous or ill at ease. She was kind and she was vivacious. To every remark made to her she would answer with alacrity, as though she already knew what you were going to say. The routine on these visits was always the same: after about fifteen minutes, tea was brought in on a Sheraton tray. The china was old and had roses on it. Miss Nicholson took a cup with me, sitting slightly apart on the hard couch, but Miss Grant took nothing. She would continue to talk while I ate biscuit and cake; when I had finished she would say, "Sarah, will you please bring my Bible to the minister." I would read a substantial portion of Scripture and then offer a prayer, expatiating upon the glories of creation, the blessed mystery of redemption, and after making suitable supplication and intercession, conclude by adverting to our hope of eternal life. At the end Miss Grant would say quietly, "Thank you very much, Mr Walls, thank you very much." Then she would be silent for some minutes.

It was always Miss Nicholson who broke the silence. On my second visit she did this with the remark, "How are you getting on with the hens?" It was one of their neighbors who had given them to me.

"Oh, John Urquhart keeps me right," I said.

"He'll do that all right," said Miss Grant, "he's a great friend of mine; he used to drive me to church when my sight first began to give out."

"I don't know what I would do without him," I added.

"Yes, the parish wouldn't be the same without John."

Although I had been the ordained pastor of this parish for only a few weeks, I was already becoming aware of how different from the life of preparation was the reality of being minister of the Word and pastor of a parish. As a student one's preoccupation and commitment was to biblical and theological study. Once responsibility for a parish had been imposed one entered into a relation with people—a personal relation. I began to understand the meaning of the word "parson." The minister was regarded not as a professional, but as their Person. The minister could not, therefore, think of himself simply as a man who provided a service for people, after providing which he could go home and enjoy a private life. A sign of the fact that the parish presumed that their minister in some way belonged to them was the keen interest that all took in what was happening at the manse. In one of his many asides, Professor Rankin had once remarked that when we got into our parishes we should be careful to light the fire at seven o'clock in the morning, even if we returned to bed. "When they see the smoke rising," he said, "they'll say, 'Oh, they're up at the manse'." Even the kindly interest of Euphemia Grant bore witness to this propensity to live in the minister's life. A parishioner—but a member of the

Scottish Episcopal Church–Sir John Dick-Lauder, who lived at Arabella House, said to my wife, "The minister and his family have no privacy, they live in a gold-fish bowl, it's worse than being Royalty." I was already beginning to feel this, and found it disagreeable.

One of our relatives was spending a few days with us, so that in the evening of the day I had visited Euphemia Grant–it was a Friday–Helen and I were able to take a walk after supper in the rough woodland near the manse. Helen spoke of this very topic–the sense of being in a gold-fish bowl, with the eyes of the parish fixed upon us. "I feel," she began, "that I am expected to be a certain kind of person, dress in a certain style, and do certain things. They don't think of me as your wife so much as your assistant. I don't really want to be the president of the Women's Guild–to take just one example–but I suppose I'll have to be."

"I agree," I said, "I don't think the minister's wife should be a kind of representative charitable lady of the parish–an ordained female deacon. I just want you to be my wife."

"And that's what I want too. Mind you, I'll play my part in the parish, but I don't want to take on an official role–but that's what seems to be expected."

"Maybe I'm over-dramatizing things," I continued, "but I'm beginning to wonder if there isn't a problem in reconciling our private life–that means our marriage–with my public responsibility as pastor of the parish. I have to be out a lot, especially in the afternoons and evenings. But it's more than that–I'm becoming preoccupied with the life of the parish, with everybody else's life."

"I know," she answered, "I feel it too, but I haven't said anything."

That night we put the parish right out of our minds. We had been almost five years married and never ceased to be as much in love as when we first met. "Whatever happens," I said, "whatever tensions arise between marriage and duty to the parish, I know that my priority will always be our marriage. I think a real marriage has to have a good dash of idolatry about it—like Heloise and Abelard. When I am with you, nothing else matters—it's an end in itself."

"And I feel the same," she whispered.

"I want to be completely with you now," I said.

"I wish we could be—that's what I want too—but I don't think that's wise. I couldn't cope just yet with another baby. Nicolas is nearly four, David is less than a year, and we're pretty hard up. We'll just have to be patient a wee while longer—not too long though."

"I hope not," I replied, and we went to sleep, after an embrace that was very hard to bring to a stop.

Next day my preparation for Sunday was interrupted by several chores around the garden, not least by the arrival of a goat—in a taxi. The young man who brought it said that he had heard we wanted a goat. How he heard I will never know, for I had mentioned the idea to John Urquhart only two days earlier. After supper I was still trying to get my sermon into final shape. I was a bit restless and began browsing amongst my books. I had recently picked up a book by Ronald Knox—*The Belief of Catholics*. I happened to alight on the part where he writes about suffering. Perhaps I was particularly drawn to this passage on account of my recent sick-visiting, maybe also because I had a premonition of mental or spiritual suffering. In College we had often discussed inconclusively the problem of suffering, but in the real life of a parish one had to go beyond mere academic talk. In this book I found a striking idea which was new to me. It was a comment on St Paul's words to the Colossians: "It makes me happy to suffer for you, as I am suffering now, and in my body to do what I can to make up all that is still to be undergone by Christ for the sake of his body, the Church" (Col 1:24).

Suffering was said to be something which, if offered to God in the right spirit, was taken up by Christ into his perfect sacrifice to become a spiritual power, helping on the coming of the Kingdom of God. In the past I had always strained to find an excuse for God's permitting suffering. Duncan MacDiarmid had put it to me in this way, that our job is to "justify the ways of God to men." Ronald Knox enabled me to see the problem in a different light: we could, and ought, to set aside the problem of why suffering came to this or that person, and dwell instead on the fact that something can be done with suffering, and that to be permitted to suffer is to be given the privilege of co-operating in a specially effective way with our Lord in his work of redemption.

I became absorbed in what I was reading and at eleven o'clock that night my sermon was still a bit raw. Next morning I was hard pressed to organize my thoughts so that I could adequately deliver to my people the oracle for the week.

9

In our parish the sacrament of Holy Communion was celebrated twice a year, in June and in November. At one time not so long ago the custom was, I imagine, to have only one celebration in the year—in the summer—as is still the norm in much of the West Highlands. When I was minister in Logie Easter people in the West still spoke of "the Communion Season," which ran throughout an octave—Monday to Monday. In preparation for the Sunday celebration there were services of worship every evening, at one of which the elders were expected to answer questions put to them, usually in the form of biblical texts, which they had to expound. At this annual celebration of the sacrament very few people would communicate. In the West Highlands the popular view was that until one was moribund one was unfit to receive Holy Communion. Reading many years later, about the fourteenth-century Cathars of Montaillou in the Arriège I was struck by the similarity of ethos there and that of the Protestant West Highlands today—or perhaps I should say yesterday. It would be wrong, I think, to attribute the ethos of the West Highlands to Calvinism. I think that its origin lies deeper in the ever-present tendency of natural religion towards some form of Manichaeism. It is true, however, that the attitude was not corrected, but encouraged by the former practice in Scotland of "fencing the tables," that is the reciting of a list of sins, warning people that they dare not approach the table of the Lord unworthily.

I am not a professional historian, but I cannot help guessing that the attitude and practice of West Highland Protestant Scotland may be a vestige of late medieval Catholic outlook. The annual celebration of Holy Communion lasting for a week, suggests Holy Week and the prescription that one must receive Communion at least once a year at or about Easter. Another interesting feature of West Highland practice was that the small group of communicants would go on a kind of pilgrimage round several parishes in succession where Holy Communion was being celebrated, receiving Communion at each stop—and also hospitality, which they did not need to arrange in advance. That the Communion season did not fall at Easter was dictated by convenience. The height of summer was a slack period in a crofting community.

In my parish in the fertile eastern coastal fringe with its large farms and the growing influence of the modern urban world, these older customs had changed. We had moved on to biannual Communion and all that was left of the Communion season was the Thursday Fast Day—which was a statutory public holiday—the Friday evening preparatory service, when new communicants would be formally received into full membership of the Church, and the thanksgiving service on the Monday following the Communion Sunday. Why the Thursday was called the "Fast Day," I was never able to discover. Another curious circumstance was that this Thursday was also a public holiday. One of my parishioners, Mr Reid, the Laird of Shandwick, an Englishman and a Scottish Episcopalian, commented: "Fast Day! Farce Day, I call it!" There was certainly no hint that one ought to fast.

In a few weeks I would celebrate the sacrament of Holy Communion for the first time in my life, and I was most anxious that the celebration would be perfect. The order of service recommended in the *Book of Common Order* was based upon the ancient liturgies of the Church. I intended to follow this order and raise up the minds and hearts of the people in the timeless worship of Christendom. But I knew that in spite of the recommendation of this liturgy, many especially in the Highlands regarded it as too "high Church." All that was required canonically for the validity of the Holy Communion was the reading of the words of institution taken from St Paul's Letter to the Corinthians, a blessing-prayer over the elements and their distribution, using the words our Lord used at the

Last Supper. The irony was that the canonical requirements implied just as "high Church" a doctrine of the sacrament as did the liturgy provided by the *Book of Common Order*. It was not doctrine that aroused people's opposition, but the outward form in which it was expressed. A liturgy was for the average Scots Presbyterian a service read from a book, and that was abhorrent—a shutting out of the Holy Spirit, who was expected to provide spontaneous prayer.

Reading through Presbyterian documents with me, a Scottish Episcopal student friend had remarked once that the Presbyterian documents were far more explicitly "high Church" in respect of the eucharist than were his own documents. The fact is often overlooked that on the subject of the eucharist the early documents of the Church of Scotland were more patient of a Catholic interpretation than some other Reformation documents. The Scots Confession of 1560, for example, wrestles with the problem of insisting on the one hand that our Lord is truly present in the sacrament of Holy Communion, while on the other hand refuting the doctrine of transubstantiation. "In the Supper rightly used, Christ Jesus is so joined with us that He becomes the very nourishment and food of our souls. Not that we imagine any transubstantiation of bread into Christ's body, and of wine into His natural blood,..." Further on in the same paragraph they write, "Notwithstanding the distance between His glorified body in heaven and mortal men on earth, yet we must assuredly believe that the bread which we break is the communion of Christ's body and the cup which we bless is the communion of His blood. Thus we confess and believe without doubt that the faithful, in the right use of the Lord's Table, do so eat the body and drink the blood of the Lord Jesus that he remains in them and they in him;..." The chapter concludes in the same vein: "Therefore, if anyone slanders us by saying that we affirm or believe the sacraments to be symbols and nothing more, they are libelous and speak against the plain facts. On the other hand we readily admit that we make a distinction between

Christ Jesus in His eternal substance and the elements of the sacramental signs. So we neither worship the elements, in place of that which they signify, nor yet do we despise them or undervalue them, but we use them with great reverence, examining ourselves diligently before we participate,..."(*The Scots Confession,* chapter XXI).

Before the celebration of Communion there would be a morning service on the Thursday Fast Day, and then the main preparatory service at which those who wished to become communicant members would be formally received. The Church of Scotland does not consider that there is a sacrament of Confirmation, but the *Book of Common Order* went so far as to use the word "Confirmation." Three weeks before the Communion Sunday I requested any who wished to become communicant member to meet me in the vestry that day after the service. I hoped that younger people would begin to resist the weight of public opinion and be courageous enough to seek admission to the Lord's Table.

In a small measure my hope was fulfilled, for as soon as I had reached the vestry John the Beadle said, "Janet Stewart's waiting outside." Before I had time to disrobe and invite the girl to come in, Ross Brennachie, close on the Beadle's heels, was already in the vestry.

He said, "Do you require us to stay, Mr Walls?"

"No," I replied, "I don't think that is necessary."

The schoolmaster, who was Clerk to the Kirk Session had also appeared. Reading Brennachie's mind, as I had not, he intervened quickly, "If anyone comes forward, I'm sure the minister will let us know in good time at the Session meeting on the Fast Day—that's the usual procedure."

"Yes, I'll do that," I assured them.

Brennachie hesitated then left, only to return almost at once to say, "I think there's someone waiting."

"Well, let's get out and leave the minister to his business," said the schoolmaster testily. Brennachie followed him out reluctantly.

All that lay behind this little interlude was to become painfully clear to me in due course, when I discovered that Brennachie still upheld the view that it was the Kirk Session and not the minister who were responsible for Church discipline, an important exercise of which was the admission of candidates to full communicant membership of the Church.

Waiting in the churchyard, too shy and nervous to come near the vestry, stood Janet Stewart, a tinker's daughter. It may be that the word "tinker" is no longer politically correct, but as we used it in those days it had no offensive connotation. The term "traveling people" was clumsy and not really accurate any more, for many of these people no longer traveled around mending pots and pans or selling this and that. There was still one family in our parish who lived in tents and did move about seasonally. In my childhood I remember seeing several tinker encampments. Indeed I had been photographed when about eight years old, standing in the entrance to such a tent. These tents did not have a triangular elevation but were rounded, shaped rather like igloos, and made of strong canvas. Most of these people in our parish now lived in cottages. Janet's family lived in a cottage built of caber and clay, that is having a wooden frame covered with a kind of stucco.

The Scottish tinkers are not to be confused with the Gypsies who live in the Borders around Kirk Yetholm. One of the theories about the origin of the Scottish tinkers is that they are the descendants of dispossessed people, perhaps even members of aristocratic families. It has been said that some of their ancestors may have been courtiers who were left stranded when James VI went off to London after the 1603 union of the crowns. The fact that so many tinkers bear the name Stewart is also suggestive. In Logie Easter I met some whose bearing was undoubtedly regal—imperious at times.

I was delighted to find Janet waiting for me in the churchyard. She was a handsome, well-mannered young woman, about eighteen years of age. Her most striking features were her flaming red hair and abundance of freckles. As soon as we began to chat in the vestry I discovered that she was intelligent and quite articulate. Alone of all the younger people in the congregation that morning, she had responded to my first preparatory sermon, in which I had tried to disabuse people's minds of the grosser forms of misunderstanding of the sacrament. I soon became convinced that she understood in general what she was about to do, but I offered to visit her at home to continue some instruction where her parents too could benefit from what was said. Her parents did not attend church regularly, although all of their children, of whom Janet was the youngest and the only one still at home, had been baptized. Our daily help, Meg, spoke of two groups in the parish: "Church Folk" and others. Although Janet had been coming to church regularly she still did not belong to the "Church Folk." Meg did not consider herself one of the "Church Folk" either. Wherein the distinction between these two groups lay was very difficult to discern. It pleased me greatly to know that my first candidate for admission to Communion was not regarded as a member of the "Church Folk."

On the following Sunday I read the parable of the Great Supper, preaching on the text: "And they all with one consent began to make excuse." The supreme insult we could give our Lord was, I told the congregation, to decline his invitation. To decline was a sign of pride. We were unwilling to accept an invitation, because in our hearts we believed that we had no need of invitation, for we had a right to go to the feast. But the parable taught us that if we decline his invitation in this life, he will close the door of the banqueting hall upon us hereafter. "None of those who were bidden shall taste of my supper."

Again I offered the invitation to come to be received into full membership of the Church at the forthcoming Communion. Still no one else came.

On the following Sunday I preached on the text: "What shall we render unto the Lord for all his benefits? I will take the cup of salvation." The argument was simple. To please God we must be strengthened by him. We cannot give unless he first provides us with a gift. The sacrament is not a reward for virtue but food for sinners. I concluded: "Except ye eat the flesh of the Son of Man and drink his blood, there is no life in you."

Still no new candidates appeared. Janet was to be the only new communicant.

On the Thursday following, that is the Fast Day, I had called the customary Kirk Session meeting to begin an hour before the noon service. Fifty minutes, I thought, would allow enough time for necessary business, but not for protracted discussion. As I entered the churchyard I heard the bus rattling along the main road, picking up the many parishioners who were off to enjoy the public holiday in Dingwall or Inverness. Mr Cooper, the Session Clerk, was waiting in the vestry, dressed as always in his fluffy Tweed jacket. On the previous day he had reassured me as we composed the agenda by saying, "Remember, Mr Walls, that the Session are here to assist you serve the tables, but the Communion is a ministerial act, and you are in charge." His comment was cheering, and I had not realized that he upheld the Auld Kirk tradition in these matters. What I failed to see, however, was that he said this in order to warn me of squalls ahead. A few minutes later Skinner arrived, having made a detour to examine the tombstone about which he was so concerned. Then came, slowly and in quiet conversation, Ross Brennachie and Hughie the Post.

The meeting began ten minutes late—a good thing, I thought. I constituted the meeting with prayer and we got down to business. No sooner had we begun than Skinner tried to raise the matter of the tombstone. He was quickly suppressed and told to keep that matter for an ad hoc meeting later. This settled, Brennachie began nervously, "If anyone has shown a desire to join the Church at these sacraments, could the minister let us know?"

There was something in his tone that disturbed me.

"Have you an agenda, Mr Cooper?" I asked.

"Yes, and that's on it; but we had better take things in the right order. First we must ask the minister to explain the Order of Service so that we all know exactly what we have to do."

"Very well, then," I responded, "I will do that as briefly as I can."

Brennachie was a bit taken aback, but could do nothing in the face of the Clerk's polite but firm ruling. I went on quickly.

"The first part of the service presents no difficulty— it's no different from any Sunday morning. When we come to the Communion proper I want to follow the Order set out in *the Book of Common Order*; if we do that we will be in line with the practice usually observed now in the Church of Scotland. According to this Order the minister and the Session retire to the vestry after the sermon, and return carrying in the elements, which they set upon the table."

It was clear that Brennachie was getting worried. He sat straight up in his chair and at last found words: " Is that not too much like a procession?"

With a speed and nonchalance that amazed myself I replied: "Yes, it really is a procession—a very short one, we proceed from the vestry to the Communion Table to set it ready for the Lord's Supper."

Brennachie said nothing. He had expected a contradiction. There was a twinkle in the Session Clerk's eye. I continued.

"After the consecration of the bread and the wine the minister receives Communion and then hands the bread and wine to the elders, who partake and then take Communion to the communicants, who are all sitting in the front two or three pews at the front of the church. They allow a short pause between the distribution of the bread and the cup."

The Clerk interposed: "This year it is Ross Brennachie and Hugh MacMillan who carry the bread and Alex Skinner and myself who carry the wine."

"Did you say that the minister receives before the Session?" asked Brennachie. "In the old days it was always the elders who received and then served the minister."

"That was before the union, though," said the Clerk, "and only in the down church."

I was beginning to learn more about local Church history.

"Well, whatever happened in the past—and perhaps there were various customs—I want to do what is now generally accepted, as set out in the *Book of Common Order.*"

At this point Skinner, who had been day-dreaming, probably about the tombstone, broke in with signs of impatience. "What does it matter if we go from A to Z or Z to A as long as we all know what we are doing, and there is no confusion. Do what the minister says and let us get on; John Urquhart will be ringing the bell in a few minutes."

Hughie the Post glanced at his watch. "The mail train is in at 12:15 and I'm on duty; I'll have to go now."

Brennachie shot a pained look at him. I realized now why they had been in close conversation before the meeting. "What about new communicants?" he asked.

"Yes," I said, "we'll come to that. There is little else to say about the Communion service—only that after the Blessing at the end of the service I will ask the congregation to wait until the elders and I have carried the residue of the elements to the vestry."

Brennachie had his hand on Hughie's arm and would certainly have spoken again about processions, this time one that seemed even more idolatrous than the former, but he was obviously filled with even greater anxiety over the topic of new communicants. "What about new communicants?" he said.

"Only one has come forward," I replied, "Janet Stewart."

"Should she not have come before the Session?" said Brennachie.

"Is that necessary, do you think?" I asked, looking at the Clerk, "she will have to answer questions at the preparatory service on Friday evening, and that should be a good test of her sincerity. I have carefully instructed her and can assure you that she knows what she is doing."

"Yes, it really is the minister's business to satisfy himself on these things," said the Clerk. "I move that Janet's name be put on the communicants' roll."

I had not expected such a simple solution. Brennachie was clearly shattered, but he had not quite finished. Meantime Hughie pleaded, "I'll have to go," but Brennachie kept a grip on him, and he sank back onto his chair.

"Are we agreed, then?" I asked.

Cooper and Skinner nodded assent, but Brennachie's face turned severe. "I know the girl," he said, "and I know the family; she's much too young, and in any case the Session should have been informed earlier on."

"Do you vote against this motion?" I asked.

"I don't like disagreeing with the minister," he replied, "but yes, on this I must disagree in conscience. I ask you, Mr Walls, to put the girl off for a good while yet. It would be a bad example."

"Aye, she very young" said Hughie, more to Brennachie than to the Chair. Will you excuse me," and he was off.

"I take it then that there are two against our enrolling Janet and two in favor. I must say that I was unaware that the Session had a say in this matter, but we can't go into that now. As things have developed in this way I will have to finish off in the same spirit, although I dislike being legalistic. I will use my casting vote and decide to enroll the girl."

The church bell was ringing now. I rose and raised my right hand to give a blessing. With a sudden and quite fierce movement Brennachie pulled my arm down.

"There's no blessing now," he blurted out, "the Session is in session until the end of the Communion service."

"I see," I said, "in that case we will do what is customary." I said a short prayer and we dispersed. I was content to concede this last round to Brennachie, believing that his satisfaction would prevent him causing any more trouble for the moment. I put on my robes and followed John into church to begin the Thursday Fast Day service.

On Friday afternoon I had a visitor at the manse—Brennachie himself. We sat down in the study and he began immediately. "I went home yesterday, Mr Walls, with a sore heart, a sore heart."

I was at a loss what to say and kept silent.

"Why, Mr Walls, why must you make all these innovations."

"Innovations! They aren't innovations, Mr Ross. The whole service is based on ancient custom and usage, and the *Book of Common Order*, which is the one official guide we have, was authorized in 1940."

"That's not so long ago; there have been General Assemblies of the Church before the one that authorized the book, and there will be others in future; why must we be bound by that particular Assembly?"

"Tell me, Mr Ross, your reasons for objecting to any of the things I mentioned yesterday."

"There is the procession, for example. I don't see why the minister has to go out with the elders to bring in the elements."

"How does that make a difference?" I asked.

"It makes it like a papistical procession."

"Mr Ross, you are quibbling; the minister should be there to lead the Session in prayer before they return."

"One of the elders could easily do that," he countered.

"Mr Ross, we had our Session meeting yesterday; the matter was disposed of, and I'm afraid it is now too late to change things."

"It is not too late, for the Session is still in session. And there is another thing that wasn't mentioned. What about the wine?"

"That has been seen to; I will donate the wine myself."

"Do you know that we use unfermented wine, Mr Walls?"

"Mr Ross, there is no such thing as unfermented wine, and unless we use genuine wine I fear that there is no true sacrament, no presence of Christ with us."

Ross rose to his feet, his normal, fixed Christian smile gone. "What I was beginning to fear is all too true: you are bringing ritualism and idolatry into this parish, and it is my Christian duty to oppose you. I think we need not talk any more about these things."

"This is a most unhappy spirit in which to approach the Lord's Table," I said mildly as I opened the door.

"That spirit was never here before you came, Mr Walls," and he made off towards his car, where his thin, gray-faced wife had been waiting. As he approached she neither raised nor turned her head.

10

On that same Friday, in the evening, we held our preparatory service. This was the service at which I intended to receive Janet Stewart into full communion with the Church. In the *Book of Common Order* this service is entitled, "The Order for the Confirmation of Baptized Persons and for their Admission to the Lord's Supper." Although officially the Church of Scotland does not consider Confirmation to be a sacrament, I had heard others describe it as "a sacramental sort of thing," just as I had heard marriage too described in the same terms. At all events it was a solemn occasion.

"A good gathering tonight," said John, as he helped me put on my Genevan gown. "Gathering" was the word John always used for a worshipping assembly.

"That's encouraging," I answered, then added, "Have you seen Janet?"

"No, but I'll have a look." He went back into the church, returning almost at once to tell me that she hadn't appeared yet.

Although it was mid-summer there had been a haar from the North Sea, so that the air was cool, and the light was dim. John had lit the paraffin lamps and also one or two stoves, the little red windows of which created a warm atmosphere. Even the slight smell of paraffin was pleasant and homely. John had successfully shepherded the congregation into the central area downstairs, and this helped create a family feeling. It was not until we were singing the second hymn that I noticed Mrs Ross, in the back row, alone. For a moment I was relieved, thinking that at least one source of antipathy was absent, and then I was gripped by a very different emotion. Why was he not here; did his absence have something to do with Janet's failure to turn up?

Immediately before the sermon, while we were singing, "Holy Spirit, Joy Divine, gladden thou this heart of mine," John discreetly ascended the pulpit steps and whispered, "There's not a sign of her." With an untranquil and ungladdened heart I quickly recast my sermon, avoiding reference to the admission of a new communicant. I concluded worship with a prayer of general supplication for us all, and gave the blessing, trying as best I could to avoid all sign of agitation,

When all had dispersed—none of the elders came into the vestry—John came in and shut the door firmly behind him. "I'm just after hearing that Alex Dooval—giving Brennachie the name of the croft where he was born—was seen going into the Stewart's house at half past six. It's him that's stopped her coming—nothing surer." His look indicated that he was ready to accompany me on an armed expedition.

"I'd better go up and see," I remarked weakly.

"Yes, catch him while he's still in it; and if you do, excuse me for saying it, Mr Walls, but stand on his neck, the bloody upstart—there's no use being soft with him!"

On this non-liturgical note our preparations for Holy Communion ended.

I set off for the Stewart's cottage, but I knew that it was not in my make-up to have a face to face fight with Brennachie. He was an old man and I could not consider rebuking him. I could argue and be firm in discussion, but I did not know how one set about disciplinary action or even if it were feasible. Perhaps I was beginning to take his point of view seriously. Had he not perhaps the right as an elder to act as he had done? He was only acting in accordance with practice still traditional in some parts of Scotland, and it was true that theoretically elders formed the court whose duty was to rule in a parish. It could be argued that it was I who was disturbing things by upholding another tradition, which also existed within the Church of Scotland. In arguing about baptism with Brennachie I had become aware of the problem of differing interpretations of scripture by individuals, now I saw that there was also a possibility of conflict in respect of the government of the Church. These were aspects of the same problem. How was unity to be acquired and maintained in the Church, and wherein did final authority lie?

When I reached the Stewart's little caber and clay cottage there was no sign of Brennachie. Janet was neatly dressed and had obviously been ready to set out for church. Her father who was crippled, sat on the one decent chair they possessed, her mother, a big tousled woman, hung back in the doorway. Janet was quite a contrast to both of her parents.

"What's gone wrong?" I asked.

"I think perhaps I am too young after all," said the girl.

There would be no use making a fuss, and so I said quietly, "Well, maybe you'll think about it next time."

"You see," said her father, "some would say she's too young, and us not being Church folk anyway might make things difficult for you."

The poor soul—he didn't relish the thought of his family being a cause of friction between the minister and an elder. For the time being there was nothing more I could do. I went home hoping that Brennachie would cause no further trouble over this Communion. How mistaken I was.

Next morning we had a phone call from Duncan MacDiarmid.

"I'm well ahead with preparation for tomorrow," he said, "how are you fixed?"

"I've already prepared." I had established the habit of preparing sermons the previous Monday or Tuesday, and in doing this made good use of Calvin's scripture commentaries, of which I had a complete set.

"Well, would you like us to come over and see you this evening?"

This was a providential relief—a ray of sunlight—I could do with letting off steam to someone. Had he heard rumors that I had had a bit of trouble? More than likely, considering the extra-ordinary efficiency of the Easter Ross jungle telegraph.

"Come over for supper at 6.30," I said.

The MacDiarmids possessed a car which made it easier for them to visit us than the other way round.

We talked of many things, and there was no lack of humor. Duncan although very conscientious never let things get him down. He told me that he had a friend in primary school in Motherwell—that must have been during World War I—who when up against trouble always said, "Aw forget it."

"That's my philosophy," Duncan told me, "for a happy life, every morning two tablespoonfuls of 'Aw forget it'."

We had got onto this subject after I told him how worried I was over the conflict with Ross Brennachie. "It'll pass," he said, "It'll pass. I don't know if I would have had the stomach to stand up to him though, like you've done. You'll go far." Indeed I was to go further than he wished. The Brennachie incident led us to talk seriously about the conflict between the two traditions, one stressing the authority of the Kirk-Session, the other that of the minister.

"You know," said Duncan, "up here at a Session-meeting it can be like facing the Sanhedrin; down in the Borders, especially if it's a former Auld Kirk parish, the minister is in complete charge."

I had just found in a cupboard an old Kirk-Session minute book, which ought long since to have been sent off for safe-keeping in the archives. We had a look at it that evening. It proved just how powerful the Kirk-Session had been even when things were changing in the nineteenth century. We picked up the saga of one poor lass who lived at Phippsfield. Over a period of about twelve years she regularly "compeared" before the Kirk-Session. The very use of this legal term reveals the power of the Kirk-Session. If you were summoned you had to compear. Time after time, then, she compeared before the Kirk-Session accused of having begotten a child out of wedlock. She was obliged to divulge the name of the father, who in his turn was summoned to compear before the Session in the parish where he lived. The girl was admonished, and having repented was "absolved of her sin, and admitted to the privileges of religion, in the name of the Kirk-Session." This meant that she could now have the child baptized.

"At least we don't do that nowadays," I said, "I doubt if Brennachie even would insist. I think he would just want to ignore such people, and he's not all that bothered about baptism."

"Quite simply they wouldn't come now," said Duncan, "notice how the whole system faded out up here just before the First World War. I think it was on the way out sooner in some parts. You read about it in John Galt's novel, *The Annals of the Parish,* don't you?"

"But all the same she must have been some girl," said Bessie MacDiarmid. Then she continued. "Nowadays they leave these things to the minister—if he's willing to take them on. On the Black Isle they tell a story about seven girls, living in seven villages quite far apart, who all had babies—off the ration—within the same week, all by the same father, and word got out who he was. The minister of the father's parish, who was a mild and gentle soul, talked to the boy. 'Peter,' he said, 'Peter, how could you do such a thing?' 'I borrowed the Postie's bike'."

And so to bed after a week of tense drama, but concluded in the delightful company of those who were to become our closest and life-long friends.

The Communion Sabbath dawned—at about three in the morning—very bright and with the promise of heat. At 11.30 a.m. I poured half a bottle of Port wine into a big silver flagon and took it over to the vestry, where I poured it into our two silver, tulip-shaped chalices, and then robed myself. If all were ready there would be less chance, I thought, of any argument or discussion taking place. I had scarcely done this, and was standing in an "I'm not very keen on being disturbed" attitude, when Brennachie entered the vestry.

"Good morning," I said.

There was no response. He laid his bowler hat on the window-sill and then spoke.

"Are you meaning to go on with this, Mr Walls?"

"With what?" I asked.

"All this ritualism; are you going on with it as you said?"

"Mr Ross," I replied, "we discussed the order of service at the Session meeting on Thursday, and all seemed to have been settled. In any case we are not doing anything that is not fully sanctioned by the Church of Scotland–and I simply do not accept your vague charge of ritualism. Indeed I don't understand it."

"Mr Walls, you know very well that you are introducing things that were not done here before."

"Tell me one thing to which you must object–in conscience."

"This procession for a start," he almost exploded. "If you go on with that there are some here today who will refuse to partake of the sacrament."

I was taken aback at this threat, but fortunately was able to hide my concern. Soon after this incident I learned that by "some people" Ross meant "my wife." But he went on.

"And even more serious–the wine. To think that the Lord's presence among us depends on having a particular liquid to remind us of his blood is sheer idolatry."

"Then if it doesn't matter what sort of beverage we use you can have no objection to not using the particular kind of wine you say was used last time."

I saw that he grasped the logic of this argument. That only made him very angry, and he showed it. Not only was the Christian smile gone, but it had been replaced by a look of righteous anger. When arguing with Ross over the doctrine of baptism I had already begun to feel insecure, for I was unable to appeal to any authority other than my own conviction. There were some definite affirmations in the Confessions of Faith, but in practice, in the day to day preaching within the Church, there was a lot of variation and ambiguity. The problem was not just how to interpret scripture, but how also to interpret official doctrinal statements as they emerged down the centuries. In my present confrontation with Ross Brennachie, the same issue arose, and a feeling of uncertainty assailed me. Was I at fault in setting so much store on achieving my fondest objective, which was to celebrate a genuine, ancient, eucharistic liturgy, one which moreover was widely used in the Church of Scotland? However, if I felt like this why didn't he also? He was simply holding onto his personal conviction. Morally, therefore, there was no obligation on me to give in to him. On the contrary I was morally obliged to prevent him ruling the roost. And so I quickly put off the "pale cast of thought" that was threatening to unnerve me and replied abruptly.

"No, Mr Ross, I'm sorry; it is too late to alter what has been agreed upon in the Session. As for your objection to using normal wine, as I have said, you are being illogical, in fact it's ridiculous. After all we're only using what our Lord used."

For some reason my concluding remark had touched him on the raw. He now responded, not in word but in action. With amazing agility for a man of over seventy he hopped round to the back of the table and deftly emptied the two chalices into the coal-scuttle by the fireplace. He retreated towards the door, trembling just a little.

"There's still some harmless wine unopened in that cupboard; and I repeat that if you leave the Church with the elders to fetch the elements, there are some who will refuse to partake. I am very sorry, Mr Walls, but it is my duty to put down idolatry." Ross Brennachie's violence shook me at first, then only confirmed me in my resolution not to yield another inch. John arrived a few minutes later to find me adding the unfermented "wine" to the now aromatic coal-scuttle. "Look at the label, John," I said, " 'Not to be drunk as a beverage,' and yet he wants to use it for Communion."

"But you're not using it now?" he asked.

"No, but Brennachie has just emptied the real stuff into the coal-scuttle."

"The...", and the word died on John's lips.

"Excuse me for telling you, Mr Walls, but that was what most of the row was about at the time of the Union. Some of the U.F.ers fought about it because in the Auld Kirk we would never have used anything but the real stuff. They threatened to keep out of the Union if they didn't get their way."

Now I realized why Brennachie had got so worked up over this issue. It was not a question of theology so much as of prestige and church politics.

"John," I said, "go to the manse when you have put me in, bring over the bottle you'll find on the study table, and fill the two chalices—and hide the bottle; it's only when he receives Communion that he'll get a fright—if he even notices.

"The very thing!" said John with a glint in his eye.

The hum-tone of the bell died away; the congregation were assembled; the elders sat round the Communion Table beneath the pulpit; John led me in, and after I had ascended the steep flight of steps to the pulpit, performed his ritual shutting of the pulpit door; there was silence—no organ voluntary, to emphasize the solemnity of the occasion.

"Let us worship God," and the Service had begun— my first Communion Service.

> O send thy light forth and thy truth,
> Let them be guides to me,
> And bring me to thy holy hill,
> Ev'n where thy dwellings be...
> Then will I to God's altar go,
> To God my chiefest joy;
> Yea, God, my God, thy name to praise,
> My harp I will employ.

A great column of song rose up from the congregation and seemed to drive away the demon of discord I had so recently encountered. In the center area downstairs sat the communicant members, about thirty of them; at the sides and in the galleries, which were on three sides, sat the adherents and the children. The church was fuller than it had ever been since I came. The prayers and psalms and scripture readings were soon over and we came to the culmination of the first part of the service—to the sermon, which on this occasion was purposely short and dogmatic.

The first point I made was that the sacrament of Holy Communion is the presence of Christ. I quoted Calvin: "(It is) the true and substantial communication of the body and blood of the Lord." The second point was that just as natural food gives strength to our bodies, so the sacramental elements give strength to our souls, and again I quoted Calvin: "They are received, not by the imagination or intellect merely, but are enjoyed in reality as the food of eternal life." The third point I made was that by our sacramental action we are brought into the presence of Christ on the Cross, so that we are assured of receiving the effects of that sacrifice. When I held up the bread and the cup after the prayer of blessing, I explained, I would be holding them up not so much for us to see as for the heavenly Father to behold, and have regard to the one sacrifice of Christ on the Cross. At this sacrament, time vanishes and Christ is offered up through the eternal Spirit to God the Father in heaven, and we are being caught up in that offering.

I had come to the conclusion that Calvin's doctrine permitted this view of the sacrament, but I admit that already I had been much influenced by a little book by Fr MacEvoy, S.J., entitled, *The Sacrifice We Offer*. Above all, however, I considered that the Letter to the Hebrews contained just such a doctrine as I expounded at this my first celebration of Holy Communion.

The congregation, I sensed, were with me; there was absolute silence and their faces demonstrated genuine attention. The elders, below me and facing the congregation, were out of my line of vision, but I had quite forgotten about Brennachie and our duel in the vestry.

The sermon over I descended and standing behind the Table read the "comfortable words." "Come unto me, all ye who labor and are heavy laden, and I will give you rest" followed by the prescribed words of invitation to the Lord's Table. I announced the psalm "Ye gates, lift up your heads," and announced that the Session would retire to the vestry to bring in the elements during the singing. Miss Fleming began to play and the elders rose and began to walk towards the vestry. My eye met Mrs Ross sitting at the end of the front pew. I moved to follow the elders. She rose, dropping her hymn-book as she did so, and moved back out of the area reserved for communicants. There was tense silence, and none stood up to begin the psalm. Miss Fleming played the tune over once more, this time very loudly, and soon all were singing heartily. The Session and I returned and laid the bread and wine on the table as the congregation were singing, "Be lifted up, that so the King of Glory may enter, Alleluia, alleluia, alleluia."

I took my place at the center of the table and read the Nicene Creed, which many thought was my own composition. Soon we had read the Pauline words of institution, and the prayers, which I had memorized, were in full flood.

"Verily holy, verily blessed art thou, Almighty and merciful God, who didst so love the world that thou gavest thine only-begotten Son, that whosoever believeth in him should not perish but have everlasting life.

"Not as we ought but as we are able, do we bless thee for his holy incarnation, for his perfect life on earth, for his precious sufferings and death upon the Cross, for his glorious resurrection and ascension, for his coming again, and for the gift of the Holy Spirit."

And so the prayer moved on from the Anamnesis into the Oblation, which to me seemed the most poignant part of the whole liturgy:

"...which memorial do thou, most merciful Father, behold, and have regard to the Sacrifice once offered upon the Cross, once and for all, a full, perfect and sufficient satisfaction, oblation, and propitiation for our sins and for the sins of the whole world."

At last we reached the climax. "Take, eat, this is my Body which is broken for you: this do in remembrance of me:...This cup is the new covenant in my Blood..."

I recited the "Lamb of God...," partook myself and passed the sacrament on to the elders, who handed first the Bread and then the Wine to each other. After a short pause they distributed in like fashion to the congregation, that is to those sitting in the front pews. The fragments were brought back to the table, there was a short prayer of thanksgiving, after which we sang Psalm 103, "O thou, my soul, bless God the Lord."

I announced that the elders would leave first. No sooner had I finished the blessing than Mrs Ross rose and left noisily. The elders began to move out, carrying the residue of the elements—all except Ross Brennachie, who sat firmly in his seat. Skinner, ever practical, picked up Brennachie's plate and we all moved out. In the vestry I gave another blessing, thus closing the Session meeting. I thanked the elders for their orderly and reverent serving of the Lord's Table.

Brennachie never appeared and the others soon went off home. John was in church removing the white linen cloths from the front pews. I did not bother to take off my gown and cassock but sat very still in the vestry, not knowing whether to be pleased or dejected. Had this been a true *leitourgia*—a common work—or had I produced something I thought was theologically and aesthetically satisfying, relying solely on my own opinion? I was uneasy, too, about my sermon. Was it true that what I said was perfectly in line with Calvin? And then the thought came to me: if what I said was true and was not in line with Reformed teaching, was I justified in claiming to be a minister of a Reformed Church? I looked at the fragments on the plates and the residue of wine in the two cups. What was I supposed to do with these? John would soon be back in the vestry so I hid the residues in the cupboard.

On Monday morning I resumed work on the holly hedge, but found it hard going. For a start the saw was not properly set; but it was not just that—I was emotionally and physically tired, and my mind was still at work trying to pull myself out of the morass of confusion into which I seemed to be sinking. Argument about doctrine and practice in respect of Holy Communion had widened the area of dispute. I could see now that there was more to it than conflict between individuals. When Brennachie claimed that he was enlightened in his interpretation of scripture by the Holy Spirit, it was no use my countering with the same claim, or even with a claim that I, in virtue of ordination, but still as an individual, had more claim on the Holy Spirit's guidance than he. What I was doing, what I had to do, was to claim that my interpretation—whether of scripture or of confessional statements—was supported by some kind of consensus, some tradition. But, then, was that not precisely what he was doing? The conflict was not between me and Brennachie, but between two different traditions. He complained that I was innovating, I that he was innovating. It seemed that all of us take our stand within some form of consensus or tradition. Then I began to ask: when is it legitimate to oppose and correct a tradition? The tradition that I was upholding had itself begun with innovation, with the rejection of the medieval Catholic tradition. Was I being inconsistent: how does one justify a tradition which originated in the rejection of tradition? And what is the relationship between tradition and the revelation of the Word made flesh? I still had a lot of thinking to do.

John Urquhart was on a late shift that day and about an hour after I had begun work on the hedge he appeared.

"Good morning," he said "what's new?"

"Nothing, as far as I know, John."

"And I didn't hear a thing myself," was his response. This interchange was another of John's rituals.

"Could you get my saw sharpened and set, John?" I asked.

"Certainly; and I'll get you mine now so that you can get on with the job." He went off immediately and was soon back with his own saw.

"That holly will make great burning," he said, "and I'll give you a hand to cut it into logs. That was a grand sermon you made yesterday, and grand prayers too."

"It's good of you to say so John."

"Oh," he continued, "you'll not mind if I just tidy up the bread and the wine that was left the way I used to do before these U.F.ers began to rule the roost?"

"Not at all, John," I answered, heartened by the thought that perhaps I would be enlightened about the Auld Kirk tradition and saved the responsibility of making a decision, "you'll find the bread and the wine in the cupboard in the vestry."

"I'll do that now," he said, "the wife ever just gave the bread to the hens and I take the Port down to Euphemia Grant."

I took little comfort in this custom, but for the meantime was willing to go along with it; and the memory came back to me just then of one of Professor Thomson's digressions in the Dogmatics class. Speaking of Calvin's doctrine of the eucharist, which is succinctly expressed in chapter XXI of *The Scots Confession*, he remarked that when he saw his housekeeper throwing the bread to the hens he felt uneasy, although strictly speaking after the action of the eucharist is over the bread ought not to be venerated in any way. His advice about the disposal of the wine was exactly in line with what John had just proposed. "But," he warned, "don't give them that unfermented stuff–it'll kill them."

I got on with cutting down the wild hedge. I felt better now, and John's saw made the work a lot easier. My recollection of Professor Thomson's remark set me thinking about *The Scots Confession*. Did the problem not result in large measure from the need to hold together two apparently incongruous statements, one which affirms that "we confess and believe that the faithful, in the right use of the Lord's Table, do so eat the body and drink the blood of the Lord Jesus that he remains in them and they in Him," along with the related, "if anyone slanders us by saying that we affirm or believe the sacraments to be symbols and nothing more, they are libelous and speak against the plain facts," and the other, which affirms that "we readily admit that we make a distinction between Christ Jesus in His eternal substance and the elements of the sacramental signs"? That is to say—I was beginning to see the problem more clearly—on the one hand the early Scottish Reformers maintained quite vehemently, especially against Zwingli, whom they abhorred, that Christ was really or effectively present in the sacramental signs, while at the same time they refused to accept transubstantiation. He is, one might say, really present *dynamically*, but his substance remains in heavenly glory. As I continued for another hour to hack away at the wild and tangled hedge, I took comfort from the fact that a distinguished professor of Dogmatics had, as a parish minister, shared my unease over the disposal of the sacramental signs.

11

It was customary at the Communion Season to have a visiting minister at one of the services. I had invited Alastair Sutherland, the minister of the adjacent parish of Kilmuir Easter, to preach at the thanksgiving service on the Monday after the Communion, and so on that Monday I had felt free to take some recreation by sawing at the hedge. The Kilmuir Easter manse was only three miles away, and Alastair Sutherland came over at about seven o'clock. He must have been about ten years my senior and had been in Kilmuir Easter since his ordination. We didn't see a great deal of the Sutherlands, although they were very friendly. His sight was very poor and to make matters worse, as the result of an accident he had completely lost the sight of one eye. Duncan MacDiarmid once said, "If Alastair Sutherland could see a bit better, he wouldn't drive half so fast."

There was a fairly good attendance at the thanksgiving; the Brennachies were both there in their accustomed pew at the front of the gallery; all went well without any incident. After the service we chatted for a while in the manse, and Alastair told me that one of the Cromarty family had asked him to conduct their wedding. The Countess of Cromarty's mansion was in my parish, but this family were heritors in Kilmuir Easter as well, that is they were landowners who paid tiends to the Church. It was from these tiends that the clergy received much of their stipends. I was pleased to learn that Alastair had been asked to conduct this wedding service.

"The couple who are getting married live mostly in England, and I think they are Church of England, but they want to be married up here, near the family seat."

"Good for them!" I said.

"You have a stole, haven't you?" he asked.

"Yes," I said. This stole, although black and adorned only with a gold St Andrew's cross at each end, was undoubtedly one of the things that Brennachie abhorred–a sign of Popish tendencies.

"Would you mind lending it to me for the wedding? It would brighten things up a bit?"

I smiled, "Of course."

"One of the parties is a divorcee," he continued.

"Oh, I see," I responded, but I didn't really see at all. I was merely slightly disturbed at the thought of co-operating in the celebration of a marriage which I would not have been willing to conduct myself. Luckily in the short time I spent in this parish I was never faced with the problem of the remarriage of a divorced person. Was there an official line on this in the Church of Scotland? I knew that ministers differed amongst themselves on the question. My neighbor was obviously quite content to officiate at this wedding. Only very much later did I realize the truth. The couple had probably requested marriage in the Church of England and been refused, and so they decided to get married in Scotland near the family seat. This is exactly what happened with the Princess Royal at Crathie.

I had been an ordained minister and in charge of a parish for only three months, but my theological development had moved on fast. Confrontation with Brennachie over baptism and the eucharist, and over the disciplinary matter of admission to full membership of the Church, my having to face up to the problem of what to do with the residual elements after Communion, and in general the immense responsibility of the ministerial office had caused the notional seeds of doctrinal problems sown in the time of academic preparation, to sprout vigorously. Where would it all lead? There was still a lot of wild hedge to cut down, and I foresaw many an hour spent at it, sawing away and wrestling all the time with fundamental problems, which I now realized would be mainly about ecclesiology. The culminating row with Brennachie over the Communion wine introduced a period of uneasy truce. I had made my point by establishing the observance of the liturgy according to the norm of the *Book of Common Order*, he had made his by obstructing my attempt to admit the tinker girl to Communion. My next and final confrontation with him was still a few months ahead, and it was, as it were, by proxy on his part. Meantime he registered his disapproval silently. At the thanksgiving service on the Monday after Communion he paid devout attention to Alastair Sutherland's sermon, but on the following Sunday and on every Sunday thereafter, sitting in the front pew in the gallery, he ostentatiously read and leafed through his Bible while I preached. There were occasions when he went off to some other parish to worship on Sunday morning. There were no further demonstrations at a Communion service. Indeed I cannot remember him attending any of the remaining four I celebrated at six month intervals before leaving the parish. On these days he probably went off elsewhere.

During that first summer in our very beautiful home, we settled in well. With John Urquhart's help I got the garden in order and producing vegetables. I asked John what I should pay him. He answered, "Mr McBain ever paid me one and ninepence an hour—that's fine. I manage to put in four hours most weeks, and that exactly pays for the rent of the cottage." I already had nine hens, but they didn't begin to lay until the end of the year. I bought a brooder and reared White Aylesbury ducklings. The following year, when one of the hens went broody, I set her on four goose eggs and reared the goslings—the three that escaped the ravages of the buzzards. We already had a beautiful, very young Toggenberg goat whom we named Griselda, and who, in spite of her youth, proved to be pregnant and gave birth to two lovely kids in August. In July I made an excursion to Drumnadrochit where I bought a cross-bred White Saanan milking goat. I hitched a lift with her on a lorry from a hydro-electric scheme and put her in the guard's van on the train at Inverness. From then on our children never tasted cow's milk until we returned to Edinburgh two years later. Our most exciting acquisition was probably the bees. John Urquhart was able to get us a swarm from a friend, and Peggy Logan, the local bee-wife from the Agricultural College, taught me how to manage them. The Logan family farmed Pitmaduthy, which adjoined our glebe. There was quite a worn track across the small field between us, for the Logans became firm friends. Helen and Marion, the wife of the young farmer, were specially close.

In spite of the idyllic environment and the support of good friends like the Logans and the MacDiarmids we were troubled by unease of mind and heart—not too violent, but persistent, a cloud on the horizon. I was not unduly worried on account of Brennachie, for I knew that the parish as a whole were behind me, but I was worried over the issues he had forced me to face. It may have been that already I had subconsciously reached the conclusions that in the end were to bring much pain upon us.

My unease was caused not only by failure to resolve the problem of teaching-authority—for I was beginning to see that this was the right way to describe my conflict with Brennachie—but also by the growing sense that we were being denied a full private life. We were undoubtedly afflicted with the gold-fish bowl syndrome. But the parishioners were not entirely to blame. I could see that the syndrome resulted in part at least from my own attitude. I was the parish Person and did feel that I belonged to the parish; and because Helen and I were one flesh and the family an extension of that union, parishioners quite naturally, and justifiably, saw all of us wrapped in the mantle of ordination. Not only I but all of us belonged to the parish. Never for a moment did I allow this awareness to dilute my affection for Helen and the family, but none the less a tension was developing. My relationship with the parish and with individual parishioners was not a professional but a personal relationship, and I could see that this forced me to live in two spheres at once—the world of marriage, and the world of the ordained ministry. It was not just a problem of distribution of time and energy, but a problem of inner disposition. I knew that the Church of Scotland regarded neither marriage nor ordained ministry as a sacrament, but in practice I was beginning to feel a sacramental rivalry between marriage and ministry. It was as though one man was trying to be a faithful husband to two wives. Marriage and ordained ministry were too alike; both required an unreserved giving of oneself; the minister was Christ the Bridegroom's representative in the parish, and his sacramental marriage and his natural marriage were both earthed in the one male body. The only way to release the tension thus caused would be to professionalize the ministry—a solution I could not accept.

On one of our visits to the MacDiarmids we must have been talking about this sort of thing. To my surprise Bessie remarked that she thought Duncan should never have married. "I think that we've hindered him: he's so dedicated, but I think he would have liked to be even more dedicated to his work than we've let him be." I was interested to learn that I was not alone in sensing this tension between marriage and the ministry, especially as the comment came from the wife's angle.

After a few months in the parish the notion came into my mind that Helen and the family should live somewhere else—perhaps in Skye—while I worked single-mindedly in the parish for spells, interrupted by visits to the family. The notion was as bizarre as it was impracticable, but it was born of a real problem.

This personal problem was no doubt aggravated by the strain of thinking through the doctrinal problems that faced me, but was not directly their product. It would have arisen even if I had remained oblivious to all that Brennachie had providentially forced me to face. I say "providentially" for I had been set onto a course of study that led in the end to the resolution of the problem. As background I had the memory of Professor Burleigh's early Church history lectures, from which I had gained a clear picture of the formation of the Creeds by the ecumenical councils; and I had begun to read the *Catechism of the Council of Trent* as well as books like Ronald Knox's *The Belief of Catholics*. Slowly the thought came to me that perhaps after all the Roman Catholic view of doctrine and of the nature of the Church would have to be given a fair hearing. In spite of my education I retained vestiges of the horror of idolatry and ritualism that had caused me to flee from the Moray Aisle as a schoolboy. It came to me as a relief, however, when I found myself saying: "The Roman Catholic position is at least a possibility."

Late on in that summer I spoke to Helen about what was going on in my head. " I wonder," I said, "if the answer is to accept the Roman Catholic position?"

"Well," she replied, "if you do, you'll have to do it on your own. There's a lot I can't swallow in Roman Catholicism."

In my family the horror of Rome had lurked in subconsciousness; in hers it lay nearer the surface. Her father was a West Highland minister, for whom the Church of Rome was still the Scarlet Woman or the Synagogue of Satan, in spite of the fact that years earlier he had been very friendly with the priest in Ballachuilish, even visiting him on his death-bed. Helen's remark did not upset me too much, however, for at this stage my proposition was tentative, and Helen was not aggressively hostile. In fact she was already reading with great interest some of the literature we had acquired, and being a voracious reader she got through far more than I did. In particular she was profoundly influenced by the life and writings of Mother Janet Erskine Stewart.

"Of course," she said, "there are some things in Catholicism that I do agree with: their attitude to abortion and contraception, for example. Some of our people are not all that convinced that abortion is wicked, and contraception is spreading all the time—even among ministers and their wives; and I think they may have a point on this celibacy of the clergy business. It's no fun being a minister's wife—and I can tell you, at times it was no fun at all being a minister's daughter. The hoops we had to jump through in Applecross to keep everybody happy!"

The outcome of our conversations on these matters was that both of us began to read carefully, trying to become properly informed about Catholic doctrine. Equally important was the fact that I was beginning to see the significance of the nineteenth-century Declaratory Acts, which affirmed that the Church alone has authority to determine which doctrines were consonant with the Scriptures. I had taken refuge in the idea that as an ordained minister I might have some authority to preach the Word, but I was not the Church. Where was this Church that could resolve disputes between Christians and between ministers concerning the interpretation of scripture, and so maintain the solid substance of the faith? How did one identify the Church, with whom rested this responsibility? I was beginning to see that the identity of the Church was the key to the solving of my problems. Summer passed very quickly. Suddenly we were in the first week of October. In Scotland, especially in the Moray Firth region, this time is often the loveliest time of the year. It can be warm, warmer sometimes than at mid-summer. The potato-harvest was in full swing. The earth was dry, like oatmeal, and the diggers purred up and down the fields, slowly narrowing the untidy, yellowish area where the decaying shaws were. Children had holidays from school–the "tattie holidays"–and squads of them were at work gathering the potatoes. Springtime is full of promise, but late autumn brings with it a voluptuous sense of consummation–and of hope.

But this delight in "mellow fruitfulness" is short-lived. Quite suddenly near the end of the month comes an abrupt change, and autumn vanishes overnight. On the first Sunday in November we awoke to see a steel sky, sodden leaves on the lawn, and to feel a damp, cold, east wind biting into our bones. The temperature was not so very low, but the humidity and the wind chilled everyone.

Winter had begun. I passed through the gap in the hedge on my way to the church, and the white holly stumps glared at me reproachfully. There was a cluster of folk at the church door, which was unusual, especially in cold weather. Something was amiss. John Urquhart enlightened me the moment I arrived at the vestry. "It's Euphemia Grant," he said, "she's been rushed into hospital in Inverness in the night; it's her heart I think."

"Has she been ill?" I asked.

"Oh, not recently. She had an attack a few years ago, but she never spoke about it. I fear it's serious, though; there's a history of heart trouble in the family; her father died suddenly just at the age she is now. There's nobody but me knows this: four weeks ago she had her lawyer in."

Skinner came in, hung his hat on a peg, and without any explanation—for he always assumed that his audience were already in tune with his thoughts—proceeded: "I was just saying to the wife on the way up, that we could run Miss Nicholson up to Inverness after dinner and visit my brother before we bring her home again. She's fair upset."

The bell had been rung and John came back for the Bible. "If she goes there'll be hardly any of us left." Once again I was reminded of the still unhealed division in the congregation between the former Auld Kirk and the former United Free Kirk.

I knew I would be expected to advert at some point in the service to the bad news about Euphemia Grant. Some ministers, I had discovered, like to make a meal of such incidents, and could become quite maudlin. I opted for restraint and inserted a brief petition for Euphemia in the intercessory prayers. During the afternoon I phoned the Royal Infirmary in Inverness and was told that Euphemia, although holding her own, was very weak. I decided to visit her in hospital as soon as possible. I cannot remember whether in those days there were official chaplains in hospitals, but it was customary for ministers to visit their own parishioners in hospital. In deciding to visit Euphemia Grant I was not just following custom: it was likely that she would die and I did want to see her again, as she had given me such encouragement in my ministry.

On the following Tuesday I took the train to Inverness and visited the hospital in mid-afternoon. The faithful Sarah Nicholson, who had come to stay with a cousin in Inverness so that she could visit regularly, was seated a bit tearful, at the bedside. Euphemia Grant however was far from any picture of misery. In those days people in her state did not have all the apparatus attached to them that one sees today. I could see her face just as it always was, alert and peaceful with a hint of a smile. But she was breathless and very weak. I knew that there was no need to beat about the bush. "You're not very well are you, Euphemia?" I said, using her Christian name for the first time.

"Indeed I'm not," she whispered.

Without embarking on any small talk, I began to read a short passage from scripture and then prayed as tidily as possible–for her concentration must have been impaired–but making sure that I spoke of the chief truths of our Faith. Finally I commended her to the Lord, asking him to comfort her in body and soul and prepare her for the joy of his eternal kingdom.

"Good-bye," I said. She replied, " Thank you, good-bye"–with a remarkably strong stress on the last syllable. That was the last time I saw her. She died peacefully on Friday.

On leaving the hospital I filled in the time before the evening train home by wandering around the town. We rarely found an opportunity to visit Inverness, and it is a town I have always liked very much. I walked along the west side of the river. The Ness is broad and deep and that day it was very full–swollen indeed, for there had been a lot of rain. When I reached the bridge, instead of turning right and crossing I continued along the west bank, heading for the suspension bridge which I could see further downstream. But before I got there I found myself at the Catholic Church. Apart from my compulsory attendance at Mass when in Hungary, I doubt if I had ever been inside a Catholic Church in Scotland. I decided to go inside this one. The open door impressed me. Inside I noticed three people kneeling quietly, obviously at prayer. This too impressed me. I sat down and shortly afterwards knelt and prayed. I prayed for enlightenment to resolve the problems that perplexed me, and for wisdom and prudence to do the work of a parish minister. Ten minutes later I left the church and continued over the suspension footbridge, which shuddered in response to my tread, and gazed down at the mysterious dark water flowing strongly down towards the sea. On the train journey homewards I marveled at the view across to the Black Isle and to the mountains in the west, their beauty enhanced by the bright grayness of the fading daylight.

Euphemia's "remains"—as the body was always called in those days—were brought home on Saturday, accompanied by Miss Nicholson, and the funeral arranged for one o'clock on the following Wednesday. One o'clock was the usual time for a funeral, for the men in the parish could attend during a slightly extended dinner-break. On Monday afternoon I visited Miss Nicholson, and conducted a short service in the presence of a few neighbors who had called. Just before I left, the lawyer from Tain appeared. No doubt Miss Nicholson would find some not unwelcome distraction in her interview with him.

On Wednesday at a quarter to one I found a crowd already gathered at the church door. I had never seen so many bowler hats before. The most unlikely people were wearing them—this was obviously the required uniform. There were several different styles of bowler, some of which dated from before the twentieth century. Many had a greenish tinge, and one or two were quite elongated. The rain had ceased but it was fearfully raw, yet no one entered the church. They were waiting for the arrival of Miss Nicholson and two distant cousins of Miss Grant, who lived in the south of England. Miss Fleming was waiting in the vestry to find out what hymns we were to sing. She spoke in whispers and then tiptoed into the church to take her place at the harmonium. John arrived, wearing a split new bowler. I sent him to bring the three ladies round when they arrived, so that they could be placed comfortably in the front pew. This done, John gave one strong pull at the bell and the congregation all came inside.

The coffin had been placed in church earlier and lay on trestles cross-wise in the narrow space between the front pew and the communion-table area. The service followed the pattern of a Sunday morning service. The center of gravity was the scripture readings and the sermon. I preached on the text: "This corruptible must put on incorruption and this mortal must put on immortality." Having dwelt on the thought that death is our liberation into supernatural and eternal life, I developed also the thought, which had been introduced to me by Ronald Knox, that the sufferings of this life are a means whereby we are permitted to become united with the passion of Christ and so be given the privilege of co-operating in his redemptive work. This union with Christ through suffering brings the greatest possible degree of consolation—the peace that is beyond this world's understanding.

Ross Brennachie was in church, but seated downstairs, as were all the others. It would have been awkward for him on this occasion to read his Bible as I preached. I observed, too, that he sat beside a severe-looking minister whom I did not know. As I developed the themes I had chosen, especially the one on suffering and union with the passion of our Lord, I thought I detected some attention on Brennachie's part. Did he smell a papistical rat? Was the notion that the believer can in some ways become united with the passion of Christ seem to connect with the doctrine of the sacrifice of the Mass? I did not allow my awareness of Brennachie's presence to distract me, but perhaps it did make me very cautious in wording the intercessory prayers. Had I said, for example, "Let us pray for Euphemia Grant," there would certainly have been some kind of eruption.

The funeral service came to a sonorous end as we sang Paraphrase 61—a metrical version of Ephesians 1:3-5—the last verse of which runs:

Saints by the power of God are kept
till the salvation come:
We walk by faith as strangers here,
but Christ shall call us home.

A stir moved over the congregation. The undertaker's men lifted the coffin onto their shoulders, and we all followed them and the three ladies out into the graveyard which surrounded the church on three sides. The pile of soil beside the grave was of pure sand. I took my place at the head of the coffin; the cords were distributed mainly to the elders, including Brennachie, for their were no male relatives, and the three ladies stood together behind me; the supports were removed and the coffin lowered; the cords slackened and were thrown down onto the coffin, and the men stood back a little; all the bowler hats were removed but held as wind-shields behind necks.

" 'I am the Resurrection and the life', saith the Lord, 'whoever believeth in me, though he were dead, yet shall he live: and whoever liveth and believeth in me shall never die'."

I sprinkled fine sand thrice on the coffin: "Earth to earth, ashes to ashes, dust to dust," and I commended the soul of Euphemia Grant to Almighty God, committing her body to the ground, "in sure and certain hope of the resurrection of the dead and the life of the world to come." Two short prayers followed and then the Trinitarian blessing. The funeral was over; we turned away from the grave, the men back to fields and steadings, I to the vestry to disrobe.

On the way back to the manse I shook hands with Miss Nicholson and the two cousins, promising to visit them next day. As I left them, an elderly widow, Mrs Melville, who farmed a small-holding at Arabella, hailed me and came towards me. She was a handsome, well-built woman, and when she began to speak her face always developed a rich smile. Today in spite of the funeral her features had lost none of their sparkle.

"I'm going to say a terrible thing," she began, "I never enjoyed a funeral so much in my life—is that wicked?"

"No, it isn't," I answered, "a funeral should always end in joy, and you pay me a great compliment by suggesting that I have made it seem so. You often hear people saying that in the midst of life we are in death, but it's even truer to say that in death we are at the gates of eternal life."

"Man, indeed you're right," she said, with a conviction that warmed my heart. "Come and see us soon."

I was about to continue through the gap in the hedge when I noticed Brennachie approaching, and with him the minister who had been at his side in church. He was tall and thin, his cheek-bones pronounced and streaked with blue veins. His trousers were a bit short and he was wearing boots. Brennachie introduced him as Mr MacDonald, minister of a parish somewhere in the north-west—or it may have been in the islands—I have forgotten the name. He was a second cousin of Brennachie's wife. We gave one another a formal hand-shake.

Brennachie stood back a little, the minister began without any preamble: "Did I understand that you offered prayer at the graveside for the dead?"

I felt like a boy who has been summoned to the headmaster's room. Doing my best to keep calm and marshal my thoughts I asked him what exactly had made him think that I prayed for the dead.

"After the coffin had been laid to rest," he explained, "you said something about commending the soul of our sister to God."

"Yes," I replied, "but I don't think there's anything improper in such a commendation; we do believe that we leave the soul in God's keeping."

"Oh yes," he said, shaking his head, "but to commend someone to God is to pray for him; and to pray in any fashion for the soul of a deceased person is obnoxious, because it is contrary to the word of God."

I side-stepped his attempt to lure me into a battle of proof texts, partly because I thought that was an unintelligent way to use scripture, and partly because I knew he would have a battery of texts ready to hand and would beat me hands down.

"Surely," I said, as calmly as I could, "at a funeral we must express our confidence that we are leaving our dead in God's keeping; and to commend their souls to him seems to me to be an appropriate way to do this."

He smiled, as though apologizing for having drawn me into an unequal theological contest, and continued.

"We do have confidence, as you say, that the righteous are in God's safe keeping, but why express that confidence in prayer as we bury a person? We do not know, for only God knows, who are the justified righteous. We may pray for all during their life-time, but at their death our prayers for them cease to have any meaning: there is no further change possible for them, their eternal destiny is sealed, 'As the tree falleth, so shall it lie'—Ecclesiastes eleven three. We cannot express confidence that this particular soul is in heaven, and so why do what makes no sense, or worse, might mislead people into thinking that we can alter the state of the soul of the person we have buried. That state has already been fixed by God."

I had said, "But," several times during his harangue. When he had finished I was not sure how to go on. Some of what he said was true, but I felt that his whole outlook contradicted the deep meaning of our faith in God's love. In desperation I began to say too much and opened myself to even more severe attack.

"Of course," I answered, "I agree that at death our eternal destiny is sealed; but does that prevent us expressing hope that the soul has gone to heaven—or is on its way there."

He drew breath with what I can only describe as a snort.

"Hope," he said, "is a great virtue, but when it goes beyond what the clear word of God teaches us, it is no longer hope, but arrogance."

At this point I moved out of the context within which we had been arguing and tried to recall what Professor John Baillie had said about "a kind of purgatory." I said that the souls in heaven could not be said to enjoy perfect bliss until they rejoiced together with all of the elect in the presence of God. It would have been better had I held my peace, for I was beginning to realize that I was not quite sure what I believed. I had found it impossible to commit a body to the earth without making some mention of the soul, but I had not yet reached a firm and coherent doctrine on this subject. All I had done by this interchange of views was to condemn myself completely in Mr MacDonald's eyes—and in Brennachie's, for he was taking in all that was said.

"As your last remarks make all too plain," MacDonald went on, "you do mean to pray for the dead, and you are infected with the monstrous Romish doctrine of purgatory, from which our land was mercifully liberated four centuries ago. I counsel you to consider where in scripture such doctrines can be found. Anything contrary to scripture is from the Devil, the father of lies. 'Thy word is truth' and 'the entrance of thy word giveth light'. I'm afraid you are on a very dangerous path Mr Walls."

I tried to pass off our argument as lightly as possible and said that no doubt we might continue the discussion another time.

"There would be little profit, I think, in doing so." With a curt, "Good day," he turned on his heel, and the two went on their way.

After lunch I put on Wellington boots and went out to work on the hedge. There were squally showers, but I disregarded them and was soon very warm. In one way the recent theological encounter had depressed me, in another way it had stimulated me. I knew that now I had to get right down to the bottom of these problems. The ever-recurring issue was that of the relation between the Church and the scriptures. In spite of what people like Brennachie and his minister accomplice said, everyone did interpret scripture according to their own light. Officially the Church of Scotland had declared and enacted long ago that interpretation was the responsibility of the Church. In my argument with Brennachie's relative I had deliberately avoided raising this question, but it was the most fundamental of all. I could have challenged him, for example, by asking why he cited Ecclesiastes but would not have cited Ecclesiasticus. Who, that is, had determined the canon of scripture? I could, following the same path, have mentioned Professor Burleigh's impish remark that Augustine believed the scriptures to be the word of God because the Church assured him that they were. There had to be an authoritative dogmatic foundation for faith. I was now sure that this must be so. But where was it to be found. I had suggested tentatively to Helen that it might be in the Roman Catholic Church. It was odd that only a few days earlier I had paid my first visit to a Catholic church—at least it is the first of which I have any memory, apart from the Hungarian episode. I had made contact with the stones and furniture of the Catholic Church. And now on this afternoon following the theological duel with a strictly Calvinist minister, which had spurred me on at the intellectual level to face up to Catholic doctrine, I made my first acquaintance with the Catholic Church in flesh and blood.

It was about four o'clock and time to stop work on the hedge. I had to concentrate to ensure that the trunk I had just cut through would fall conveniently inwards, and my back was towards the lawn, so that I did not see two figures approaching across the lawn from the drive. As the tree fell safely to the ground I heard a guttural voice say, "Good-day, I am the camp-leader." I looked round and saw two men dressed in earth-brown battle dress with green diamond patches on the knees. They were the camp-leader and another member of the Prisoner of War camp which was located in our parish, at Marybank, about two miles from the manse.

   The two German prisoners-of-war followed me into the study. The camp had been established at Marybank in our parish quite recently, and the men, who were now working on farms, were all ordinary soldiers of the *Wehrmacht.* The more politically problematic prisoners were all in the Watten camp in Caithness much further north. The leader, whose name was Hans, explained that he hoped to organize appropriate Christmas festivities at the camp and had come to ask my help, which I was very pleased to offer. There were many difficulties to be overcome—how to obtain flour, for example, which would be required to make *Lebkuchen.* In the end a hundred-weight of flour was provided by Jockan the Miller, who said that he would study the regulations and find a loophole—typical Highland attitude to government regulations. Hans said that the men would like to make toys for every child in the parish. There was plenty of wood to be picked up here and there. The parishioners, when I told them of the scheme, rallied round generously. The Women's Rural Institute agreed to organize things, and in due course all that was needed for a traditional German *Weihnachtsfest* had been provided. Besides the flour, which was probably the most essential item, there were thirteen cockerels as well as many other odds and ends.

   Helen brought in coffee and some cake, and Hans introduced his companion, "This is Hubert Nitsche, our Catholic padre."

   Until now Hubert had spoken little; now as we drank coffee he played with the children, who had been allowed to join us. They took to him at once, especially Nicolas, who was now four years old and very sociable and talkative, and Hubert for his part seemed to be very much at ease with them. Meantime Helen and I and Hans discussed minor details of the projected Christmas festivities. The forenoon was almost over, and so Helen invited the two men to stay for lunch. Hans had to return to the camp to complete work schedules, but Hubert was free until late afternoon when he was to be picked up by a lorry which would take him on to Watten, for he had to serve all of the camps in the north-east. Hans said he would direct the driver to call at our manse.

"Will you stay then?" asked Helen.

"I would like to," he replied, "if it's no trouble."

"None at all, we like having visitors." And so Hubert Nitsche stayed to lunch, and for the first time in our lives we talked to a Catholic priest.

He was a youngish man of medium height, with clear, smiling eyes. Because of his dress, we could not really take in the fact that he was a priest, or indeed any kind of clergyman. Under the neutrality of his anonymous uniform he had been able to enter our house without arousing any of our preconceived notions of what a priest was like. We accepted the fact that he was a Catholic priest in a theoretical kind of way, while being impressed only by his personality, which was quiet and self-effacing and at the same time striking.

"How is it," we asked him, "that you have no official dress or badge or something?"

"In the German army I was a conscript medical orderly. After capture, when it became known that I was a priest, I was permitted to celebrate Mass and hear confessions, and in the end to move about from one hostel to another if I could find transport. It's all very unofficial and haphazard, but it works quite well."

He proved to be a delightful guest. After lunch he and I retired to the study. He sat very still, smiled, and listened. He was one of the most composed people I had ever met, and if he had any problems of his own he never mentioned them or gave any sign that he had any worries at all. But I had problems, and before I realized it, I was trying to explain to him what troubled me, and was asking for his comments.

"My trouble is," I began, "that I do have strong convictions, but am not sure if I have the right to demand that the congregation share them."

"Do your convictions contradict the official beliefs of your Church?"

"Well, I'm not sure. You see, it's difficult to find out what the official line is on various points."

"But is there no confessional statement, no catechism?"

"There was. In the seventeenth century the Church of Scotland held firmly to the *Westminster Confession of Faith* in detail. Now we have liberty of opinion on such points of doctrine as do not enter into the substance of the Faith."

"That seems sensible enough to me," said Hubert.

"Yes," I replied, "but what is the substance of the Faith? It seems that in practice we have liberty to decide what that substance is. It has not been defined."

"I see the difficulty now," Hubert answered.

I began to feel the benefit and stimulus of having someone to talk to about these problems instead of merely having to soliloquize as I sawed away at the hedge. The thing that had already struck me was that instead of making any criticism of the Reformed point of view and commending the Catholic viewpoint, he seemed to be trying to think along with me and make out as good a case as possible for the Reformed position. I continued.

"When I left college I believed that through ordination I would receive grace enabling me to be sure of what I might teach as the substance of the Faith, but now I find no such assurance, and am at times opposing what are clearly the accepted traditions of the people, and also the views of other ministers."

"I agree with you," said Hubert, "that ordination gives grace to preserve and teach the Word of God. But, as you say, something must be wrong when a minister finds himself opposing tradition, for tradition is the product of the exercise of that same ministry of the word in earlier times; it is the work of the same Spirit and if tradition varies the Spirit must be contradicting himself."

"That is exactly what the Scottish Reformers wrote in their very first Confession in 1560," I exclaimed, 'The Spirit of God, who is the Spirit of unity, cannot contradict himself'."

"Absolutely right," he replied.

"I think the Church of Scotland is aware of this," I went on, "because in the Declaratory Acts it states that the Church is the sole judge of what is in agreement with the scriptures. I take that to mean that the Church is custodian of a public interpretation, a tradition, one could call it, to which the individual believer and minister must conform."

"Yes," my guest answered, "the Holy Spirit dwells in the Body of Christ, in the Church as a whole. How does the mind of the Church of Scotland as a whole express itself?"

"I suppose ultimately through the General Assembly or through the majority vote of the presbyteries."

"The authoritative proclamation of the traditional, public belief of the Church of Scotland would then be found in the successive declarations of these courts?"

"I suppose so," I said.

"And if these show a harmonious sequence, then you would have something to turn to as the official teaching of the Church of Scotland, and you could determine whether or not your private convictions were in agreement with this."

"This is precisely what worries me," I explained. "The kind of things that recent Assemblies have approved would not have been accepted in past ages. The biggest difference between past views and today's views is, however, a difference in attitude towards the Confession of Faith itself, which implies a change in attitude towards those responsible for teaching doctrine. In the seventeenth century and even later people were content simply to accept the Confession—as many of the Free Church people do today—but the Confession itself states that 'all synods and councils since the Apostles' times may err and many have erred, therefore they are not to be made a rule of faith.' But this statement about the fallibility of councils was made by a fallible council, so where does that leave us?"

"In other words," said Hubert, "the Church of Scotland originally accepted the principle that the teaching Church possesses no absolute authority. I can see that this view was necessary in order to justify the break with the medieval Church; but now the Church of Scotland is adopting a Catholic position, attributing to the Church the competence to define what is in accordance with scripture. I can see that it must do this in order to counteract the disintegration of doctrine in the face of liberty of opinion. And I can see your problem too—the problem of identifying this Church or organ within the Church whose word can be trusted."

"Exactly," I agreed.

This was the first time that I had found someone who understood my problem and took it seriously. Once or twice I had raised the subject with Duncan MacDiarmid, whose response was to say jocularly, "I'm only a simple servant of the Lord; I try to show people that God cares, and I leave these theological problems to others."

With Hubert's ready ear and clear head conveniently here in my own study, I decided to go on.

"Tell me," I asked, "in your Church are you as a priest troubled by this sort of problem?"

"We do have the problem of sorting out what is ephemeral and local in opinion and practices from what is central and enduring. I would say, however, that it is a soluble problem. We can be sure what is—in your phrase—of the substance of the Faith; and in matters of dispute there is an ultimate contemporary court of appeal, a proper magisterial authority."

"Now that is precisely what I want to know about. What is that proper authority? In the Church of Scotland we seem to have reverted theoretically to the Catholic view that the Church must and can teach, but have not given flesh and blood to any organ of authority. How do you, in the Catholic Church, work this out in practice?"

"The foundation is, of course," he began, "the Incarnation—'the Word was made flesh and dwelt among us.' The fulfillment of the Incarnation came at Pentecost when our Lord poured out his Spirit upon the apostles. Immediately St Peter went out and began to tell men and women what they must do to be saved. 'Repent and be baptized and receive the Holy Spirit,' he told them. The other apostles likewise went out and taught the Faith, baptized, confirmed, and celebrated the eucharist.

"If anyone were to ask, 'What is the substance of the Faith?' it was the apostles who would answer—they were the proper authority; and they spoke as a college, as one man, their unity guaranteed by the leadership of Peter to whom the Lord had said, 'When you are converted, strengthen your brethren.' Potential disunity was resolved by Peter's intervention, as at the Council of Jerusalem when 'there was much disputing over it until Peter rose and said to them...'.

"The first decade or so after Pentecost shows us the essential form of the Church. Peter and the apostles taught the Word of God unambiguously with the authority of Christ. But the Lord had said, 'I am with you until the end of the world,' not merely until the end of their lives, and so the apostles, in virtue of the charism they possessed knew how to provide for posterity. They appointed successors to teach and to govern in the Churches they founded, and gave them their own apostolic power through prayer and the laying on of hands. The Pentecostal Gift endured in the consecration of the bishops, the Spirit remained active in the flesh and blood of the Church. Peter's charism, which was to maintain unity, continued to be effective through the Bishop of Rome.

"But as well as ensuring that the Word of God would endure in the preaching of the Church, the apostles did something else. They or their associates committed the salient facts of the gospel to writing. Eventually, about the fourth century, the Church through councils and synods decided which books were truly apostolic in origin. They could do this by reference to the substance of the Faith which they possessed in living tradition. After this we had, for good, the canon of scripture. The appointment of successors in the person of bishops and the production of the New Testament were complementary actions of the apostles and so there is no opposition between scripture and tradition."

"The impression amongst Protestants," I interjected, "is that Catholics rate the scriptures secondary in importance."

"The scriptures certainly are not inferior to tradition," he replied, "but I understand what is behind the impression you mention. The fundamentals of the Faith are first known through oral tradition, through what the mother teaches her child, through the catechism learned in school. The Bible, on the other hand, is the store-house from which the adult Christian draws nourishment for the deepening of his spiritual life. This order recapitulates the historical order: first came the apostolic preaching—the *kerygma* as scholars describe it—then came the written word of the New Testament to develop the Faith already established."

"In a way, then," I said, "when the Church of Scotland asserts that the Church is the sole judge of what is in agreement with scripture, it is accepting the same idea as Catholics accept."

"Except," replied Hubert, "that the function of Pope and bishops is not merely to produce digests of scripture or commentaries on scripture, but to uphold a tradition that emanated from the same source as scripture, that is from the Word made flesh."

"I see; the substance of Faith, preserved in the tradition upheld by the unified college of bishops in communion with Peter's successor, is the touch-stone which can keep scripture scholars on the right lines."

"Yes," replied Hubert, "study of the scriptures must always be carried out from the standpoint of faith, and the substance of the Faith is guarded at all times by the Pope and bishops, just as Peter and the apostles taught and guarded the Faith in the first generation of Christians."

I recalled Professor William Manson's affirmation that scripture scholarship must always proceed from the standpoint of faith–exactly as Hubert had put it–only Manson's words had struck us as a discovery, whereas for Hubert it seemed to be taken for granted.

"And one thing more," I continued, "do you maintain also that once traditional teaching has been clearly expressed, particularly in dogmatic formulae, that teaching cannot be altered?"

"Yes," he answered, "although in one sense doctrine is still developing, for our Lord said that the Spirit would lead us into all truth, but once a doctrine has been crystallized, as it were, into clear dogmatic statement, it cannot be altered. 'The Word of God endures for ever'."

It was already almost dark when one of the Agricultural Executive Committee's lorries rattled over the gravel in front of the manse, and the driver sounded his horn. Assuring him that he would be welcome any time we said Good-bye to our guest, and he set off on his sixty mile journey to Watten.

After Hubert had gone and when the children were in bed Helen and I had a very great deal to talk about. Helen had a theological mind and already understood perfectly what was going on in my head, for we discussed everything. She was aware of my desire to find an authority greater than personal conviction, and my insecurity affected her too. More than once she had told me that something was wrong, that my work was sapping my energy more than it should, that I never relaxed or showed an undivided mind in my family life. I seemed always to be making an effort to hold the Church together in my imagination, as though trying to conjure it up by an act of thought.

That night I recalled as best I could Hubert's description of the structure of the Church.

"Do you see what it means?" I asked Helen.

"Yes: it means that the Catholic Church believes in itself, which is more than we do."

"I never thought of it in that way; but it's true, and that's why I'm exhausted trying to find firm ground to stand on."

"But if the Catholic Church has an unbroken tradition—which includes the production of the New Testament—going right back to the apostles," said Helen, "and other Churches don't or can't claim to have it, we have no right to keep going on our own."

"Well, what's keeping us from accepting the claim of the Catholic Church?"

"If you had asked me that last April, when we first came here," said Helen, "I would probably have said that nobody can expect us to swallow all that superstition, but now I wonder. What is all that superstition anyway?"

"Certainly the bits of Catholic teaching that I have come across," I answered, "don't seem like superstition. What I have read in Ronald Knox and in the *Catechism of the Council of Trent* makes a lot of sense to me. And Fr MacEvoy's presentation of the Mass as the making present of the one historical sacrifice of Calvary has opened up a whole depth of spirituality I just didn't know about before."

"There's another side to it all too," added Helen, "the moral aspects of faith. We don't get much official support from the Church of Scotland for our abhorrence of contraception, for example. And the Church of Scotland seems to be a bit shaky on the question of the indissolubility of marriage. The Catholic Church is quite clear on these issues. I didn't tell you," she concluded, "that last Sunday evening while you were in church I listened to a service on the radio from a Catholic Church. In his sermon the priest used the phrase, 'We Catholics believe.' Could you get up in the pulpit and say, 'We Protestants believe?' "

"I could say, 'I believe,' " I replied, "but not, 'We believe.' That about sums up the problem."

We had started a train of thought that was to gnaw relentlessly at our minds for several months to come; we had set in motion a critical phase in our spiritual and material lives. Next morning early we took breakfast from a tray in our bedroom, and this became the pattern of our daily life—breakfast in our room and endless discussion, testing out our thoughts and also trying to face up to and solve the material problems that we might have to bring upon ourselves, for we could not disguise the fact that if we followed the present direction of our thinking to its conclusion, I would become jobless and all of us homeless. For me a subsidiary problem began to emerge. Had I a right, as a married man, to prejudice the well-being of my family, even at the dictate of conscience. There was Helen to think of and Nicolas and David, and now Helen was once again pregnant.

For the time being, however, I had to separate in my mind my private problems and the duties which I still had to and could perform. Whatever happened I could at least preach what I believed to be sound biblical teaching, and I could baptize children. And there was preparation for Christmas with the added interest of the POW camp *Weihnachtsfest*.

The scheme we had worked out with the camp leader proved a great success. Visiting the camp one day I saw that already they had produced several toys, very imaginatively designed and beautifully painted. I think some of the men must have been professional toy-makers. A week before Christmas there was a Christmas party for the children of the parish. The POWs not only made toys, but also decorated the hall in flamboyant German style and provided a very convincing Santa Claus.

The camp *Weihnachtsfest* took place on Christmas Eve—quite late. Helen and I were invited. We not only enjoyed the meal, but also the atmosphere. We saw the Christmas Tree lit, candle by candle, each one in memory of a different category of absent friends and relatives. When it was all over we walked home through the birch glades where the trees, normally so silver-white, appeared yellow against the deep, crisp snow. Once home we pulled out our Christmas Tree from the stable where it had been hidden from the children, decorated it and set out the presents beneath it, and then fell wearily into bed.

The children woke very early and soon the sitting-room was littered with Christmas wrapping paper as the presents were uncovered. Unfortunately I had to rush off in order to conduct a short service in the camp at 10 a.m., after which I came home for the children's Christmas service at noon. This was quite short—by Highland Presbyterian standards—and at two o'clock we had our family Christmas dinner. We had never been very keen on Turkey and so we had a gigot of beautiful local lamb.

Later in the afternoon I thought it would be appropriate to call on two or three of the house-bound sick. I could not risk cycling, but a walk would do me good anyway. First I visited Donald the old reprobate—whom I rather liked—taking a couple of bottles of stout with me. He was sitting on a chair by the fire, dressed in all the garments he could muster—even an overcoat and bonnet. I greeted him, read part of the Nativity narrative from St Luke, said a very short prayer, gave him the stout and departed. Mrs MacKay whom I visited next was very weak. I was glad I had come because she died shortly afterwards. There were one or two elderly people with whom I stayed only a short time. I passed by the house where Euphemia Grant had lived and had decided to make for home when, half a mile further on I saw Miss Fleming our organist lurking in the porch of her house, obviously on the look-out for me. She had spotted me on my way out. She pleaded with me to come in just to take a cup of tea. I had to agree, and received indeed not just tea, but a glass of Port wine. I wondered if this was some of the wine left over from the November Communion—had John the beadle included her in the elderly? I was glad to have it. Miss Fleming was a kind-hearted lady, but the epitome of gentility, and much given to adulation of the clergy. I was quite embarrassed by her eulogy of the "beautiful children's Christmas service. You must just have a gift–that's what it is, a gift." I got home at last to discover that Nicolas had abandoned the toys he had been given and was giving his whole attention to a six inch nail which he was hammering into a block of wood in the scullery.

On Sunday after Christmas the service was an adaptation of the Nine Lessons and Carols. We sang the old favorite Christmas hymns, the children of the parish sang carols they had learned, and there was a surprise item– a solid phalanx of POWs seated in the gallery sang, *O du fröhliche* and *Es ist ein Ros' entsprungen.*

On the four Sundays in preparation for Christmas I had been at ease, in spite of private problems. I had preached a series of sermons, building up expectancy of spirit appropriate to the season of Advent. I had tried to enter into the mind of John the Baptist as he called out: "Prepare ye the way of the Lord." At last with the ninth lesson of the Christmas service came the grand finale: "And the Word was made flesh and dwelt among us." But when it was all over and when the parishioners had commented– as is the custom in the Church of Scotland–on the excellence of the sermon, the beauty of the service, especially of the children's singing, I retreated to the manse, exhausted and–sad to say–a little depressed. "The voice of him that crieth in the wilderness, 'prepare ye the way of the Lord....' " These words still echoed through the parish, which lay around me like the wilderness of Judea. That which we had expected, had longed for, didn't seem to have come to stay. Where in this parish was the real Presence of him we call "Emmanuel–God is with us"? With the Jews of John the Baptist's time we had looked forward to his coming; but we had, it would seem, overshot the stable at Bethlehem, so that now, instead of having him with us for good we were looking back across two thousand years, anticipation transformed into nostalgia. For a moment, by an immense effort of imagination, we had recalled the image of the Word made flesh, cradled in the arms of his mother; and then as the words and the music died away, so did the image fade in our minds.

Christmas had come and gone, leaving us caught up in the orbit of an everlasting Advent.

13

A week later the parish livened up to celebrate Hogmanay and the New Year. All work stopped at 5 p.m. on Hogmanay—the last day of the old year. From midnight first-footing and carousing went on until well into New Year's Day, and trailed on for several days thereafter. We could not entirely escape this pagan festivity, which had an up-side in its encouragement of good neighborliness. On New Year's Day at about ten o'clock we saw John Urquhart marching stiffly up the drive, his breath condensing below the drooping points of his mustache. It was seriously cold. A freak drop in temperature had taken place suddenly towards the end of November, normally very cold, but this year the reading had fallen below freezing to 15 and 13 degrees Fahrenheit on two successive nights; and the frost never gave way until the following Easter. The hill sheep had a very hard time of it that winter.

"A Good New Year to you!" John declaimed the moment we opened the door.

I made the ritual response, "The same to you and many of them." According to strict usage the second phrase, "many of them" should be said solemnly with a drop in the voice, in order to avoid presumption in the face of providence.

"Come into the study where the fire is," I invited.

"Never mind the fire," said John. "I've something here that will warm you up. Get a glass now—and one for the wife too."

John was already jovial, and from his pocket he produced a half-bottle of Dalmore malt whisky.

"It's a shame to drink your whisky, John, and it so hard to get—at least the genuine article like Dalmore."

"Scarce indeed! Not to everybody, though, but you'd think Gobbie at the Shandwick Inn was giving it away—the fuss he made with me."

Helen came in. "Good morning mistress, and a Good New Year to you and the bairns," he shouted, waving the bottle in the air.

We wished each other health and happiness and took a nip of John's precious elixir.

"I ever came to the manse first thing on New Year's Day," he explained, "not that all of the ministers would take a dram, mind you. And I hope that it's many a long day before I stop coming to first-foot you. Will you not be seeing about a layer here?"

"Goodness me, John," Helen exclaimed, "you don't want us in the graveyard yet!"

"Indeed no, but I hope that's the only way you'll go out of this parish. Well, I must be off now; I've all the wife's folk to visit west the Post Office." John invariably included a point of the compass in any topographical statement. He also maintained the quaint Highland mode of accentuation. For him, "post office" became "postóffice."

When he had gone I went out, despite the cold, and sawed away at the hedge. Our neighbor, Alastair Logan, was taking a leisurely walk round his farm, looking at the sheep he had enclosed on turnips and kale in the glebe field adjoining the manse. "My, you're hardy working out in this weather," he said. "But you're coming on; keep it low till it fills out, then you'll get the shelter of it—for many years to come. It was let go far too wild before you came."

It was almost nine months since I began work on the hedge. I was a third of the way round, and the pile of cut branches was quite high, but I decided that I would wait until the work was finished before I set it alight. The thicker trunks would be saved for firewood. I went in for lunch, and in the afternoon resumed my study of the *Catechism of the Council of Trent*.

Not until fully forty years later when I visited the Church of Guardian Angels at Brixen in the South Tyrol did I realize how persistent and precise had been the working of the hand of providence in my life. The unexpected appearance of the POW Catholic chaplain was an example. I had broken the back of the work on my hedge, and had in parallel broken the back of my theological research, but so far I had relied upon reading and soliloquizing; now, at a critical stage in my progress had come a real-life encounter: soliloquy had changed into dialogue, and the meeting with Hubert proved to be a catalyst that stimulated the final movement from tentative to firmly held belief.

In principle Helen and I had both reached the conclusion that the Catholic view of the Christian Faith and of the Church was correct. The gap between the revelation of the Word made flesh and the effective impact of that Word in succeeding generations I had at last seen bridged by the continuity of the apostolic voice in the magisterium of the Catholic Church. This was the voice that had resounded throughout the Mediterranean world in the first century, had deposited a written testimony to that Word in the books of the New Testament, and had guarded and proclaimed the substance of this revealed truth from time to time in the work of ecumenical councils, bequeathing to us great and enduring symbols of the Faith such as the Nicene Creed. To act upon the recognition of that principle was another matter. Emotionally and socially we were living within a Presbyterian ethos; Presbyterian blood still ran in our veins. Besides this we had a strong sense of responsibility to the Church of Scotland, to this parish in particular. Would it be right for us to make a decision about abandoning the Church of Scotland solely for the reason that it satisfied us personally—even if that satisfaction had to do with conscience?

Helen and I resolved the problem temporarily by going into a kind of free-wheeling that would allow us time to consolidate our thinking. We set about reading diligently;

my chief text until now had been the *Catechism of the Council of Trent*, but soon I became absorbed in John Henry Newman's *Apologia Pro Vita Sua*. I could scarcely believe that another person had experienced about a hundred years ago exactly what I was experiencing now. We were fortunate, in that active dispute had ceased. Ross Brennachie had registered his disapproval and then withdrawn from warfare with me; none of the other elders had a theological axe to grind; people accepted the rule that baptism would be performed in church, and I set about expounding scripture through the Sunday sermon, in the belief that I was providing a genuine spiritual diet for the people. My happiest moments were at baptisms when I was quite sure that whatever my problems, whatever the deficiencies of the Church of Scotland, a child was being received into the Body of Christ. And all the while we got on with our own lives, not insensitive to the parish, but in a strange, hidden way, detached from it. Although I was no longer burdened with any public theological dispute, and had found a reasonable *modus vivendi*, inwardly we both continued to engage in a severe struggle—the search for the answer to the question: what must we do? All around us the land was held in the grip of the severest frost for many years; the earth was already frozen to a depth of about eighteen inches. We too were frozen into a state of indecision; we enjoyed remarkable clarity of mind, but suffered a paralysis of will. We knew that eventually a thaw had to come, and the prospect frightened us.

The awkward predicament in which we now found ourselves did not, however, prevent us from living a full life, and in the country, life can be very full indeed. There was much coming and going between us and the Logans, our immediate neighbors, and the MacDiarmids in Alness. There was a thriving Women's Rural Institute in which Helen found great entertainment and made many good friends. The community activity which aroused the greatest enthusiasm, however, was drama. During that first winter we had already attended several productions in Tain, when in the course of a week we not only saw excellent performances from about eighteen parishes, but listened to first-class adjudications from distinguished people, including Eric Linklater, who lived at Pitcalnie in the adjoining parish. In the barber's shop in Tain on the Monday following the Drama Festival I marveled at the animated and knowledgeable argument that was in progress concerning the performances and the adjudications. There was nothing dull about life in Easter Ross.

Our domestic life, too, ticked over pleasantly enough. Just before New Year's Day one of our nine Rhode Island Reds laid her first egg—on the south exposure against the wall of the house, in the snow. Thereafter we had a plentiful supply of eggs—but deposited in the nests in the stable. I had at times too much to do looking after poultry, goats, bees, and the garden. Because we had no car and because of the severe weather, we did not travel much. Friends visited us. A regular visitor was Dr. Auchterlonie—one of the celebrated St Andrews clan of golf professionals and club-makers. His ostensible reason for visiting was to check Helen's blood-pressure—in January she was four months pregnant—but his time was mainly spent doing *The Scotsman* crossword with her and drinking tea. Helen could do this crossword in about half an hour. I suppose that the prospect of the birth of a child distracted us from the task of making up our minds how to act, now that we held the view we did about the nature of the Church. At the same time it must have increased our anxiety.

Easter passed and the Communion Season was upon us again. This time there was no upheaval and things went quite well—but still no sign of Janet Stewart. The Thursday Fast Day service was conducted by Robert Begg, minister of Tain. He was very solemn and parsonical—he even wore on occasion an old-fashioned shovel hat. In the intercessory prayer he prayed for all manner of people and intentions, reaching a dramatic and sobbing climax with a prayer for "all at the manse, and especially for the infant of a day."

Christopher had been born on the previous evening, while I attended a meeting of the local branch of The Bible Society. David's birth had been plain-sailing, and Helen had said that if all child-bearing were like that then there wasn't too much to worry about; but with Christopher, born five years to the day after his elder brother, Helen was back in the same predicament. Not only was he, as his brother had been, an anterior occipital presentation, but the cord was wound several times round his neck. Dr. Auchterlonie told me that it was the skill of the midwife which had saved Christopher's life. " I doubt Helen won't want to face that again for quite some time," he said.

The midwife was indeed first-class, and a bit high-class. On leaving us she was on her way to Foulis Castle. She didn't like eating with us in the kitchen, particularly if Meg, our daily help, was there too.

It was only a few weeks after this that my grandmother visited us and died in our manse only an hour or two after having held her youngest great-grandchild in her arms. Later on in the summer we paid a visit to Helen's family in Skye. It was a long journey—by train to Dingwall and then to Kyle of Lochalsh, by ferry over to Kyleakin, and then by car to Torrin. For young people this ought not to have been too exhausting, but we had burdened ourselves with much gear. First there were the two older boys plus the baby; but we had also a large pailful of raspberries, having been reluctant to let the crop go to waste, and in addition we had a nucleus hive of bees, which Peggy Logan, the Bee-wife, had helped me to take from my now thriving hive. A quiet buzzing came from this nucleus and disconcerted other passengers in the train, who did not see the box tucked away under the seat. The day was very, very hot. As we walked from the train to the ferry in Kyle one little bee was able to squeeze its way out from under the lid and disappeared over the sea to Skye. For a moment we held our breath, expecting this to be the herald of a mass exodus, but all was well. We had covered about half of the final stretch by car when one of the children had to get out quickly to be sick. By the time we arrived in Torrin we were not in prime condition. It was a perfect summer, not a cloud in the sky for three weeks, and Loch Slapin alive with mackerel. The bees were transferred into a hive. In the evening I was reading Newman's *Apologia* and Helen's father asked me what my book was. I told him and he said, "That would be a book he wrote when he was an Anglican." "No," I replied, "it's his explanation of why he became a Catholic." Helen's father made no reply. Free of the burden of bees and raspberries our journey home at the end of August was much less arduous.

As the year moved on through autumn and towards the chill of November we became more and more at home in Easter Ross and happier every day in the companionship we enjoyed there, in spite of the fact that in our hearts we were becoming increasingly conscious of the need to make a break with the Church of Scotland. Every morning we followed the same routine. Very early, before the children demanded attention, we would take a breakfast tray up to our bedroom and discuss the prospect of my leaving the ministry and finding another job, and of our finding somewhere else to live. There were so many hypothetical questions that we became exhausted. The nature of our problem made it necessary for us to keep it to ourselves. There was no one we could turn to for advice. The way in which we worked together on this deep problem was indicative of the way we felt about marriage. Within a few years we had developed a firm sense of total unity, of unreserved giving to each other, physically, mentally, and spiritually.

In clearing our minds we had been helped by our first conversation with Hubert, the POW chaplain, and we had met him again on two occasions, but very briefly, for he was never able to stay long in our parish. We noticed that he never urged us to become Catholics, but simply answered our questions, and of course he was unlikely to be able to help us solve the practical problems that lay ahead. As we approached our second Christmas in the parish Helen suggested that we get in touch with Hubert, tell him that we saw no way out except to seek reception into the Catholic Church, and ask him if he had any ideas about what we might be qualified to do if we did become Catholics. On my next visit to the camp, when I hoped to discuss the arrangements for Christmas, I asked Hans to let Hubert know that I would like to see him.

"I've just heard that he won't be back," he said, "he's been repatriated—went straight home from the base-camp last week and couldn't get up here to see us."

At Christmas we got a beautiful Christmas card from Hanover. On the card as well as the usual Christmas greeting were a few lines, thanking us for the hospitality we had given him in Scotland, and giving us what proved to be the best possible advice.

"Pray to the Holy Spirit always. Please pray for me and I will remember you at the altar." It was signed—not "Hubert" but "Fr Apollinaris, O.F.M."

We had never neglected to seek the enlightenment of the Holy Spirit, but after receiving Fr Apollinaris' card our devotion to the Holy Spirit became more formal. I learned the old-fashioned prayer to the Holy Spirit by heart and said it every morning. To this day—fifty years on—I begin every enterprise with the threefold recitation of this prayer. Very soon, in January of 1948, our minds were made up. We now believed that the Catholic Church governed by the Pope and the bishops in communion with him, was the one visible Church, founded by our Lord. But a daunting hurdle had still to be jumped: when and how were we to make the break with our present way of life? We knew no Catholics and, living as we did in relative isolation, were unlikely to be able to make any contact with the Catholic Church. Our pain was made greater every day by our ever increasing friendship with those around us, so that what made us afraid, as we looked forward to what now seemed the inevitable result of our decision, was not that we would have to leave our home—we could face up to paying that price for the pearl we were sure we had found—but the knowledge of the deep and inexplicable wound we would have to inflict upon this loyal and affectionate congregation. Apart from arousing the clear-cut opposition of Ross Brennachie, nothing I had ever said in sermons, or done in the parish, had displeased anyone. They regarded me as very sound. It was as though I was able to carry them along with me theologically. And I was about to abandon them.

At the beginning of February Helen and I walked round the manse policies as it was getting dark. "It will take me about six months to finish cutting the hedge," I said, "and that will be the dead-line. When the whole thing is cut I'll set a light to the heap of branches; the dry holly leaves will fairly explode—that'll be the sign for us to go."

I don't know whether that dramatic image released the tension or just made us all the more afraid, but I did keep on working regularly at the hedge, slowly coming closer to the end.

In July we went on holiday to stay with Helen's aunt and uncle in Fort William. Their house was opposite the Catholic Church. Uncle Isaac was the parish priest's doctor and auntie Jessie a great friend of his housekeeper, a Barra woman, whom we had already met during our honeymoon. Our Fort William relations, simply because of where they lived, were our only oblique connection with anything Catholic, and now for the first time this began to mean something to us. As we had experienced some years earlier, in Lochaber there is a very happy relationship between Catholics and Protestants. Probably their common Gaelic culture has something to do with this, and also the fairly even balance in the two populations. Uncle was a Lewis man and in that island Protestants do not look favorably upon Catholics, but uncle was a-typical. For him, a lapsed Free Presbyterian, a light—almost the light of sanctity—shone upon old Monsignor MacMaster.

"If it hadn't been for some idiot of a Spanish doctor telling him he had a weak heart when he was in the seminary at Valladolid, the Monsignor would have been an archbishop now—he might well have been the Pope!"

Such was his admiration of his patient. And auntie Jessie had much the same mind.

"He's a fine old man; he lives only for the Church; the Church is everything to him; and Meshagh (that was the housekeeper) won't let the wind blow on him." And she would go on, confessing an admiration for the Church too, "I always go over to midnight mass at Christmas; the atmosphere is wonderful—the church is so big and the people are so small."

During this holiday we paid regular visits to the church, persevering in prayer to the Holy Spirit. I think that on one occasion we were introduced to Monsignor MacMaster by Meshagh, who asked us to dinner, but we never breathed a word to them or to our relatives about the impending crisis in our lives. In the last week of our stay in Fort William we met an eccentric character who was staying as a guest in the Church of Scotland manse at Kilmonevig. His name was Gabriel Marlowe, a novelist who wrote film scripts in Hollywood. He was American but born in Austria, and he was a Catholic convert Jew. I think it was because we knew he had no links with the world in which we lived that we began to tell him something of our predicament. He was most sympathetic and seemed to understand the theological route which had led us towards the Catholic Church. When I tried to explain how I had found no sure doctrinal ground upon which to stand, he said, "Yes, I think a good Reformation slogan would be: 'And the Word was made flesh, and the Word was misunderstood.' " Our conversation turned however to mundane topics. We told him that if we left Logie Easter we would have a problem finding somewhere to live.

"I have a friend in East Lothian, who might have somewhere for you on her farm," he told us, "I'll give you her address."

Gabriel Marlowe was our second live contact with Catholicism, and through the East Lothian contact he had given us we were led to our third and very important encounter with Catholics in real life.

Our summer vacation lasted into the first week of August. Gabriel Marlowe offered to put us up for three nights in his house in Edinburgh; our Fort William relations were happy to keep the children for a few days; and so we set off for Edinburgh, intending to look for somewhere to live in the south. We still had said nothing to anyone except Gabriel of our final objective. Gabriel's friend in East Lothian was Isobel Walker, a daughter of Johnnie Walker of whisky fame. She owned the farm of Stonypath in the lower slopes of the Lammermuir Hills, at Garvald in East Lothian. We arrived at her house in the early afternoon and were taken to see an empty farmhouse which also belonged to her. It turned out in the end that there was no suitable accommodation here for us. I had already decided that I would probably have to follow a course of teacher-training in Edinburgh and would have to live in the city. Our journey down to Stonypath had not been fruitless, however. We had begun to realize that we were on the move, and it had another more specific result.

After tea, Isobel Walker said, "Would you like to go and see the monkeys?"

"What monkeys?" I asked.

"The Cistercian monks," she replied. "They came here two years ago from Roscrea in Ireland–they're my immediate neighbors."

We walked through a grass field, down to the stream, then up a steep slope onto a field which must have belonged to the abbey, for we saw a young monk in brown overalls trying to persuade a calf to get out of the barley. At last we were on a lawn with a Eucalyptus tree and saw before us the red sandstone facade of a Scots Baronial castle. Thirty seconds after we rang, the massive door swung open and Father Alphonsus, dressed in a habit which could have gained him a commission as an advertisement for a whiter than white detergent, gripped each of us firmly by the hand and said, "Welcome to Nunraw."

What impressed us by this visit to Nunraw was not the conversations we had with Father Alphonsus and Father John and the Abbot, although these were helpful, but the welcome. Monks were a species of men quite unknown to us, and yet we felt perfectly at home. They told us a little about their manner of life and its rationale, and I think that even on that brief visit we sensed the sign of something that transcends this world. When we spoke about the problem we had faced and the way we thought it could be solved they did not seem to be surprised or indeed excited. In confirmation of a remark I made about the need to be sure of the substance of the faith, the Abbot simply commented that it was true, that the Catholic Church did not go back on anything once it had been authoritatively defined. Like Fr Apollinaris they did not take up polemic argument and did not attempt to convince us. Fr John said, "I'm glad I'm not in your shoes; but we'll pray for you, and you must pray to the Holy Spirit. He will give you the answer."

At Nunraw we had picked up some interesting literature about the origin of the Cistercian Order and about St Bernard of Clairvaux. This reading put more flesh and blood onto our concept of the Catholic Church. Above all, however, we had made contact with the concrete reality of the Church, and moreover in the distinctively Catholic form of the monastic life. At first we had been attracted by ideas, by doctrine, now we had glimpsed the visible shape of the Church. At this point in our development it became appropriate that we make a physical move towards that Church.

We returned home via Fort William, and by mid-August we were back to what appeared to be normal operations in the parish. On the first Sunday after our return from holiday I preached on the text: 2 Peter 1:20, "No prophecy of Scripture is of any private interpretation." My sermon was a résumé of the arguments that had brought me to believe the Roman Catholic Church to be the true Church. I did not explicitly state that this was so, but described the marks of the Church in a Catholic manner and firmly refuted the notion of an invisible Church. I would have been happy had a deputation come to me in the vestry afterwards to demand my resignation on the grounds that my views were not consonant with Reformed teaching, but no such thing happened. On the contrary, Skinner, on coming into the vestry, said, "The wife was just saying that the minister's preaching better every week." And outside, as she was getting into her car, Mrs Melville said, "Man, you've a powerful delivery; you'll be off to one of those swanky charges in Edinburgh soon."

On Monday morning I calculated that one more week's work would complete the trimming of the overgrown holly and hawthorn hedge. Then, to keep true to my resolve I would have to announce my departure, not in the way Mrs Melville had imagined, but out of the Church of Scotland altogether. The more successful I seemed to be, and the kinder people were to me, the more acute did my agony become. Was there no other way out?

That evening I discussed the issue with Helen.

"What if I am suffering from a subtle delusion?"

"Why on earth do you say that? You've been thinking this out carefully for many years—more years than you realize; and I've been thinking too—and I don't feel deluded. What interests me most is the moral teaching of the Catholic Church; and I appreciate more than you do, I think, the idea of celibate clergy. Being a minister's wife's just unreal."

"Yes, but am I allowed now to act just as an individual? I have a responsibility, and the people look to me for teaching?"

"But it makes no sense if you can't teach them the whole, solid truth—only that makes sense. Otherwise you're leading them up the garden path. If there is only one true Church then you've got to be right in it to receive its benefits."

My final gambit was: "As long as there's a vestige of truth in the Church of Scotland, must I not for the time being at any rate, teach what I can and baptize the children? After all there is a unity in our common baptism; doesn't that justify me carrying on here as minister?"

"You know that's sheer nonsense. Of course there's unity in baptism, of course the new life's given in baptism, but a child has to grow, hasn't it? You can't be content to stop the faith at the initial stage, as if you could stop a child from growing into an adult. The faith has to become fully formed; and I'm convinced that can't happen within the restrictions of the tradition we've been brought up in. And you're convinced too. I know it."

14

Work on the hedge took a little longer than I had estimated; it was after the middle of September before the last straggling branch had been cut. As I finished off the last few yards my mood was different from what it had been when I began the work two and a half years earlier. It is true that there was an acid feeling in my stomach—fear at what lay only a matter of days away. And yet tension had gone. Newman wrote of the sense of rest or relaxation he had felt when finally he accepted the whole teaching of the Catholic Church. I had the same experience. It was not that suddenly every question had been answered, every problem solved, nor that I saw the prospect of a life wherein all that I required would be handed to me without any effort on my part; but I felt stimulated now to continue the journey into the search for truth with a confidence I had never known before. I had found a sound and habitable house in which to live, a house that was adequately furnished and equipped. There would be plenty of hard work to do, but now there was a place in which to rest and be fed.

In another way too I was beginning to sense relief. I would be free to let go responsibility for this parish, would be loosed from the bond of personal relationship I felt for this congregation, a bond which from the start I had felt to be sacramental and so similar to the bond of marriage, that there had been within me a rivalry between the two sacraments. I was convinced too that marriage is a sacrament. The strength and spiritual efficacy of that sacrament had been shown to us in many ways, not least in the unity of mind and heart that had enabled us so quickly to resolve the fundamental problems of the nature of faith and the shape of the Church. I could now look forward to devoting my life wholly to realizing the full potential of this sacrament.

As the moment for setting alight the huge heap of branches drew near, I found myself summing up the conclusion we had both come to in a simple manner. I knew—for I had read Church history—that the members of the Catholic Church were far from perfect, that spiritual treasure is contained in earthen vessels, but I found myself addressing to Peter the words he had addressed to our Lord, "To whom shall we turn?" No Church other than that ruled over today by the successor of Peter claimed to speak the word of truth with the same authority that Peter had claimed in his own day. The words of the first letter of St John pointed towards the Church in communion with Peter's successors: "It is as eye-witnesses that we give you the news of that life, that eternal life, which ever abode with the Father and has dawned now on us. This message about what we have seen and heard we pass on to you, so that you too may share in our fellowship" (1 Jn 1:2-3).

The revelation of the Son of God had to do with seeing and hearing and handling and passing on; and the claim to have seen, and to possess the competence to hand on with dogmatic certainty, was neither an arrogant scandal nor an optional extra for those who are temperamentally addicted to authority. It is necessary for spiritual health.

All of the cut branches had been piled up in one place near where I started cutting the hedge, and where new growth was already showing. By now the holly leaves were quite dried out. My mind was made up. On a Wednesday afternoon at the end of September I stuffed some dry holly leaves into the bottom of the heap and put a match to them. They exploded into flame, and soon all of the leaves were blazing. As the initial blaze died away a fire kindled in the small branches at the bottom of the pile, and soon there was a terrific bonfire that threatened to scorch a nearby beech tree. I became concerned too lest sparks should ignite stooks still standing in the field next the church. Luckily there was no damage. At ten o'clock that night there was a glow that shed a warm light across the manse lawn.

By the end of the week I was in a state of great agitation. I would have to announce on Sunday my intention to offer my resignation to the Presbytery at their October meeting. I decided that I ought first to make this known to one or two individuals. I telephoned Mrs Melville. Her response was: "I'll not believe it till I hear it from the pulpit."

"You'll hear it tomorrow," I assured her.

"Then I'll still not believe it."

I went down to see John Urquhart. He was out, so I told his wife.

"It's no true," she said, with a nervous giggle.

"It is though; and you'd better tell John in case he gets a shock tomorrow."

"He'll get a shock all right," she said, "and he'll say plenty."

How simple it would have been had I been able to disappear quietly from the parish before morning. Morning came and I had to go through the gap in the shorn hedge and face the congregation. I trembled in the vestry. I had eaten nothing and it was now noon. Skinner came in, hung up his hat, breathed deeply but said nothing and went out. John came in, a wild look in his eyes.

"What nonsense is this?" he muttered.

"It's quite true, John."

"You're not going, though!" he gasped.

"Yes, John, I am."

"You'll not get leave to!"

John led me in and the service began. While the psalm was being sung I observed the faces around me. It was evident that some had heard the news, some had not. As the service gathered momentum I got into my stride with a picturesque theme from the Old Testament; the strain was eased and I began to have the sensation of once more living within the Old Testament dispensation–a prophet uttering an oracle. In the sermon I did not advert to what I was about to announce. Perhaps some who had got wind of my intentions were beginning to think that after all they had been treated to one of those rumors to which we were well accustomed; but before the concluding paraphrase I said: "Will you please wait for a moment after I have pronounced the benediction; I have an announcement to make." The tension returned immediately.

After the blessing the congregation sat down; I stood still, gripping the sides of the pulpit, my palms wet, and finding it hard to breathe.

"I have a distressing announcement to make. Tomorrow the Presbytery meets, and I will ask them to allow me to demit my status as a minister of the Church of Scotland. My reason is simply this: I can no longer subscribe the formula by which all ministers are bound."

I left my books in the pulpit and hurried down the stairs and into the vestry. No one moved at first and there was dead silence. It was reported to me years later that an old retired gamekeeper, whom I had not known to be a remnant of the Auld Kirk congregation, stood at the church door, waving his fist and shouting: "That's your damned elders for you; they drove Forbes to the drink, Mr McBean into the wilderness, and now they've driven Mr Walls out of the Kirk." It was true that all of the remaining elders had formerly been in the United Free tradition, but untrue that they had ganged up with Ross Brennachie, against me.

Skinner came into the vestry and said: "This is a terrible blow you have struck us."

"I'm sorry it's so sudden," I replied, "but I have considered my decision very carefully and it would be dishonest of me to stay."

"Well, maybe the Presbytery will change your mind for you," he said firmly.

John came back. "I'm no right at all today," he began, "but the Presbytery won't hear of it, so you can just put the idea out of your head."

"They won't do that John," I said quietly.

I had still to face the Presbytery, but the worst was now past.

The Presbytery met in Tain five miles away. There were about twelve parishes in our Presbytery, so that the number at any sederunt was usually about twenty–a minister and one elder from each parish. We sat in a room of the parish church halls, on hard, backless benches facing the Moderator and Clerk who sat behind a heavy, varnished table. Three tall, narrow windows at the back of the room had movable panes high up, but these were closed. The room was both cold and stuffy.

We sang a psalm and the Moderator said a long prayer. Minutes of the last meeting were read and business arising from them discussed. Then came great sheaves of printed matter from the Church Offices at 121 George Street in Edinburgh. We waded through these interminable recommendations and regulations from our bureaucratic headquarters–flippantly referred to as "one two one" or "the Vatican" or even–by the impious–as "the kingdom of God limited."

At last we discussed local affairs, and when it drew near to four o'clock members were glancing at their watches. One gentleman dared to yawn. The end seemed in sight and my muscles were tensing and flexing and I was looking for my opening when Robert Begg, who always played such a prominent part at the Synod, and who had prayed at our Fast Day the year before for "the infant of a day," rose solemnly.

"Mr Moderator, fathers and brethren," he began, giving an elastic bend to his knees, "the business of this meeting has served as an excellent example of what I make bold to call the preoccupation of the Church with purely technical and administrative–yes–bureaucratic matters. Surely, fathers and brethren, we ought to introduce into our meetings discussions of much deeper, spiritual value. I have no desire, my friends, to detain you long this afternoon, but I would like to suggest that at our meetings in future we have read a theological paper on some topic of practical, pastoral interest. There are many topics on which we–I am sure I speak for all–would gladly seek light." One of the elders meekly nodded assent. "And I feel sure," he continued, "that regular discussion of serious subjects, carried out in the spirit of fellowship which we enjoy here, would do much to help us all."

The Clerk was becoming irritable, but Robert was not to be stopped. "If I may crave your forbearance, gentlemen, for one more minute, I would suggest that the first subject we address should be baptism, or more precisely our baptismal practice. I have in mind, of course, what I have on previous occasions described as 'the baptismal disgrace' the abominable practice of baptizing children whose parents never darken the church door. When I first came here I was weak, compliant with the requests of these spiritual pilferers; but now, Mr Moderator, I am adamant, I refuse to baptize. And now I ask that we discuss this matter and agree on a plan of concerted action." Slowly he pushed the tails of his clerical frock coat aside and sat down, a serious frown on his countenance.

Duncan MacDiarmid shifted his position and gave me a hint of a wink. The Clerk fumbled with papers, obviously unwilling to let the discussion go any further, but the Moderator, instead of merely thanking Robert, himself responded.

"A very important point Mr Begg. I'm sure we all agree with you. It is a great scandal that nominal Christians and even pagans should..."

"Excuse me, Mr Moderator," interposed the Clerk, "it is not in order for the Moderator to take direct part in discussion from the chair. If anyone wants to comment on what has been said I would ask him to do it briefly, otherwise we must move on to closing the business."

A quiet west-Highland minister, whom I did not know very well, rose and with a very clear voice said, "I am naturally as vexed as Robert Begg is by careless parents, but I am also disturbed by the rough and ready remedy which Robert Begg has suggested. I think that the grace of baptism must not be denied to any child under our care. A child is not to be penalized for the sins of its parents. Our task therefore is to improve the situation by seeing to the education of parents. I may delay a baptism for a time, but I baptize all children and believe that if someone has faith, even if only the minister, the baptism is effectual."

Having delivered his tidy little speech in a cultured Highland voice he sat down as briskly as he had risen.

"Is there any further motion?" asked the Moderator.

"There is no motion before the house; we're not even having a debate on this at the moment," interrupted the Clerk.

"Is there any further discussion then?" asked the Moderator.

"Moderator, fathers and brethren," said a burly, red-faced man in a yellow raincoat, "I am no theologian like the two gentlemen who have just spoken, but I feel that we should view this matter from a more practical point of view. The arguments so far have concentrated on the child. Well, what is the effect on the child? Do we really know? What we must consider is the effect of the baptismal ceremony on the parish. Will the people be edified or not? There is much to be said on both sides. Perhaps each case ought to be settled on its merits."

"Are we not beginning at the wrong end," piped up a very old minister. "It's all very well asking who ought and who ought not to receive baptism; but what we really need is an up-to-date statement on baptism and in particular on infant baptism. I wonder if it is wise to keep up the practice of infant baptism. Baptize children by all means if their parents want it, but might it not be better to wait until later in life and let those baptized be responsible for their own actions? I must confess that when I baptize a baby I am a bit worried."

The Clerk was now making an attempt to bring the meeting to an end, but without success. A cheerful Glasgow man was now beginning: "At our last Communion I found a man who had never been baptized and I didn't know how to handle the situation. Perhaps the Presbytery can enlighten me."

Another minister, dressed in a very pale gray suit rose and took up the last point. "Mr Moderator, I feel that much of what is being said is vain philosophy. Theology is not religion, and true doctrine does not necessarily lead to heaven. The problem posed by the last speaker is surely no true problem to the spiritually-minded. The Lord is ever present to those who call on him; he is present in both sacraments, and surely the greater sacrament includes the lesser."

"We are getting nowhere," the Clerk intervened, and our time is up. "I move that at our next meeting we ask our most recently inducted minister to read a paper on baptism."

All eyes turned on me. Now I had to rise. For half a minute I could say nothing, then I almost whispered, "I cannot. Mr Moderator, fathers and brethren, I wish to demit my status."

Complete silence. Duncan MacDiarmid almost fell over backwards. Robert Begg, always in command of the situation, rose authoritatively and said: "The answer, gentlemen, is that we cannot accept this demission."

The Clerk, who of all those present, did have a grasp of Practice and Procedure, and was competent to conduct a meeting, asked quite simply.

"Mr Walls, would you state your reason for making this unexpected request."

"Yes," I replied, "I am no longer able to subscribe the formula."

"In that case," said the Clerk, "we must appoint three of our number to confer with you in order to ascertain that you are acting with full responsibility, and to report their finding to us in two weeks."

"This is absurd gentlemen," shouted Robert Begg, "the formula is so all-embracing and allows such liberty of interpretation of doctrine, that surely anyone could sign it."

"That is beside the point," said the Clerk, who was on the point of missing his bus home. "Whom do we appoint?"

There was now no question of any other competent business. The Moderator closed the meeting with a rather perfunctory prayer and we began to disperse. Almost all tried to make some kind of friendly and neutral remark. They hoped that my mind would change after my conference with the little committee.

"You're not going to join the Piskies?" asked Duncan.

"You're not losing your faith?" asked another.

"If it's financial trouble," whispered a third, "I'm sure I could help–I'm on my own you know."

As I was leaving, one minister, who had crossed swords with Brennachie on several occasions, said, "What's all this, you're not caving in to Brennachie, are you?"

"No! no!" I assured him, "it's got nothing to do with that. I simply cannot subscribe the formula."

"Oh, damn the formula!" he shouted, "I don't even remember what it is. There's far too much red tape nowadays."

For one thing I was most grateful. No one seemed to suspect what my positive views were. This was a great blessing for the interest of the press was never aroused, and we got through this crisis without any contact with the media. Taking refuge in the negative reply: "I cannot subscribe the formula" was like saying, "I take the fifth amendment."

In two weeks all would be formally settled. Then we would have to leave our parish and manse. We had to work fast. I paid a flying visit to Edinburgh and found lodging with my maternal grandmother, who was still alive. I told her that I had decided to turn to teaching as a profession. My contact with her gave me an inkling of the almost impossible task I would have in explaining my action to relations and friends. I had for the moment to put that worry out of my mind and set about applying for a mature student grant and enrolling at Moray House, the Department of Education at Edinburgh University. Back home at the manse we tidied everything up and I sold our hens, the goats, the incubator and the brooder. We kept the hive of bees and they traveled to Edinburgh with us in the removal van.

The last week spent in the parish was harrowing. Parishioners called in the evenings, asking me to change my mind. At the end of the week a little deputation from the women of the parish came and gave Helen a cheque. "It's just a minding," they said, and Helen wept.

On Sunday I did my best to preach at noon. The horror of that occasion has blotted out from my memory all of what I said. I canceled the evening service. At the end of the service I had to shake hands with everyone. To my surprise Ross Brennachie had come to this service, and I was glad that he did. He was the last to come and say farewell. I thought that now he looked quite old, in spite of the firmness of his step. He was not smiling, but he shook my hand in his customary very serious way.

"I hope that you are doing the Lord's will, Mr Walls," he said.

"I think I am," I replied.

"Well, perhaps it's all for the best. But what will you do now?"

"I don't know yet, but I'll probably turn to teaching."

He turned away, hat in hand, a worried look on his face, and walked to his car, where his wife was already seated, her eyes cast down, but seeing all that was going on.

Early in the evening John, dressed in his Sunday suit, rang the door-bell.

"Well," he snapped, "have you thought better of it?"

"I still think the same, John," I answered.

"Listen," he announced, "some of us have got up a petition, and we'll take it round the parish and get it signed by everybody. Will you stay then?"

"John, there is nowhere I'd rather stay than here, but a petition will do no good, for my leaving has nothing to do with the people. I can't sign the formula, which means I don't believe the right things."

"You can believe anything you like!" he exploded, "you're the minister and it's nobody else's bloody business what you believe. Will you not stay?"

"I cannot stay, John."

He turned on his heel, tears in his eyes, and marched off muttering imprecations against everything.

The following Wednesday the removal van arrived at 8 a.m. There was a thin layer of snow on the ground. By eleven the house was empty; Meg was there, weeping noisily, helping Helen put the final touches to things. At one o'clock we left and went across the field to the Logans for lunch. Marion was very quiet; Alastair said, "Laddie, you're no wise." Helen and the children remained with the Logans and I went into Tain to the Presbytery meeting. The business was soon completed, with very little emotion, thanks to the Holy Spirit, I believe. The committee of three reported that they believed me to be of sound mind and that my decision had been responsibly made. Begg once again brought his big guns to bear, insisting that nonetheless they ought not to accept my demission. The Clerk quietly pointed out that if my reason was that I could not subscribe the formula it was not a case of granting my request but of their asking for my demission of status. With an ill grace Begg held his peace.

My demission of status was accepted and the meeting over except for the final prayer and the farewells. I had demitted status fully convinced that the substance of the Faith could not be found with full assurance within the Church of Scotland, but I ceased to be a minister, and said Good-bye to this Presbytery with deep affection in my heart for the Church of Scotland and in particular for these men, my colleagues, to whom I caused great distress. My dissatisfaction with Reformed ecclesiology in no way lessened my sincere admiration for these men, nor constrained me to belittle the effectiveness of their ministry, which each one carried out according to his conscience. After all, the tree of my faith had been planted and nourished for many formative years in the soil of the

Church of Scotland, and although it had blossomed fully only when I found the one visible Church, its roots were in my Reformed past, and I will never despise these roots. In a final prayer the Presbytery of Tain commended me to the keeping and the direction of Almighty God; and after the blessing had been pronounced everyone shook me warmly by the hand, saying that they could not understand why I was doing this, but that they knew I must follow my conscience.

In silence Duncan MacDiarmid drove me back to Logie Easter.

"When you're down at the Assembly next year will you come to see us," I asked.

"You may be going off," he said, "but you've not seen the last us."

I was comforted by this remark, and indeed we had most definitely not seen the last of the MacDiarmids.

I asked Duncan to let me off at the end of the manse road. I looked at the house and walked round the summit of the little manse hill, surrounded by the severely trimmed hedge, now sprouting new growth. Only two and a half years earlier I had surveyed this place in the warm light of a spring evening, rejoicing in our first real home, rejoicing even more in being sent here to begin a life's work, breaking the Bread of Life to the people. Now this all appeared to be collapsing in tragedy. How could it be that in seeking my own salvation I had to withdraw from my responsibilities to this people to whom so recently I had felt bound as in a form of wedlock? But it was only an apparent tragedy. As I looked up to the rough croft land rising towards the mountains in the west, and over the fertile plain towards the coast, I recalled the kindness and loyalty of my one-time flock; I realized that I was acting not merely out of consideration for my own peace of mind, but for their sakes too. Trying to minister the truth to them, I had discovered the inconsistency of the Reformed tradition, and had been led to find the full assurance of faith in the Catholic Church. Therefore, although I could not convey the fruits of this discovery directly to my parishioners, it was for their good as well as my own that I followed my conscience now. For a time there would be bewilderment, vexation, even sadness; but soon a new and—I was sure—worthier, minister would come to serve this people. He would teach from scripture according to his lights and he would baptize the children. Almighty God would not abandon this flock; and I would now have a deeper, though hidden, ministry to perform. My life must be dedicated from this moment to prayer and sacrifice for the return of the fullness of revelation to this flock and to the whole of my beloved country. My action in resigning this charge and demitting my status as a minister was not abdication, nor did it express contempt for the Church of Scotland or for its people and ministers; it was a fresh and fuller offering of myself for the people I had been called to serve.

Surveying the parish from the vantage point of the manse hill, I commended the people to God—as the Presbytery had commended me—and I prayed that in this life many would discover the full assurance of faith as I had, and that we all, persevering in good faith, would be reunited in heaven. The very misunderstanding which my action produced, and the suffering—the greatest I had ever known—which that action produced, would be offered up to God on behalf of my former parishioners.

I crossed the stile and walked through the glebe field to the Logans. After supper Alastair drove us to the station. Penance began with a night train journey to Edinburgh. The train from the north squealed to a halt in Kildary station; John Urquhart was on duty and helped us heave the heavy trunks into the guard's van; he came back to the carriage and slammed the door shut, giving the handle a half-turn to lock it; his brown eyes were swimming again.

"If only I could have locked the pulpit door on you!"

Then he raised his green paraffin-lamp and waved out the train.

15

Early on a cold October morning we arrived by taxi from the Waverley Station at my grandmother's house in Findhorn Place. Paying the taxi made the first dent in the sixteen pounds–proceeds of the sale of our hens and equipment–which was all we had in the world. In the next few years we were to suffer a lot of privation, but that material inconvenience was as nothing to the mental agony we had to suffer during the first few months of our transition from the Church of Scotland to the Catholic Church. We found it almost impossible to tell people, especially our relatives, the reason for my leaving the ministry. In those days–the late forties–becoming a Catholic in Scotland was incomprehensible and to many people morally reprehensible as well. We said nothing to my maternal grandmother, but being very perceptive she smelt a rat even before she spotted Father Walter Glancy calling on us one morning. "Who was that?" she asked, frowning with one eyebrow raised. Then when Nicolas went off to St Peter's school the cat was out of the bag. She said nothing, but the atmosphere was unpleasant. A similar tension developed when we met old acquaintances, although with genuine close friends it was not so difficult. Very awkward were those occasions, at first fairly frequent, when I had to be interviewed by officials–on seeking entry to the Department of Education, for example, or on applying for an education grant. Without fail the question would be asked: "What was your previous employment?" And the matter was never left there, for my reply provoked more questioning, because the interrogator could never make sense of it. When in the end I was accepted at Moray House, the teachers' training college, the term had already begun. My late arrival caused no serious problem except in the P.T. class where I presented myself without all of the standard gear. The instructor treated us all as though we were in Primary Seven but I, recognized as a late-comer, who moreover wore a gray, not a white shirt, and black, not white, gym-shoes was commanded to stand aside in a corner. Our pathway towards the doors of the Catholic Church abounded in humiliations.

It was not long, however, before things began to settle down. We were both received into the Church by Fr Walter Glancy at Sancta Maria Abbey, Nunraw, on 23 December 1948. As we left the little chapel–an adapted Nissan hut–Helen whispered, "I got quite a fright–now I really am one of these people." Intellectually she was convinced, but emotionally she still belonged, much more firmly than I did, to her Protestant past, and in particular to her West Highland background and family; but we got used to the shock which our conversion had caused, to ourselves and also to those who knew us, and quickly began to form a circle of Catholic friends. The three boys were conditionally baptized a few days later in St Columba's, Edinburgh.

Although she did not in the least approve of what we had done, my grandmother never created any difficulties, and the rest of my family were not at all distressed. A great sorrow was that Helen's father never approved, and his anger on hearing of our conversion was so vehement that he put his health at risk. We were told that he had rushed out to walk in the Skye mountains, and returned having ruptured a stomach ulcer; Helen was deeply disturbed and a year later developed a nervous breakdown from which she took fifteen years to recover. Our old friends, to whom at first we may have appeared as curiosities, never treated us with anything but kindness. Top of this list were the MacDiarmids, who kept their promise and came to stay with us often, usually at the time of the General Assembly. Very soon it became clear that, after the initial awkwardness attached to informing others of our having been received into the Catholic Church, our problem was not the way we were treated, but that of how we ought to respond to the kindness and affection that was shown us by our former friends and colleagues.

During our last few months in the parish of Logie Easter I had already become aware that our conversion was not an escape from dark error into the bright light of truth, but a progress from the incomplete to the complete, from concepts to living realities, and so I had formed an attitude towards the Reformed Church that was perfectly in line with the ecumenical theology which a decade or so later was to be formulated in the Vatican II documents, *Lumen Gentium* and *Unitatis redintegratio*. It was another thing, however, to live out this theology in the situations presented by life, for the Catholic Church had not yet underwritten the emergent ecumenical theology in guide lines or canonical formulae. Living in this vacuum was difficult. For example, in this period after our reception into the Church but before Vatican II, my brother and sister both got married. There was no great difficulty about our attending the weddings, but we were required at least to inform our parish priest, because strictly speaking we would be attending heretical public worship; and although permission was immediately given we for our part did feel uneasy worshipping in a Reformed Church. Another occasion caused me great unease of conscience when I was urged to resume my connection with the Edinburgh University Singers who were giving a recital within the context of an evening service in a Church of Scotland. I did so, but was not fully convinced that the charity of my helping the choir out when they were short of a tenor outweighed my fault in attending heretical worship. Today, fifty years later, few Catholics and certainly no Protestants will understand the scruples I have just mentioned, but then they were real.

Why was the state of affairs like that? If we recall what things were like in those days between the Catholic and the Reformed Church—and there are some people who can do this—and if instead of dismissing it as a piece of nonsense we try to understand the reason behind it we can learn much. In the early twentieth century the general impression was that Protestantism and Catholicism were mutually exclusive, were enemies. From the Protestant viewpoint the image of the Scarlet Woman was still powerful. Had I myself not been influenced by it when I fled from the "ritualism" of St Giles'! And so it was reasonable for Protestants to denounce Catholicism and impede its development where possible. In the nineteenth century organizations like the Society for the Promotion of Christian Knowledge had overtly carried out this policy. Such zeal was one of the reasons why the Catholic Church so vigorously fought for the provision of Catholic schools, for it was no illusion to think that the state education system could be used as an agent in the destruction of the Catholic faith in the young.

The protectiveness of the Catholic Church, expressed in regulations forbidding Catholic attendance at Protestant worship makes sense when seen against the background of organized proselytism by those who in good faith abhorred the Catholic Faith. Helen and I were fully convinced in our profession of the Catholic Faith, but at the same time we could appreciate the feelings of apparently bigoted Protestants. More than that we could see the possibility of a new relationship forming between those who for centuries had been like enemies. We were still obliged, however, to live within the canonical framework that had grown out of centuries of enmity, and that was irksome. It was not long, however, before the irksomeness began to wear off and we found that our unusual position of being Catholics whose roots were deep in a Presbyterian past, which we still respected, imposed upon us the responsibility of becoming the nucleus of an ecumenical movement.

While Vatican II was still several years in the future I was being asked by Catholic societies to give them talks not just about our conversion, but also about our background, for there was already amongst the couthy Catholics of Scotland a desire to understand better those whom we described as "our separated brethren." Whenever I gave such talks I always urged the audience to refrain from bristling up at offense, and realizing that it resulted from ignorance to try to pay their Protestant brethren the compliment of assuming that they were kindly disposed to their Catholic brethren. I was firmly convinced that real ecumenism depended upon spiritual and moral relationships between believers and not upon what my friend Jim Whyte called "ecclesiastical joinery."

The desire to overcome bigotry was evident too among Protestants. I recall one occasion when during the early days of our being Catholics a non-Catholic society asked me to talk to them. This was a group of former pupils of my old school. The Heriot Club met in Gladstone's Land in the Lawnmarket where I spoke on a more philosophical plane about the difference between the Catholic and the Reformed view of revelation. The discussion that developed mainly between myself and a brilliant mathematician, who had been Dux of the school in my final year, showed that the arguments of the future were likely to be not between the Catholic and the Protestant traditions, but between those who believed in revelation and the possibility of its being grasped by men and women and those who believed that the mind of man is locked within itself and able to see no further than the physical world around us. This meeting taught me also the importance in ecumenical dialogue of a sense of humor. Although there was no atmosphere of animosity as the meeting began I sensed that an over-serious or pious approach would be quite out of place. I presented myself to them as "an old boy made bad" and the outburst of hilarity proved to me that I was right in suspecting that there had been a little tension, but that now—to mix the metaphor—the ice was broken. All of these early encounters with both Catholic and Protestant groups were but the herald of much bigger developments that were to follow in the sixties and seventies.

The prospect of ecumenical advance is made possible by the fact, stated in Vatican II documents and stressed in several statements by recent popes, that there is much held in common by all mainstream Christian communities. In the first paragraph of the concluding chapter of his *Apologia pro Vita Sua* John Henry Newman wrote: "I was not conscious to myself, on my conversion, of any change, intellectual or moral, wrought in my mind. I was not conscious of firmer faith in the fundamental truths of Revelation, or of more self-command; I had not more fervor; but it was like coming into port after a rough sea; and my happiness on that score remains to this day without interruption."

At first it may seem odd that Newman, having previously firmly believed in what he calls "the fundamental truths of Revelation" found it necessary to seek reception into the Roman Catholic Church. What difference did that make? My own experience helped me to understand Newman. I had found that in old-fashioned Church of Scotland tradition, that is the element in it which could be traced back to its origins in Calvin's theology, the fundamental truths of Revelation had indeed been preserved: belief in a transcendent God, in the mystery of the Trinity, in the mystery of the two natures in one Person in Christ. One might say that I found, as Newman had found, the substance of the Nicene/Chalcedonian creed preserved within Christian communities separated from the Roman Catholic Church. What I, like Newman, had discovered was that this Belief was not a proposition or set of propositions, existing in some philosophical milieu, and offering themselves to the grasp of individual believers, but that it was an heirloom handed down by the living Church, depending for its own unity and credibility upon the sustained unity and visibility of that Church. Moreover, like Newman, I had discovered that the one visible Church was the agent required for the development of that Faith, so that it could be presented in a meaningful way to succeeding generations, and applied to the changing conditions of mankind. This need for development and application, in my opinion, would be necessary especially in the realm of morals, to teach which the Church also held a mandate from the Lord. In our generation the need for the latter aspect of the Church's activity may be more apparent than it was in Newman's time, for today the undermining of the Christian Faith seems to begin in the field of ethics, and the Church's magisterium is attacked chiefly when it speaks on moral issues. Newman saw that the fundamental truths of Revelation, including moral truths, with which he was already acquainted, are safe only when guarded by the living unified Church, for the Spirit of Christ—who as the *Scots Confession* says, is the spirit of unity—lives not in formulae or texts, but in the living Church. A hundred years later than Newman I came to see that one required not only to believe in fundamental truths, but also by faith to recognize the one visible Church as the Pillar of Truth. This was the new element in Newman's vision, as it was in mine. It was not that one added a new doctrine, that of the Church, but that one began to live in the Church.

The first sentence in the paragraph of Newman's *Apologia* to which I referred above, reads thus: "From the time I became a Catholic, of course I have no further history of my religious opinions to relate. In saying this I do not mean to say that my mind has been idle, or that I have given up thinking on theological subjects; but I have had no variations to record, and have had no anxiety of heart whatever."

Like Newman, since my becoming a Catholic I have no variations in belief to record, for the Church still professes exactly the same faith as she ever did, as the recently published *Catechism of the Catholic Church* proves, but I cannot say, as Newman did, that "I have had no anxiety of mind whatever," for the Church, in a way that perhaps Newman could not have foreseen, has become infected with views, and unsettled by movements which are out of tune with her true nature, so that Catholics have had to struggle to distinguish what is authentic from what is spurious. Because my reception into the Church took place as this period of turmoil was just beginning, I find it fitting, as Newman did not, to continue writing the history of my theological development. This history tells not of any change in belief, but describes my attempt to sort out the true from the false in what has been going on in the Church over the past fifty years. Help in this work of discernment has not always been given by those from whom it might have been expected.

Our first experience was of course our reception into the Church. For us the most important element in this ceremony, and that which demanded most effort on our part, was making a confession of sins and receiving sacramental absolution in the sacrament of penance. Probably it is the recollection of the seriousness and effectiveness of that occasion that underlies my present sorrow at the way this sacrament is misunderstood and neglected today. This neglect is one of the serious errors that has been allowed to grow in the Church, encouraged greatly by the failure of pastors to stamp out the erroneous view that there is an effective general absolution given at penitential services. The teaching remains unchanged, that for a Catholic who has committed grave sin, the ordinary means of reconciliation with God and with the Church is through the sacrament of reconciliation, which involves individual confession of sins and the reception of absolution. The faithful are encouraged to confess venial sins also, so that they may increase in grace.

On the other hand, while our reception was deeply moving, there can be no doubt that the present method and rite of reception is much sounder than the one which we experienced. Today the Church has reverted to the more ancient custom of receiving adults through the conferring of the three sacraments of initiation, baptism, confirmation, and the holy eucharist in that order, the priest being given faculties to confirm for the occasion. If the person has already been validly baptized, the sacrament of penance is celebrated at a convenient time before the reception. The present method also ensures that the one received is confirmed before receiving holy communion, which was the rule until about a century ago, but today is not universally applied in the case of children. The Church has still much thinking to do on this problem.

In our case we were not confirmed until the following spring. We received Holy Communion for the first time at the Christmas Midnight Mass in the chapel at St Raphael's Hospital, where Fr Walter Glancy was chaplain. On this occasion after we had received Holy Communion and the Mass ended, we were confused when quite suddenly Fr Glancy turned to face the altar and began to celebrate Mass all over again; not only that, but he did the same again and said a third Mass. After the three Masses were over we were entertained to a meal by the sisters who ran the hospital, and during the meal we questioned Fr Glancy, who explained that on Christmas Day a priest could offer three Masses. As docile neophytes we accepted that it must be quite in order. Even so, we were a bit disappointed on account of what seemed to us a kind of quantitative approach to devotion. Today I can rejoice over the liturgical improvement embodied in the rubrics, which I re-read only a few days ago, and which lay down that the three Masses a priest may celebrate on Christmas Day must be said separately at the proper times—midnight, dawn, and during the day.

There is one practice which I encountered even before we were received, and about which I felt exactly the opposite from the way I felt about the stringing together of the three Christmas Masses: I was edified by it. St Patrick's Church in the Cowgate is only a quarter of a mile from Moray House, the College of Education, where I now studied. During the lunch-break I often paid a visit to this church. On 2 November I found a great number of people praying there, and many of them were making repeated short visits. Our instruction had already begun and I asked Fr Glancy about the practice that I had observed in St

Patrick's. He explained that the devotions I had seen were those attached to the gaining of indulgences, on this particular occasion being offered on behalf of the souls in purgatory.

I began at once to study carefully the doctrine about indulgences—a good start, I thought, for what doctrine could be farther removed from Reformed thinking! Even before I had discovered the authentic teaching about indulgences, however, just seeing the industry of ordinary people at prayer in this way impressed me. They were practicing their faith. St Paul had told the early Christians that they must work out their salvation in fear and trembling. The people I saw in St Patrick's were certainly working at something, and the accent was on prayer, which is a sign of faith. The exposition of the doctrine of indulgences I then found most interesting. At New College Professor Hugh Watt had made quite sure that I knew all about the dreadful superstition and simony connected with the sale of indulgences, but I had not heard anything about the doctrine that had been thus debased. I do not remember which text-books or catechisms I used in 1948 in order to become properly informed on this subject, but the essential points I learned then have been reproduced even more clearly in the new *Catechism of the Catholic Church*. The fact that the doctrine is still to be found in this authoritative document indicates that the doctrine has by no means been discarded by Vatican II, as many imagine. What, then, is the teaching of the Church about indulgences?

In defining an indulgence the new *Catechism* quotes an earlier pronouncement of Pope Paul VI:

> *'An indulgence is a remission before God of the temporal punishment due to sins whose guilt has already been forgiven, which the faithful Christian who is duly disposed gains under certain prescribed conditions through the action of the Church which, as minister of redemption, dispenses and applies with authority the treasury of the satisfactions of Christ and the saints'* (n.1471).

I realized that the first thing one must get clear about indulgences is that they do not effect the forgiveness of sins. Having grasped that fact it then struck me that indulgences were the answer to an objection, a sneering objection indeed, which I had heard directed not at the Catholic Church in particular, but at all Christians, the complaint that is, that by accepting forgiveness for sins, even the most heinous, we "get off Scot-free." Underlying the concept of indulgences I saw the problem of reconciling God's mercy with his justice. Only God's forgiveness can open up again the prospect of reconciliation with God and one's fellow men and women, but there is left over damage to be repaired, and God's justice requires that the repair be carried out. I don't mean reparation that might be required through having damaged another, but rather the damage done by the sinner to himself. By fulfilling the conditions, and performing the prayers or actions, required for the obtaining of an indulgence, the sinner or someone acting as his intercessor, is making a contribution towards repairing the damage done to his own soul by his sin.

The new *Catechism* contains interesting and important articles on "The punishments of sin," which elucidates the thought behind my phrase "damage to be repaired."

> *To understand this doctrine and practice of the Church it is necessary to understand that sin has a double consequence. Grave sin deprives us of communion with God, and therefore makes us incapable of eternal life, the privation of which is called 'the eternal punishment' of sin. On the other hand every sin, even venial, entails an unhealthy attachment to creatures, which must be purified either here on earth, or after death in the state called Purgatory. This purification frees one from what is called the 'temporal punishment' of sin. These two punishments must not be conceived of as a kind of vengeance inflicted by God from without, but as following from the very nature of sin. A conversion which proceeds from a fervent charity can attain the complete purification of the sinner in such a way that no punishment would remain (n.1472).*

The forgiveness of sin and restoration of communion with God entail the remission of the eternal punishment of sin, but temporal punishment of sin remains. While patiently bearing sufferings and trials of all kinds and, when the day comes, serenely facing death, the Christian must strive to accept this temporal punishment of sin as a grace. He should strive by works of mercy and charity and the various practices of penance, to put off completely the 'old man' and put on the 'new man' (n.1473).

To grasp the meaning of the doctrine of indulgences, equally important as understanding the concept of temporal punishment due to sin, is an understanding of the importance of the communion of saints, of the fact that there is a sharing amongst all of the members of Christ's body of their spiritual gifts, all of which gifts flow from the infinite merits of Christ. These gifts are known as the Church's "treasury of merits," and the Church has a measure of competence in the sharing out of these gifts amongst her family, just as a mother might share out good things amongst all of her children.

An indulgence is obtained through the Church who, by virtue of the power of binding and loosing granted her by Christ Jesus, intervenes in favor of individual Christians and opens for them the treasury of the merits of Christ and the saints to obtain from the Father of mercies the remission of the temporal punishment due for their sins. Thus the Church does not want simply to come to the aid of these Christians, but also to spur them to works of devotion, penance and charity (CCC n.1478).

The industry of those I saw at prayer in St Patrick's only a few days after leaving Logie-Easter was a response to this spurring on by the Church to works of prayer, penance, and charity. The worshippers, having in those days been thoroughly catechized, were under no delusion that they were buying forgiveness. They were making the effort, required of Christians, to lay claim to the treasures of grace available for them, so that they might come closer to that state of sanctity which would enable them to see

God as he is, and the Church was guiding them along this road. Besides the prayers or other good works prescribed, the conditions laid down for the obtaining of an indulgence are most demanding. If one seriously fulfills these conditions one is already making great progress along the pathway of prayer, for to gain an indulgence a person must examine his conscience, make a confession of sins, and receive sacramental absolution, being firmly resolved, by the grace of God, to avoid not only grave sin, but also venial sin. He must also receive Holy Communion. To seek to gain an indulgence is the same thing as to seek perfect sanctity. In seeking an indulgence on 2 November, moreover, the worshipper is engaged in a sublime act of charity: he is offering this indulgence, that is the remission of temporal punishment due to sin, on behalf of a soul in purgatory, who cannot pray for himself.

In November 1948 I saw many Catholics doing just that in St Patrick's in the Cowgate, and was reminded of St Paul's exhortation, reproduced in one of the Scottish paraphrases: "Thus faith approves itself sincere, by active virtue crowned."

16

My grandmother's house in Findhorn Place was a fairly large self-contained villa, in which we occupied the ground floor. There was a small garden at the front and quite a long garden at the back, at the far end of which we kept six hens, which we had been able—I can't remember how—to bring with us from Easter Ross. In the middle of this garden, facing due south, was our one hive of bees, which had been comfortably transported with our furniture in a removal van. I know that we remained in this house until at least May 1949, because it was in the garden there on a warm spring day that Helen saw the two younger boys assisting the bees by stuffing daffodils into the entrance of the hive. Both boys were covered from head to foot in bees. Helen, who was quite fearless in situations like this, ran out and stripped both youngsters naked and brought them into the house. No one received a single sting, and the bees, having made their point, continued happily foraging in the sycamore trees, which abound in the south side of Edinburgh.

Later that year in nearby Upper Gray Street we found more suitable accommodation in a bungalow belonging to St Columba's Church. Here too was a garden in which we installed the beehive and the six hens, but as livestock was now proving a burden, I gave the bees to Raymond McCluskey, and one night at Christmas I wrung six necks and gave the birds as Christmas presents to friends who were visiting us.

By the time a year had passed after our reception into the Catholic Church, awkward explanation of what we had done ceased to bother us, for most of our friends and acquaintances now knew of our action, and we had very quickly entered a new world. One evening in the Catholic Chaplaincy in George Square I met the Church historian Father Philip Hughes who suggested that I write memoirs of my Presbyterian past because, he said, it would all fade very soon from my memory. He was right, for although I have never lost my sympathy and respect for the Reformed tradition, especially as expressed in the lives of ordinary devout folk, nor has my affection for my friends ever diminished, I soon discovered that my mind-set had changed; I did not view the things of faith in the same way as my Reformed Church friends; and so in spite of friendship and mutual respect, a gulf had opened up between us, and this saddened me.

Not only did Helen and I now live within a new mental and emotional framework, but we inhabited a new world, becoming occupied with making new friends and getting used to the practice of the Catholic Faith, through participating in the liturgy and in popular devotions. We were helped in this process by Nicolas who attended St Peter's school in the adjacent parish. By following his religious education and by our contact with the activities of the school, we were initiated into the alphabet of Catholic practice and worship.

During the year 1949-50 when Nicolas was in Primary 3 we learned a great deal, for that is the year when children are prepared to receive Holy Communion. We now learned of a popular devotion which was another expression of the need to do something to prove the sincerity of our faith. "What must we do to be saved?" people had asked St Peter at Pentecost. We learned that the children in Primary 3 were doing something: they were being encouraged to pray in church on nine successive Saturdays (a novena of prayer) and to mark a particular petition on a card which was put in a box in the church. I could see very well how such a practice—"holy book-keeping" as my friend Bill McKechnie called it—could become superstitiously used, but used sensibly it had the great merit of teaching the children that God does invite us to make our requests known to him, and that we must persevere in prayer.

It happened that the MacDiarmids were in Edinburgh at the time when Nicolas was engaged in this little devotion. Bessie MacDiarmid, who had brought another minister's wife with her to visit us, asked Nicolas what he wanted to pray for. He showed her the card on which he had ticked off: "For grace to make a good confession." "That's very good," she said, whereupon her companion asked, "Is Grace his sister?" "No," she replied, "he doesn't have any sisters," and changed the subject.

Our time spent in the little house next to St Columba's Church lasted until spring 1951 and we benefited greatly by our closeness to the sanctuary. It was easy to pay a visit to the church and pray before the Blessed Sacrament. On Sundays besides the celebration of Mass there was also a devotional service in the evening. Normally this began with the exposition of the Blessed Sacrament and ended with Benediction with the Blessed Sacrament. By attending these devotions and by our private visits to the church we learned of the importance of the doctrine of the real presence, and also in some measure the art of meditation.

Meditation was also introduced to us through the Rosary. Sometimes the Rosary would be recited in the presence of the Blessed Sacrament at these Sunday evening services, but I did not find the public recitation of the Rosary so helpful as when I prayed the Rosary on my own. Even before being received into the Catholic Church I had not thought it improper to ask the faithful departed, especially those of great virtue, to pray for us, and so the notion that Mary, the mother of our Lord could pray most effectively for us presented me with no problem.

Devotion to Mary is commonly regarded by Protestants, however, as a major stumbling-block in the way of taking Catholic doctrine seriously. Why is this so? I can think of several ways in which Protestants might take issue with the Catholic Church and insist on maintaining their separation, without any need to make an issue of devotion to the Mother of God. It is precisely because she is truly the Mother of God that devotion to her is justified and fitting. I always presume that my Reformed Church friends profess the Creed of Chalcedon and accept too the earlier councils, including that of Ephesus in AD 431, which described Mary as *Theotokos*–"The Godbearer." Further, I see in St Luke's Gospel a hint of genuine feminism in his presentation of the young Mary as a woman with a mind of her own, who weighed up what the angel was saying–discerning the spirits–giving her consent to become the mother of the Holy One of God only after she was sure that his proposal harmonized with the pattern of God's previous dealings with his chosen ones. Mary's deliberate, active co-operation with divine grace serves as the model for the response of every believer, for grace is not irresistible, but must be grasped willingly. Moreover, because of her free consent to become the Mother of God, she deserves our gratitude. She was no puppet on a string.

So much then for her role as chief human co-operator in God's plan of salvation by offering herself as the conduit of the eternal Son into this world; her role as intercessor should become evident to us if we think realistically about her motherhood. Knowing that she was genuinely his mother helps us to take seriously the fact that our Lord is true man as well as being true God. This fact is sometimes obscured by a crypto-monophysitism that often passes for orthodoxy. Such a tendency can be corrected by imagining the Child in his mother's arms. What is the first image that a baby sees? Its mother's face. Who is the first person it identifies? Its mother. And so it was with Jesus; in his sacred humanity the first person he saw and knew was Mary, and as a baby he cried out to her and instinctively asked her help. If he was happy to ask for her help why should not we, his adopted brothers and sisters do the same? For we are his brothers and sisters: on the Cross Jesus said to John, "Son, behold your mother."

It must be noted, however, and noted well, that Mary acts not as primary agent, but only as intercessor. At the first sign, when he let his glory be seen, Jesus enjoyed the co-operation of his mother. She said to her Son, "They have no wine," and then to the waiters, "Do whatever he says." She made the request, but it was Jesus, not she, who turned the water into wine.

Within the context of the Rosary, prayed in private, my devotion to Mary, the Mother of God grew. I discovered too at a very early stage in my Catholic spiritual development, that this form of devotion came more and more to depend upon the Bible. Before proceeding to say the prayers attached to a particular mystery I would pause for a few minutes to allow the scene to come into clear focus. This led me to read the passage in scripture which recorded the event, and as I did this I found that more and more material would come to mind. The Annunciation scene, with which the Rosary opens, is a fine example of this: one cannot meditate upon it without being reminded of similar incidents of angelic annunciations described in the Old Testament, and of the episodes touching on unusual conceptions granted to devout women. The Annunciation of the conception of our Lord is set against a rich Old Testament background; and the same can be said of all of the fifteen mysteries of the Rosary. Through the Rosary, therefore, I had almost effortlessly entered the world of meditative prayer, a world in which the worshipper is drawn into the presence of our Lord through a concentration on actual places, persons, and conversations, all provided for us in the text of the Bible. Many years later when I read *The Spiritual Exercises* I discovered that this was in essence the method of meditation taught by St Ignatius of Loyola.

A great deal of the discursive theological work that led us into the Catholic Church had been done before we were received, but so much remained to be done, for understanding the Faith grows through prayer. Guided by the excellent religious education our eldest child was receiving at St Peter's primary school, and through joining in the normal life of a parish our private and public prayer-life developed steadily. In private prayer–apart from the practice of meditation associated with the mysteries of the Rosary—we were greatly helped by *A Simple Prayer Book*. This inexpensive little book is by far the best prayer-book I have ever seen. It is re-issued periodically, but while the language is kept up-to-date the content of the prayers never changes, and most of the prayers can be said and understood by all but the youngest children. It is, therefore, an instrument that fosters family unity in prayer. Most important of all, having it always at hand reminds us that prayer, though it need not be lengthy, must be regular. Neatly and clearly set out in this little book is a scheme of prayer for morning and night, as well as prayers for many occasions and a guide to the practice of Confession, as well as short devotions in preparation for, and thanksgiving after, receiving Holy Communion. With this unpretentious manual to guide us we not only established a firm prayer-pattern for our own lives, but were able to do the same for our children. When Nicolas died tragically at the age of twenty-two I found amongst his belongings a worn-out copy of this book, which he had held onto since his days in St Peter's primary school.

St Columba's was quite a beautiful little church, tastefully furnished. It had a semi-circular apse with the altar recessed in the apse. This was before the days when an auxiliary altar would have been placed nearer the front seats to allow the priest to celebrate Mass facing the congregation. Aesthetically the building had not been impaired by a breaking of architectural unity. While we were not unimpressed by the aesthetic qualities of the church, we were more attentive to the reality of the celebration of the Mass. As a Presbyterian minister, although facing the congregation when celebrating the Lord's Supper—a stance which was a tactical device of the Reformers in their attack upon the doctrine of the sacrifice of the Mass—I had already begun to believe that the eucharist was more than a mental commemoration but was a making present of the sacrifice of the Cross; it was a sacrifice, but because there could be no other sacrifice than that of Calvary, the eucharist was that sacrifice. In the Masses we were now attending in St Columba's the doctrine of the sacrifice of the eucharist was very clearly expressed. When the priest raised up the consecrated bread and wine at the end of the Canon of the Mass, presenting them, not to us but to the Father, in the words, *"Per ipsum, et cum ipso, et in ipso, est tibi Deo Patri omnipoténti, in unitáte Spíritus Sancti, omnis honor et gloria, per omnia sæcula sæculorum,"* we were, in this sacramental mystery, through faith, present at the Son's offering of himself on the Cross to God the Father. More than that, we were being caught up in that sacrifice and our offering of ourselves had become pleasing to the Father, through its association with the sacrifice of his only-begotten Son. At this point in the Mass I always had a sense of solidarity with the celebrating priest. He, by his special commission, consecrated the elements and presented them in our name, but we were literally right behind him. In those days during 1949-51 when we worshipped in St Columba's, Upper Gray Street, I rejoiced in this unambiguous expression of the Catholic doctrine of the sacrifice of the Mass.

My experience of the Catholic Church was further extended during the period 1949-50 by my being asked to help in the choir at the Jesuit Church of the Sacred Heart in Lauriston Street. As a family we remained embedded in St Columba's, but I went off on Sunday forenoons to sing at the 11 a.m. Mass at Sacred Heart. In those days this was known as the Solemn High Mass when the ordinary of the Mass would be sung either in plainchant or in some Baroque polyphonic setting. Through this connection I got to know several of the Jesuit fathers, notably Fr James Christie, who was parish priest at the time. My education was helped on a lot by the conversations I had with him and with others, and I took a great liking to the Jesuits. I once asked my friend Bill McKechnie, "Why aren't all priests Jesuits?" To be fair I must add that I had a high regard also for the Dominicans whom I knew at the university chaplaincy in George Square, but I did not have so much contact with them. It is of no significance, I am sure, but at that time in Edinburgh I observed that whereas the Dominicans, no doubt as a symbol of their being mendicant friars, took no pride in the cleanness of their shoes, Jesuit shoes were always highly polished. I was slowly learning about the diversity that is embraced in the Catholic Church.

A decisive consolidation of my Catholic belief began in August 1949 when, having completed a year's training at Moray House and gained a teaching certificate and a Diploma in Education, I was given a post in St Ninian's Primary School in Restalrig, where I taught for two years. There is probably no better way to become thoroughly initiated into the ethos of a community than by working in a school which serves that community, and is a mirror of it. In those days the Catholic ethos was clearly articulated in the religious education program of a Catholic school. That program was not confined within the time-table of religious instruction, but spread out into the framework of prayers in class, in the dining hall, and in the encouragement of extra curricular activities. There were school Masses on special occasions, and supervised visits to the church to allow the children to make their confessions.

Doctrinal instruction was not left to chance. There was a detailed syllabus for each year, which included Old Testament history, doctrines of the Faith, which were to be explained to the children according to their intellectual capacity, and then learned in the encapsulated form of the Catechism. Quite a bit of time was spent in learning and singing hymns, and also the plainchant versions of parts of the Mass—the *Sanctus* and the *Agnus Dei*, for example. The children learned also some of the plainchant melodies of the Latin antiphons of our Lady—the *Salve Regina* and others. I discovered to my astonishment that the children loved these antiphons. Once when we had an inspection the priest doing the job asked the class what they would like to sing. They opted for one of these antiphons. "That's beautiful," he said, "what else can you sing?" And they offered a second. The next time he asked them, yet a third antiphon was suggested. "Can't you sing any ordinary hymns in English?" he asked.

Decades later I asked a tough little teenager what had impressed him most on his visit to the Cistercian Abbey at Nunraw, and he replied immediately, "That thing they sing at the end of Compline." He was referring to the *Salve Regina.*

As soon as Helen and I had left the parish of Logie Easter at the end of 1948 a great burden was lifted from our spirits. We were now at rest in belief; the Church was a home not a debating hall; but in a particular way for us the stress upon our marriage was removed. The conflict between my personal bond with the parish and the personal bond of marriage had gone.

Now it may well be that in the Reformed tradition, which does not regard the ministry as a sacrament, the relationship between minister and people can and should be other than I had conceived it, so that it would be possible for a man to provide a valuable ministry within the Church and yet not find that his ministry became a rival to his marriage, but I could not think of the ordained ministry nor practice it in any such way. It may also be true that some married people are not so passionately in love with each other as we were, so that in the case of a minister and his wife the tension between being parson and being husband might not be so acute as we had felt. Now that I was free from a pastoral bond, that I had felt to be sacramental, we were confirmed in our conviction that marriage was our vocation.

By now much care had to be directed to the three young children. This claimed time and energy, but we never experienced any diminution in the affection we had for each other. It never occurred to us that the impulse to make love had been just a ruse of nature to encourage procreation. True, we had never imagined that love-making could be justified apart from its procreative potential, but we believed also, and our experience confirmed, that personal union was perfected by the carnal "knowledge" that is at the heart of marriage. When first we had fallen in love the thought had struck me that such passion is something that stands on a pedestal, inviolable, never just a means but an end in itself. As our marriage progressed I did not give up this notion. It seemed that marriage is a kind of justified idolatry, as when one shows reverence for an icon. Married love is a great icon of the love of God, the love of Christ, the Bridegroom, for the Church, his Bride. The unicity, apart from which marriage would be meaningless, is directly linked with the oneness of the Godhead:

> *Listen Israel: the Lord our God is one God.*
> *You shall love the Lord your God with all your heart,*
> *with all your soul, with all your strength (Deut 6:5).*

Marriage, which in the Christian view is a sacrament of the love between God and mankind, must therefore possess the quality of exclusive worship. And so in worshipping each other as images of God who made us, a married couple are able, therefore to abandon themselves to that passion, described in the Song of Songs, without diminishing their love of God.

> *Set me like a seal on your heart,*
> *like a seal on your arm.*
> *For love is strong as Death,*
> *jealousy as relentless as the grave.*
> *The flash of it is a flash of fire,*
> *a flame of God himself.*
> *love no flood can quench,*
> *no torrents drown (The Song of Songs 8:6-7).*

Not only is the worship of God unimpaired by the whole-hearted devotion a married couple give to each other, but through their devotion to this icon of divine love, they are led closer and closer to understanding the love of God and the meaning of union with God, the Person of all persons.

No matter how deeply interested a man or woman might be in other necessary pursuits—work or play—none of these pursuits may be permitted to assume more importance than marriage itself. Life provides many delights, but for a husband and wife there should be no delight that can match the delight of their being together. All activities must work together to support the marriage. And this is true even of the procreation and care of children. Care of the family is not a substitute for married love, but part of it and a factor in its growth. When the family are grown-up and have gone off to lead their own lives the parents remain, and their love remains. True married love endures from the springtime of Romeo and Juliet until the winter of Darby and Joan.

In the history of the Church the meaning of marriage has sometimes been misunderstood. Within the first year of our life as Catholics an unsympathetic acquaintance sneered that now we would be expected, perhaps ordered, to have several more children. The notion was not uncommon that the Catholic Church saw marriage as a means to one end, the procreation of children. Helen and I had never thought like that, and we did not perceive any blindness on the part of other Catholics to the fact that the union between spouses is also an end of marriage. There was no problem here: marital intercourse may be regarded as a means, but a means that leads to two ends, on the one hand new life, and on the other, the deepening union of the persons. Neither of the ends may be claimed to be superior to the other for both are joined in the design of nature, and in the exercise of married love, the means, that is sexual intercourse, may not by the human agent be directed to the fulfillment exclusively of only one of these ends.

Unfortunately the realization that the unitive aspect of marriage is an end in itself has led to the separation of the two ends, so that some feel justified in switching off the procreative potential so as to allow intercourse to proceed unrestrained by considerations of whether or not it is prudent to conceive a child at a particular time.

In the early fifties, when we were becoming acclimatized to Catholic life, it was generally accepted by Catholics that to disconnect artificially the connection between intercourse and procreation was a serious disordering of nature, and therefore gravely sinful. Even before we were received into the Catholic Church we held that view. It was difficult, we have to admit, to remain true to our conviction, for there had to be some fairly long periods of abstinence which did not, however, weaken our marriage but strengthened it. When prudence dictates that family size ought to be restricted, and this is achieved by the periodic abstinence that a natural method of avoidance of conception requires, it seems that nature grants a bonus by giving a deeper dimension to love. Marriage is a sacrament, and a sacrament carries within it the merits of the sacrifice of Christ. Without a sacrificial element—and abstinence from immediate gratification is a sacrifice that nature provides—marriage would lack its link with the Cross. Contraception pulls this cross out of marriage.

17

Our tenancy of the house in Upper Gray Street expired in spring 1951. There was an old house, used as a lawyer's office, for sale in Dalkeith about seven miles from the center of Edinburgh. We were able—I don't know how—to get a loan and buy this property. One Saturday morning I went out to see the place, taking the children with me. We got off the bus about half a mile short of Dalkeith and walked the rest of the way into the town. Along the side of the road trees had been felled, and I still recall the superb scent rising from the sap that was oozing out of the base of the trunks. They were oak trees.

Dalkeith was and still is a very pleasant little town. Originally a market town set in agricultural Midlothian, it had also become the home of a coal-mining community, and was linked within a network of mining villages. The main street, with the medieval Church of St Nicholas on the north side, was very wide as in market towns all over Europe, and at the east end, a bit removed from other buildings, were the massive gates of Dalkeith Palace, a residence belonging to the Duke of Buccleuch. The palace demesne although very large was entirely encircled by a high stone wall, which could, however, be penetrated at several points, and I used to lead my sons on expeditions through the woods and thickets to collect rose-hips, which at that time were marketable, or else simply to pretend that we were fugitives being pursued by Sioux Indians. On one occasion Christopher, the youngest and having an over-efficient imagination, became terrified, thinking that his skull was about to be split by a tomahawk.

These expeditions and others to an allotment took place some time after we had settled into this home. At first the going was very rough. We had to suffer tradesmen intermittently working in the house for months before the place became properly habitable. At one point in the proceedings the men departed, leaving a heap of sand in the middle of the kitchen floor. It was Helen who suffered most from this move to Dalkeith, for she spent all day in the house, which although a good house, was in a dreadful state, and surrounded by higher buildings, so that to see the sky one had to go outside. Even then one had to crane one's neck, for the street was very narrow. The house did have the advantage of being central and close to shops; indeed the two adjoining properties belonged to a grocer and a baker. The baker, who made the best high-pan loaf I have ever eaten, had his bakehouse about three yards from our back door.

Shortly before we left Edinburgh Helen had shown signs of phobia. She discovered that she became afraid when she found herself in a lift; but she was not just claustrophobic, for a similar panic had once come upon her when she was out shopping, so that she had to hurry home. The move to Dalkeith aggravated her condition; very soon she was suffering quite frequently from severe migraine, which could last for five days at a time, and she now felt trapped when she entered a building or a bus. Handling this problem was an important factor in the way we now had to manage our lives. There seemed to be no adequate medical or psychotherapeutic help available. Things began to improve and life became gradually more normal after we got back to Edinburgh in 1957, but especially after our move to Morningside in 1961.

Having found a place to live in Dalkeith I now had to try to find work there. I was lucky. There is a Catholic primary and secondary school in Dalkeith. I learned from the parish priest Dr. John Ward that there would be a vacancy in the primary school there after Easter. I applied to Midlothian Education Authority and was coolly told that if they had anything they would let me know. Dr. Ward was astonished when I told him of this.

"But they are desperately needing someone," he said, "and I think they need a secondary teacher as well."

So it turned out, and in due course I was offered a job in the primary school. I had learned, too, something about the arrogance and love of power that can infect bureaucracies.

The primary school at St David's, Dalkeith was pleasant as a school but abominable as a building; it was falling to pieces. I continued teaching as I had been doing in Edinburgh and although the school and equipment were sub-standard, the setting was pleasant. At lunch-break the children would run wild in the "High Woods" on the banks of the river Esk, and when they returned the classroom would reek of the wild garlic they had crushed with their shoes. I always got home for lunch for it took only seven minutes to walk. Most of the children were healthy and well cared for. Miners are very good to their children. There was a sprinkling of children from Nazareth House in Lasswade.

One officious but sweet little girl stands out in my memory. She was called Sadie, and she opened and shut the door for me when I entered or left the room. No one else ever dared usurp her function, for which, I think, she had been appointed by my predecessor. One day the children were being allowed to read a book of their own choice. Sadie had two books on her desk.

"What book is that you're reading, Sadie?" I asked.

"It's not a book, Sir," she replied soulfully, "it's a volume."

On the last day of the summer holidays after my first term in this school, a letter was pushed by a pupil through our letter-box. Once again I became aware of the high-handedness that can affect our educational bureaucracies. The letter was brief, signed by the headmaster, and it read, "As from the beginning of the autumn term, you will be employed in the secondary school as a science teacher."

The plan, of which I had no inkling, had already been conceived, I suspect, when I was offered the post in the primary school. The authorities knew that it was almost impossible to get a qualified science teacher to replace the person who was to leave in summer, but it would have been difficult for them to appoint me, unqualified as I was, directly to that post, but they were able because of the primary vacancy to get me onto the staff and then slide me unnoticed into the science department. The authority also benefited financially, for I received the primary salary, which was less than the secondary salary. The only semblance of competence which I possessed, which the authorities must have noticed, was my excellent school record in physics, dynamics, mechanics, zoology, and botany, and a merit certificate in natural philosophy from the university. But I had almost no knowledge of chemistry. I protested to the headmaster, who paid no heed, but remarked that I would find it an invigorating challenge to have to teach science.

St David's secondary school—a junior secondary—was situated low down close to the river Esk on the north side of the town, a little upstream from the abattoir. It carried on a child's education for three years after the primary stage. That is to say, the pupils were aged roughly 12 to 14. As a comprehensive school it served pupils of all academic abilities, but each year contained three streams: the literary; the domestic/technical and the modified. It was hoped that pupils in the literary section would continue their education at a senior secondary school. I never bothered to find out the method by which children were selected for a particular stream. There was a certain amount of self-selection at work. One boy said to me: "If you can get bad marks you get put down into technical and then you don't get any homework."

Whether or not I rose to the challenge proposed by the headmaster, I don't know. There were black spots and bright spots in the two years I spent teaching in this junior secondary school. I became class master of one of the literary classes, which meant that as well as teaching them science I was responsible for their religious education.

I enjoyed teaching these slightly older children and found the operation worth the effort, for there was amongst the children enthusiasm for their faith. Only a small minority of the children came from families who had lapsed from the Faith. As in the primary school there was a detailed syllabus to be followed, and through teaching these older children I learned how to relate explanation of the Faith to its verbal formulation. I saw an analogy to this relationship in scientific method, which had been so thoroughly dinned into me at school. First one discovers the meaning of a natural phenomenon by experiment, and then one is able to encapsulate the reality of nature in a formula, for example, the principle of Archimedes. In learning about our Faith, unless we can capture its realities in words, the reality tends to disappear into the air–like a kite without a string. No doubt the syllabus provided for us at that time could have been improved, but the method of catechesis was sound.

With science, I would not claim that my teaching was entirely successful. The literary class, that is the children with a higher IQ and a more academic bent, could cope with experiments, and I was happy enough when we were dealing with physics, but chemistry was a problem. On one occasion I nervously invited the class to make an act of contrition, and within seconds the retort had hit the ceiling. I had no experience of working with hydrogen.

Things went quite well with the domestic/technical classes, but with the modified stream one was in a different world. Because I was unqualified to teach science I was given every class in the modified stream, the reasoning being that I would be good enough for them. The problem was not simply that the children in this stream were of lower intelligence, but that their capacities and needs had not been properly considered, one sign of which was that they had to make do with an unqualified teacher. The regulations prescribed that this group receive science lessons for so many hours each week, and so they were confined for one and a half hours twice a week in a very small room, equipped with a small sink and one Bunsen-burner, and subjected to a watered down version of the academic science course.

At first I set them to do experiments, but the freedom of movement required resulted in chaos, for scientific study through experiment demands both high intelligence and also thorough self-discipline. I abandoned all attempts at experiments—there was no equipment in any case—but to my astonishment discovered that the pupils in the modified stream, especially the boys, were delighted to work at arithmetic which continued the sound education they had received in primary school; and they could see and feel proud of their results. Another thing that kept them content, especially the girls, was to have a story read to them. I was forced to devise my own program.

I felt a little uneasy because of the cavalier way I began to treat the official syllabus, but my conscience was calmed when one of my superiors said to me:

"Don't worry what you do with them so long as you keep them quiet; none of them can make anything of science anyway."

In the summer term I had the bright idea that I should take the class outside to the "High Woods" and the "Low Woods," and have a look at things botanical. With some this proved highly successful; and those who were totally resistant to any kind of education enjoyed an opportunity to fool around harmlessly in the fresh air and sunshine. Unfortunately these expeditions had to cease; the headmaster, who surveyed all things from a window high up in the old building disapproved and told me that they ought to be in the classroom. So we went back to stifle in the smallest room in the school for one and a half hours twice a week.

In spite of the positive side to the work I was doing in St David's secondary school, I was not really satisfied, and so began to consider alternative kinds of work. Some form of teaching seemed to be the right field, but my having been shunted into the science department had confused things. It occurred to me that I should try to get back into primary teaching. Perhaps I could become a country *Domine?* This idea appealed to me, and we were attracted too by the thought of getting back to the kind of life we had known in Logie Easter. We had also discovered that when we got away from town and into the open country Helen's phobias slackened their grip.

For several months we scanned the advertisement column in *The Scotsman*, on the look-out for a post in a Catholic country school. Several did appear; I remember applying for a post in Chapeltown, Braes of Glenlivet. All our efforts were in vain. Sometimes the application was not even acknowledged, and if it were, I had no luck. Eventually we learned from someone who was in the know, that the kind of school I was after was normally a one-or two-teacher school, to which the authorities would always appoint a woman, as the girls had to be taught sewing. I wondered if the reason might not have been that a woman's salary was less, in those days, than a man's. In the end I gave up the effort to find a country school.

Then out of the blue the scene changed. The Scottish Organizer of the Converts' Aid Society died, and I was asked if I would take over his work. I traveled down to Twickenham and was interviewed by Freddie Chambers and his wife Pat, and taken to meet Fr Gordon Wheeler, at that time parish priest at Spanish Place. I enjoyed my visit to Holmes Road, Twickenham very much, for I was so hospitably treated. I was offered and accepted the job. Over the next twenty years during which I worked as Scottish Organizer of the C.A.S. Helen and I paid several visits to Twickenham when we attended Annual General Meetings of the C.A.S. in London, and we had a glimpse into a world that was very far from the one we inhabited at home. I got the impression that in England, especially in the Archdiocese of Westminster, there was developing a Catholic establishment, or perhaps the desire amongst Catholics to become assimilated into the Establishment.

With hindsight one can estimate the value of the course of one's life. Over a period of twenty years, because I had to visit as many Catholic parishes as possible in order to raise money for the C.A.S., I got to know nearly every inch of Scotland, an accomplishment which has not only given me enormous pleasure, but proved endlessly useful.

In particular I got to know Glasgow–knowledge denied most Edinburgh men. This knowledge was not limited to topography; I met the people and discovered the unique Glasgow sense of humor. Sometimes I traveled on the busses, where much of the action is. One dark night I asked the Clippie, that is the conductress, to let me know when we reached Peat Road. She nodded, but in the end remained silent and I was taken several stops beyond my destination. On the return I remarked to a man at the bus-stop that the Clippie hadn't told me when to get off.

"Her mother tellt her no tae speak tae strange men," he replied dryly.

Another time when the bus on which I was traveling was zigzagging at some speed, I whispered nervously:

"I hope he knows what he's doing."

"Huh!" said the Clippie, "There's nae tread on the tires; we were nearly aff the Jamaica Bridge this morning."

A friend told me of a bizarre incident when a bus, coming in from the south side of Glasgow, ground to a halt. The driver jumped out of his cab and came round to the back of the bus.

"Can onybody tell me the way to West Nile Street?"

The entire bus-load, helpful as only Glaswegians can be, immediately began to give him directions. When the confusion settled down the driver went back to his cab and the journey continued. The Clippie, who had remained at the back silent and unconcerned, manicuring her nails, now put away her nail-file and muttered:

"Twenty-wan years on this route, an' he still gets lost!"

Most important for me, however, during these years of traveling the length and breadth of Scotland, were my contacts with the parishes and with the clergy. I gained a first-hand insight into the Church as it really is and became acquainted with priests as they really are. All of this provided me with a living commentary on the parable of the drag-net that hauled in fish of all kinds–good and bad. I was fortunate, though, for I think that I found more good than bad, and while I found that the good were not yet adorned with halos, I found also that the bad weren't quite so bad after all. Most of the priests upon whom I called were welcoming and hospitable, and I found their conversation enlightening. There were some disappointments: now and then I would call at the presbytery attached to a colossal parish in the west where the parish priest was likely to be also a canon. Some of these presbyteries were impregnable fortresses, the entrance blocked by a portcullis in the form of a housekeeper. Even in those cases, once entry had been gained the scene could change. Once–and it was not in the west–having got in, I found it much harder to get out, such was the loquacity and hospitality of the incumbent.

With many of my clerical contacts I had only an official relationship, but there were some who became very close friends. Fr John McFaul, when I first met him, was the senior assistant priest in the very large parish at Possil Park. During the time he was there the Church of Scotland were much concerned with the celebrated "Bishops' Report." There were four assistant priests–called "curates" in those days–in St Teresa's, Possil Park. I used to call Fr McFaul "the bishop in this presbytery," for he was *de facto* the boss. The parish priest was never to be seen, for he "enjoyed" poor health. In spite of this the whole show ran smoothly, and the curates, Fr McKinnon, Fr MacLeod, and Fr Broderick "not S.J."–as Fr McFaul always explained– all spoke kindly of their invisible head, telling anecdotes about his obsession with railway time-tables. At length the parish priest died on a day when I happened to be paying a visit to that parish. It would be a good idea, Fr McFaul remarked, for them to embalm and conceal him, and go on running the parish as before. Fr McKinnon said that the rumor was already circulating that this was precisely what had been going on for several years.

Through contacts such as I had with Possil Park and our later visits to the Gorbals where Fr McFaul became parish priest, I saw the human face of the Church, and gained deeper understanding of the mystery of Christ's presence in this earthen vessel.

In this new work I was free, and had opportunities, to serve the Church in diverse ways. As before, but now over a wider area, I was sometimes asked to give talks about the Reformed Church, which demonstrated a growing awareness amongst Catholics of the importance of seeking unity among Christians; and I was able to write articles and letters to the press, and I began also to translate German Catholic theological books. In the twenty years I worked for the Converts' Aid Society I must have translated about twenty theological books, including Josef Lortz's classic: *The Reformation in Germany*.

In a haphazard way all of my activities were beginning to feed into ecumenical work. My interest in this had already begun while we were living in Dalkeith, but it became much more explicit after we moved back into Edinburgh in 1957. The Second Vatican Council was still a few years in the future, but the atmosphere in both the Reformed and the Catholic Church had changed a great deal during the short space of nine years since we left the Church of Scotland. Friendly personal contacts were more common than before, and in our particular case we discovered that without conscious effort, we had become a link between many Catholic friends and many Protestant relations. Our move back to Edinburgh heralded a phase in our lives in which ecumenical enterprise was to play a large part.

18

In the spring of 1957 we received a phone call from Mrs Wright in whose house in Saxe-Coburg Place we had lived immediately after our marriage. She told us that the Misses Ross, who lived in No. 14 Saxe-Coburg Place, were looking for a tenant to occupy the upper two flats of their house. If we were interested–and we were–she would speak to them and introduce us. During the two years we had already spent in Saxe-Coburg Place we had never met the two old ladies, but we had seen them, particularly the older Miss Ella, who now and again would skip out into the square with a little shovel to retrieve horse-dung after the milk cart had passed; and we had heard a great deal about them.

As we were soon to see for ourselves, the Misses Ross lived the most well-regulated of lives–as if in a convent with a community of two. They kept to a strict time-table for meals and enjoyed a frugal but nutritious diet. They ate porridge and toast in the morning, a "proper" three course dinner at one o'clock, tea with sandwiches and fruit-cake at 4:30 p.m., and at seven in the evening a banana, a boiled sweet and a glass of milk. A daily woman came in to do heavy work and help cook the dinner; the two ladies took it in turns, week about, to go shopping in the forenoon or to work in the garden. On Sunday they made their way up to St Giles', the High Kirk of Edinburgh.

We applied for the tenancy of the flat, and in due course were interviewed by their "man of business," one of the distinctive breed of Edinburgh solicitors, whom a friend of ours described as "the wind and watertight club." The way he conducted the interview allowed us to learn something about the ladies' religious orientation. When he had covered essential points he asked, casually, "And where do your boys go to school?" a question which can be used as a circumlocution for, "What is your religion?" In this case it was being so used; he asked to be excused for a moment, and left the room. We guessed that he was telephoning the Misses Ross to inform them that we were Catholics. He returned almost at once with an exaggerated apology for having had to leave us. The business was quickly settled and we were sent off to meet the Misses Ross.

We found them to be utterly charming—not at all what one expects of Edinburgh spinsters. The first remark made by Miss Joanna, the younger of the two—she was only about eighty-six—was:

"Do you know what the silly man said to us on the phone? 'Do you have any objection to their being Roman Catholics?' "

"Well," I said, "no doubt like all lawyers he was just being very cautious."

"I thought he was better educated than that, and that he would recall how closely associated our father had been at one time with Fr Power, S.J., when the pair of them were examining a bone found in St Giles' to determine if it were an authentic relic."

One of the things that our friendship with the Misses Ross taught us was that among devout Scots Presbyterians who have a sense of history, the feeling towards the Catholic Church is vastly different from what is popularly imagined. The attitude of those ladies had also been molded by their long association with the High Church tradition upheld at St Giles'. They were true Auld Kirkers, and one sensed that in their eyes the aulder the Kirk, the better.

Those ladies demonstrated also how wrong it is to equate Scots Presbyterianism with Puritanism. The Misses Ross were zealous and strictly principled. In her young days Miss Joanna had been active in voluntary social work, which she performed with considerable legal acumen. She brought actions against several Rachmanesque landlords in the Royal Mile, in defense of the really poor. Their religious and moral strictness did not prevent them, however, from leading interesting and very cheerful lives. Helen was once asked to help them get suitably dressed for a champagne party at Christmas time; along with former tenants of the flat we were on more than one occasion invited to what they called "a tenants' ball," when they entertained us to Madeira brought to them by their niece, a doctor, who occasionally came up from London to visit them. At one of these parties I heard Miss Joanna say: "Don't give Ella too much Madeira; she's got a very poor head for liquor." Another time when Helen and I were paying a visit downstairs, we heard great thumps and vibrations overhead. We apologized for the noise. "I don't hear any noise," said one, "and in any case," said the other, "the boys have a right to live." They learned too that David was learning to play the bagpipes, and we asked if the sound disturbed them. "Of course not," they said. After that Miss Ella would sometimes ring our bell and say, "We don't hear any bagpipes; I hope you're not restraining David by making bogies out of us."

Towards the end of our stay in this flat Miss Ella took ill and was for a few days confined to her bedroom in the basement of the house, where she lay on a tiny narrow bed. Helen would go down and sit with her from time to time, when she noticed a small crucifix hanging above her bed. The alert little Miss Ella saw that Helen's eye had glanced at the crucifix.

"Yes," she said, " that was a gift to our father from one of his Catholic friends. I like to keep it there; as we come nearer to the end, the Catholic in us begins to come out."

The Misses Ross also stimulated our sense of the past, for they told many anecdotes set in old Edinburgh, and often connected with their father, who was a distinguished architect and archaeologist. With his partner McGibbon he had compiled several volumes on Scottish domestic, ecclesiastical, and castellated architecture, volumes which are still regarded as authoritative. So often did the ladies begin a tale with "Our father," that we used to refer to him as "Our father, which architect in heaven."

"Our father" had come home one day after a spell spent in research in the reading-room of the central library in George IV Bridge, and told his wife and daughters that the opposite side of the desk had been occupied by Robert Louis Stevenson. As I had spent much of my study time while at school and at the university in that same reading-room, Miss Ross' tale made me feel that even I could claim a flesh and blood link with R.L.S.

Living now conveniently in the heart of Edinburgh, having made a host of Catholic friends lay and clerical, and being once again comfortably in touch with our non-Catholic friends and relations, we found ourselves thrust into the ecumenical movement which was already stirring in Scotland. I am sure this stirring must have been growing in several places, but we became closely associated with a development that proved to have wide repercussions.

Fr Jock Dalrymple, then an assistant priest in our parish of St Mary's Cathedral, told me that he had been discussing with Dr Ronnie Selby Wright, minister of the Canongate Kirk, how they might co-operate, for at times they found themselves thrown together in pastoral concerns. Could some kind of liaison be formed between Presbyterian and Catholic clergy? I suggested that a beginning could be made by having informal meetings for a few people with a view to promoting mutual understanding. He asked me if I would be able to do something about this, and I said that I would.

First I discussed the idea with my brother-in-law the Rev Roddie Smith, minister of the Braid Church in Edinburgh, and with Fr James Quinn, S.J., and shortly afterwards wrote to these two and to Fr Jock Dalrymple and to Dr Ronnie Selby Wright and to Fr Lawrence Glancey and to Rev. Campbell MacLean, who like Roddie Smith, was one of my relations by marriage. The letter I wrote was simple and made no attempt to describe what we might be about: I invited them to come to our house on a certain date and partake of a "theological glass of whisky."

The first meeting of this group had no agenda, but the talk soon revealed that there were many topics that could profitably be examined. Campbell MacLean invited us to come in a month's time to his manse at Cramond, and offered to read a paper on a book by Bornkamm, which he happened to be reading at the time. In the discussion at that second meeting the Catholic practice of Confession—the sacrament of penance—was mentioned several times, and Ronnie Wright suggested that it would be helpful if we were enlightened on the doctrine of that sacrament. A third meeting was arranged and James Quinn was given the task of expounding the doctrine of the sacrament of penance. And so this little seminar progressed, meeting roughly once every six weeks.

This venture must have begun sometime in 1958, and it continued all the time we lived in Saxe-Coburg Place. More important than the enlightenment gained by the members of that particular group was the fact that it was the parent of a dialogue which subsequently spread more widely and still continues.

An important consequence of these informal meetings came about in autumn 1960 at Sancta Maria Abbey, Nunraw. Helen and I and the family paid regular visits to the monastery, where we had been received into the Church, and during one of our visits the Abbot, Dom Columban Mulcahy, told me of a plan he had in mind. In essence his plan was an expansion of the idea behind our little seminars.

"Sure," said the Abbot, "it would be a great t'ing if we could get together some of our priests and layfolk and some ministers and elders and what not from the Presbyterians, and have a sensible talk and discussion, and a meal and a social chit-chat."

"That would be great," I said.

"Now," he went on in a more conspiratorial tone, "it shouldn't be a hole in the corner affair—a bit more official like—but d'ye see, we couldn't really expect the bishops to do much about it. That might be a bit too official and they'd have to carry the can if anything went wrong."

"Yes, they do have to ca' canny," I agreed.

"Well now," he proceeded, "as the chairman of the Council of Major Religious Superiors in Scotland I'm kind of semi-official, but I'm not in the lime-light like the bishops, so I wondered if I couldn't fix up something, and I'd like to ask your help."

"What have you in mind?"

"Next April," he explained, "we will have our meeting of Religious Superiors in Craiglockhart Convent, and I t'ought we might invite a few of our separated brethren to lunch. I have in mind Bernard Leeming, S.J. to give a talk in the forenoon. We want to hear him ourselves anyway—he's top class on this whole ecumenism business."

"That all sounds excellent to me. Go ahead with it."

"But d'ye see! I don't know how to set about inviting the chaps; I don't know who ought to be invited. I wondered if you could advise me."

"Rather than try to advise you myself," I explained, "I could introduce you to those who really can advise you."

I thought immediately of our little seminar group, and forthwith arranged to take Ronnie Wright and my brother-in-law Roddie Smith, who was Convener of the Inter-Church Relations Committee, down to discuss this plan with the Abbot.

Following this meeting with the Abbot invitations were sent out to ministers and elders of the Church of Scotland, and on 6 April 1961 one day of the annual conference of Major Religious Superiors in Scotland was devoted to entertaining quite a large number of Presbyterian clerics and others in the Convent of the Sacred Heart at Craiglockhart, Edinburgh.

The spiritual content of the entertainment was provided by Fr Bernard Leeming, S.J., who in a masterly fashion presented a view of ecumenical theology within the context of Catholic ecclesiology. What he said foreshadowed the doctrine that soon after was to be expounded in the Vatican II documents on the Church and on Ecumenism. His lecture was instructive for the Catholics in the audience, and by the non-Catholics present was warmly acclaimed. In his lecture and in the questions and discussion which followed, the notion was beginning to be expressed that the conflict between, for example, the Reformed and the Catholic doctrine of justification was probably based upon misunderstanding, and could eventually be overcome. As we now know, in Germany joint statements have made which remove that misunderstanding.

A strong sense of hope and the beginning of several important personal links grew out of this meeting that day. In the course of discussion that day, Dr Rudolf Ehrlich, one of the Edinburgh ministers, a refugee from Nazi Germany, and a theologian of high repute, reminded us that there were still serious problems to be faced. One of his colleagues described Rudolf Ehrlich as a reincarnation of Martin Luther, to whom he bore a physical resemblance. He was nothing if not clear and forthright in expressing his views, and he still spoke with a slight guttural accent, which increased the weight of his utterances. On this occasion, after expressing deep appreciation of the value of Bernard Leeming's lecture, he added:

"Let us not forget, however, the sixty-four thousand dollar question: even if we achieve convergence on substantial theological matters, what are we going to do with the Pope?"

Our physical needs were catered for by the sisters, who provided an excellent lunch. A very good time was had by all, and as we departed Mgr Paddy Quille, at that time parish priest at the Cathedral, and a man who never allowed himself to be oppressed by problems, exclaimed:

"That was the best party we've had since the Reformation—long may disunity flourish!"

A few weeks later a Glasgow minister—it was suspected—tipped off the press about the meeting at

Craiglockhart, and there appeared in the newspaper whose owner had, for personal reasons, an ill-will toward the Catholic Church, a double-page spread about the "secret meeting" at Craiglockhart at which wine had been poured by nuns. The whole thing was presented as a Catholic plot, and infused with an atmosphere of Renaissance Orgie-Borgias.

No one bothered too much about this, but it encouraged those who had organized the event to plan in future on a national scale and in a more public way. On 26 April 1962 the Major Religious Superiors arranged a similar meeting in Dowanhill Convent, Glasgow, but this time the guest-list was prepared with the help of the Presbytery of Glasgow, so that there could be no talk of secrecy.

These two meetings were valuable, most of all because they stimulated the formation of local groups and the formation of local Councils of Churches. Less than a year after the Craiglockhart meeting in April 1961 the first of a series of meetings took place in Edinburgh at the University Staff Club in Chambers Street. The University Staff Club was chosen because it was ecclesiastically neutral ground—and it served first-class wine and cheese. The programs at these meetings were like that of the Craiglockhart meeting. A paper would be read on a theological subject, and discussion would follow. Equally valuable was the informal conversation that took place and the personal contacts that were made. Because Scotland is a small country and so many people know each other, the ideas that were expressed at these Staff Club meetings, and the ethos engendered there, spread quickly throughout the country. There was also an atmosphere of optimism which helped to keep things going. The close-knit texture of Scottish society is a factor that must always be taken into account when analyzing intellectual or spiritual developments in the country.

In his essay on the Scottish Enlightenment, David Daiches points to this factor as one cause of the rapid and thorough growth of that movement: "But most of the men of the Scottish Enlightenment shared a common optimism about the ability of eighteenth-century man to bring new and helpful insights into all aspects of the human condition. Most of them knew each other; many were close friends; some were related by marriage. All were stimulated by enormous curiosity and a determination to find new answers to old questions."

This close-knit texture still characterizes Scottish society and was undoubtedly a factor in the rapid development of ecumenism in Scotland. The scene as it had come to be in April 1961, the time of the Craiglockhart meeting, was vastly different from the scene of 1948, when we were first received into the Catholic Church, and the change had been effected almost entirely through personal friendships and even blood relationships.

At first the Staff Club meetings were attended by Presbyterians and Catholics, but it was obvious that the other Churches ought to be invited, and they were. At one meeting I overheard Fr James Quinn, S.J. introducing Graham Hardy, minister of Palmerston Place Church to Canon Rogers of the Scottish Episcopal Cathedral, also in Palmerston Place, and explaining impishly: "You see, we are the bridge Church."

The way in which inter-Church relations grew—through direct personal friendship—stressed the human element in the process. Mutual respect was soon a reality and there was much bonhomie. But the strength of these realities was already concealing an incipient danger. Was the serious problem of division amongst Christians to be perfectly solved solely by mutual respect and charity? Again it was Dr Rudolf Ehrlich who at one of our Staff Club meetings introduced the subject of the Church's Magisterium. It was commonly agreed, he told us, that the Roman Catholic Church took its Magisterium seriously, but he added, few Catholics and probably no modern Presbyterians realized that the Reformed Church too acknowledged a magisterium. The problem was to identify the magisterium and define its precise place in the scheme of salvation. In other words, he was reminding us, the problem is not just what are our doctrines, but on what authority do we proclaim them. He could see that the specter of indifferentism was materializing out of the "ecumenical spirit."

From this time onwards I found myself much occupied with ecumenical affairs, in particular with things that began to happen in the parish to which we moved in the autumn of 1961. The Converts' Aid Society had bought a house in Nile Grove in Morningside and installed us as tenants; and so we bade farewell to our dear Misses Ross in the north side of the city. One of the last things I remember about our adventures in Saxe-Coburg Place was our departure in a Volkswagen Beetle on a pilgrimage to Lourdes, shortly before our moving to Morningside.

The Beetle, which we treated as if it were a pony or a mule, had the engine behind and the "boot" in front. The "boot" was not designed to contain large suitcases; we therefore packed all our luggage in small containers and built these into what space there was, and into every available cavity within the car itself. When this operation was complete there was an enormous weight of stuff in the car; then we packed in the human cargo—and there were five of us, all fully grown adults: Helen and me and Nicolas, Mary MacPherson—a friend of Helen's from Kyle-of-Lochalsh—and Dominique Margot—a French youth with whose family Nicolas had spent the previous summer. In mid-forenoon, after the near despair that accompanies this sort of effort, we moved off, and at eight o'clock in the evening arrived at Saffron Walden, where we spent the night.

Next morning, via the Blackwall Tunnel, we sped on to Dover and crossed to Boulogne, from which port we made our way to Rouen, to spend the night in the hotel beside the Gros Horloge. It was a pleasant hotel and the mighty clock most impressive; in fact, it impressed us all through the night with its chiming and the incessant clicking of the movement. Before settling down for the night, however, we were taken proudly by Dominique to a restaurant, where he promised we would get a proper French meal. It was indeed a splendid meal, but Dominique was a bit crestfallen when he learned that the specialty of the region, which he insisted we order, was well-known to us—skate. In the morning I found the French hotel custom of serving breakfast on a tray in the bedroom most agreeable.

Next day the journey down through Evreux, Le Mans, and La Flèche was pleasant and interesting; as we drew nearer to the Loire valley, for the first time in my life I saw vineyards, and was most impressed. We reached our destination in the late afternoon.

Dominique's home was at Le Pré, a little country mansion a few kilometers east of Saumur. His father was a colonel in the *Cadre Noir*, the crack cavalry regiment with the Lippizaner horses. He and his wife gave us a warm welcome. I could see that they—and Grandmère who lived with them—were very fond of Nicolas, who had stayed for six weeks with them the previous year, and who spoke French fluently. There were two little girls, Marie Odette and Marie France, and the older—Marie Odette, about six,— was very bright indeed. She observed immediately that I was trying to learn French and began without any shyness to point to objects and, for my benefit, distinctly pronounce their French names. On one occasion she must have spotted a slight twitch of my nostril as the car was being filled with petrol, for she said very clearly, "*ça sent l'essence.*" Marie France, aged three, clung to Nicolas in smiling adoration.

That evening we were entertained to dinner in their home on the little estate. Everything we ate and drank came either from their own little estate or from the land not far away. An exception was a bottle of vintage Bordeaux, which was sipped sparingly from small glasses, whereas the carafe wine from a vineyard down the road was quaffed with greater abandon from large glasses.

The Margots had the use of an army-flat in the town of Saumur, and there we stayed over the weekend.

On Sunday after Mass we were taken to see the Loire Valley–chateau Azay le Rideau, chateau Chinon, and the celebrated *caves* at the vineyard of St Nicolas de Bourgueil. In the evening the Margots took us back home again for an evening meal at Le Pré. Apologetically they explained that on Sunday they never prepared an elaborate meal, and hoped we would be content with a simple boiled egg. Of course we would be content! We discovered, however, that a boiled egg in the Loire Valley is far from simple. "A simple boiled egg," strictly interpreted, meant that the egg would be the only item requiring to be cooked. It was augmented with an unlimited supply of bread and butter, and a superb salad; there was also some cheese in the background, lest we should feel deprived of protein; and instead of wine, there was Normandy cider.

On a warm and sunny autumn morning we wrenched ourselves away from the glowing hospitality with which Saumur had blessed us. In the town, window ledges and street borders were ablaze with the bright colors of petunias. Madame Margot fetched a chamois and, having wiped away the layer of dead insects from the wind-screen of the Beetle, tore the chamois in two and presented me with one half, saying: "Like St Martin of Tours' cloak."

The journey south was full of interest, but very, very warm. We were struck most of all by the long straight stretches of road, lined with tall poplars. Somewhere between Saumur and Angoulême Nicolas said, "I have an announcement to make: we have just completed eight miles of this highway without making the slightest turn." For us another intriguing feature was the unmodernity of the layout of the little towns and villages. They were bottle-necks of cobbled streets that ensured speed reduction. As yet there had been very little post-war reconstruction so that there was an air of dilapidation in many villages; even so, the mood of the country was far from gloomy.

We had been unsure how long our journey would take and so had planned to stay the night in Pau, and proceed next morning to Lourdes. Thus we arrived in the forenoon at Lezignan-Lourdes, about two and a half miles outside the main town, and received a warm welcome from Madame Biscaye, the little dark-haired Basque *patronne* of the small hotel which had been recommended to us by the French wife of one of our Edinburgh friends, who had also written to Madame Biscaye introducing us to her. The three days we spent there were memorable. The rooms were comfortable, the food excellent, and the cost amazingly small. But there was something extra, perhaps because of our having mutual friends, although I think that in the end it was because of the sympathy we felt with the people and the place. It was like being at home with friends and family; on our last night, joined by Madame Biscaye and her husband, and by two young couples from Perpignan, we had a quiet ceilidh round the dinner-table.

The object of our journey was not just to visit France, but to make a pilgrimage to Lourdes. While still in the process of examining the Catholic Faith, Helen and I had both heard of the apparitions at Lourdes and had been impressed by the story of St Bernadette. We had noted, too, that although there were one or two authenticated miracles which were important as signs and reminders of God's power and love, the dominant theme of the cult of Lourdes was that of care for the sick and the consecration of suffering, for the sake of the redemption of the world.

In a way I had been discouraged from attempting to go on pilgrimage to Lourdes, by the picture I had of excited crowds of miracle-hungry pilgrims, something quite out of harmony, I believed, with the authentic message of Lourdes; but now we met with the reality, and it was totally different from what I had imagined it might be. Even at those celebrations where huge crowds took part there was no atmosphere of hysteria, but rather of fervent, quiet prayer. As for the commercialism which is sometimes said to attach to Lourdes, when one has entered the Domain, the town and all its noise and trinkets seem a thousand light-years away. Divine peace and reassurance pervade the Grotto and its surroundings.

In the afternoon, after we had taken part in several public devotions, I went on my own to the Grotto, at a time when few others were there. It was then that I most deeply appreciated what Bernadette had learned. I prayed effortlessly, as though prayer were being sucked out of me. We had almost too much to pray for, and I needed help, for we had come to France not just in order to visit Dominique's parents and bring him home, and we had come to Lourdes not just out of general interest and devotion, but because Nicolas was very ill. In May an X-ray examination had revealed that he had Hodgkin's disease, and the prognosis was that he was unlikely to live more than three years. He himself did not know this, and the medical advice we got was that we should await further developments before informing him. By the time we set off for Lourdes he had recovered from his first spell of radio-therapy and seemed quite well—indeed at Lourdes he worked as a *brancardier*, helping the sick, as he had done a few years earlier, but for us the expedition was overshadowed by the very dark cloud of our knowledge of his true condition.

It was natural, therefore, that we should have given much thought to the meaning of Lourdes, and to the place of miracles in the scheme. During that short visit our belief that the seeking of miraculous cure is not the prime concern of those who make pilgrimage to Lourdes was confirmed. We did pray for a cure for Nicolas, but we learned to pray for much more than that. In my short time of prayer alone at the Grotto I found deep peace. The message of Lourdes is not about wonder-working, but about the triumph of the Cross; and the high point in St Bernadette's life was its ending when she came to know and accept that miracles were not for her; her suffering and death were to be consecrated and become prayer for others.

19

On our homeward journey from Lourdes we followed a more easterly direction, traveling first along a minor road until we reached the *Route National.* As we sped along towards Toulouse, through the ancient Visigoth kingdom, the vista towards the hazy Pyrenees brought to mind the epic of Ronceval, and Roland and Oliver. I longed to be able sometime to return and visit that enchanted part of Europe. Through Montauban and Cahors we traveled, surprised to find the road through the Massif Central so hilly and winding until, after a strenuous day's driving, the little black Beetle deposited us safely in the town of Brive.

Next day we had an easier run down into the Loire valley. Between Chateauroux and Blois we spotted a hoarding with the legend:

FRIGIDAIRE -
MACLEOD, PÈRE ET FILS–
GENERAL ELECTRIC–BLOIS

We reversed in order to read the address, which was inscribed at a lower level, and arriving in Blois about twenty minutes later we found the place. Would Helen discover that this MacLeod was a distant cousin? Nicolas went into the showroom and came back to tell us that indeed M. MacLeod–the name pronounced by his informant in the Gaelic way–was the proprietor, whose grandfather had settled in the Loire valley after the First World War, but unfortunately he was not available, for that very day he was off getting married. We proceeded, sad that we hadn't been able to speak to this MacLeod, but happy to know that there must be quite a lot of MacLeods enjoying life in this gentle Vouvray country. Late that evening we reached Meulan on the outskirts of Paris, where we spent a very pleasant night with M. and Mme Bellet, with whom our second son, David, had spent the summer, and whose son, Patrique, spent the following summer with us. By finding exchanges for our three sons we tried to ensure that the Auld Alliance would be kept alive. I do not remember the details of the journey home, but eventually we did get back and shortly after our return moved to Nile Grove in Morningside.

Morningside suffers from wicked misrepresentation of being very snobbish and unfriendly. It is true that in the late nineteenth century and early twentieth century there had been a move by the Edinburgh aristocracy–that is the legal profession–from the New Town to grand villas on the slope rising up from the Braid Burn to the Braid Hills. This, the southern part of Morningside, which I called "chateau country," was only part of modern Morningside, and no longer set the tone of the place. Morningside for us turned out to be the friendliest place in which we had ever lived. For a start it has a fairly distinct physical definition: there is a straight street–not much more than half a mile long–running downhill from Church Hill to Morningside Station, which contains every necessary shop, and where people are meeting each other, day in day out. The larger shops–the Coop, for example–were often the scene of lengthy conversations. Helen once entered the Coop during winter in broad daylight, to emerge only after it was pitch dark. And there were the more formalized means of communication, a theater, a cinema, a dance-hall, four pubs, and several church halls. Morningside was a very friendly and comfortable place to live.

Still, however, even among its humbler inhabitants, it retained an air of gentility. Fr James Rae, who had recently come as assistant priest to St Peter's parish, and who turned out, as we discovered much later, to be a distant cousin of mine, our having common Orkney ancestry, told us of a visit he paid to an elderly lady who lived in a little flat in Morningside Road. He was instructing her in the Catholic Faith, and asked if she could remember how to bless herself in the name of the Trinity. "O yes," she said, "In the name of the Father, and of the Son, and ... O, I'm afraid I've forgotten the other gentleman's name."

Our pleasure at finding such a congenial place in which to make our home, could not but be overshadowed by the cloud of apprehension hanging over Nicolas' future. We tried to accept the advice given us, to put the matter out of our minds until symptoms began to reappear, and meantime got on with our lives. As well as traveling around Scotland, working for the Converts' Aid Society, I had begun to work as a translator of German theology. At about this time I was working on *The Holy Places of the Gospels*, by Klemens Kopp.

For physical and psychological recreation, Helen and I would go up to the Braid Hills and play golf. There are two municipal courses on the Braids, and for Edinburgh residents the green fee in those days was only a few pence; and they are superb courses with springy turf growing on volcanic soil. The greens, especially on No. 1, are large and were perfectly kept by an enthusiastic young head greenkeeper. For a few shillings one could have lessons from Mr Houston, a canny old unpretentious professional, whose advice, I believe, was sought even by celebrated golfers.

We both took six lessons from him and our golf improved unbelievably. One day Helen failed to observe one of his basic instructions and hit a poor shot. He exploded, but with restraint:

"Huh!, ye rascal, ye've done it again."

He would encourage us to use the three iron, and to begin the down-swing very gently. When we showed surprise at the ball traveling two hundred yards in a straight line down the fairway, after we had carefully obeyed his instructions, and swung very gently, he would say:

"There's nae need to hit further than that; and if ye can dae it yince, ye can dae it again."

Sometimes after three hours concentration on a piece of translation I would go up at 11.30 a.m. to Braids

No. 2 with three clubs—it took only three minutes to get there—play for an hour and be back, refreshed, by one o'clock. Besides the pleasure of playing golf, from the Braids one got an exhilarating view over Edinburgh and beyond across the Forth to the hills of Fife. When entertaining visitors from abroad, I always took them up to the high ground beside the eighteenth hole at the Braids and proudly pointed their eyes northwards to see the whole city laid out below and then I took them to the Ferry Road at Goldenacre and pointed their eyes south across the level ground to take in the panoramic contour of the Royal mile.

The congeniality we felt in Morningside derived from several circumstances. There were the physical and social qualities that I have described. Besides these we now dwelt in a convenient house and in a place that was accessible to friends and relations. Although some years before, our relations with Helen's father had been most unsatisfactory, by the time we moved into Nile Grove, we were on very good terms with the rest of the family. In fact, Dr Roddie Smith, who was married to Helen's older sister, Mona, was one of my chief contacts in ecumenical work, and the Church of which he was minister stood at the end of our street. The Smith's manse was only about five hundred yards from our house. As well as having Helen's relations close to us, my sister had now come to live in a flat opposite St Peter's Church, which was only half a mile away.

Our sense of being rooted and more at home in the world was returning, and a powerful factor in creating this sense was our becoming immersed in the life of St Peter's parish. The church building was impressive, neo-Romanesque in style, wherein the liturgy was celebrated with dignity. On Sunday there was low Mass at 9 a.m. and a solemn high Mass at 11 a.m., sung in Latin by a very competent choir. In the evening there were devotions with a sermon and Benediction of the Blessed Sacrament. Fr Walter Glancy, who had received us into the Church in 1948, was now parish priest here, assisted by Fr James Rae and Fr Willie Loftus. Fr Loftus was elderly, a late vocation who had studied at the *Beda* in Rome. My little nephew, who lived opposite St Peter's, liked Fr Loftus, who kept his pocket full of sweets which he gave to the children who played around in the courtyard. Because of his seniority, our nephew called him "the prime minister" at St Peter's. Very important, however, for our development, and especially for mine, considering the course my life was to take in the end, was a pastoral venture initiated by Fr James Rae. He began to form Bible-study groups, and he asked me to help him. A number of important things were learned from these study-groups. Although it was clear that some expertise–even academic–was needed on the part of those leading the study, insight into the meaning of scripture would often come from a relatively unlettered person. There was a complementarity between the scholarly and the prophetic contributions. Similarly we learned about the relationship between individual searching for the truth and the normative teaching of the Church. Sometimes our discussions seemed to recapitulate the doctrinal history of the Church. A speculative hare would be started and then followed. Sometimes the speculation ran into a cul-de-sac, and was seen to be erroneous but having given it a good run for its money, we found ourselves better able to understand the orthodox formulation provided by the Church.

Having settled in our new habitat we found that two forces were forming our life and way of thinking. First as a result of our being immersed in an active Catholic parish–and for my part as a result of theological progress through the work of translating–we became more and more confirmed in our adherence to the visible Church cared for by the apostolic college centered round Peter. At the same time, as a result of our having reconnected both socially and physically with our Presbyterian past, we were becoming increasingly aware of the importance of seeking common ground with the Reformed Church and with members of that communion.

In Morningside, even before Vatican II, there had been considerable ecumenical activity, chiefly connected with the Church Unity Octave, when a joint service would be held in one of the Churches. After the meeting at Craiglockhart Convent in April 1961 the Abbot of Nunraw began to make many contacts, especially with Presbyterians. As yet the rules for ecumenical worship had not been clearly set out, so that when the Abbot was invited to preach at an ecumenical service during a Church Unity week, the propriety of his doing so was questioned. Archbishop Gordon Joseph Gray was not only the ordinary of the diocese, but also a resident in our district, and he was a friend of my brother-in-law, the minister of the Braid Church, and so it fell to me to discuss this problem with the Archbishop. Very properly he was cautious, foreseeing possible implications for the issue of intercommunion. I explained that the service at which the Abbot would preach was not a eucharist, and although the principal Sunday service in a Presbyterian Church could be regarded as corresponding to the Catholic Sunday Mass, this ecumenical service was an evening service and need not be regarded in quite the same way. I agreed with his Grace that there might be risks, but stressed the fact that such participation by the Abbot would greatly advance the cause of mutual understanding and respect among Christians in Morningside. The Archbishop in the end agreed that we should go ahead with the service, and the effects of that service justified his decision. By the end of the sixties a quite extraordinary and theologically sound ecumenical movement began to thrive in Morningside. I am told that it continues today.

There were other times when I had cause to discuss similar matters with the Archbishop. On one of these occasions I argued for enthusiastic ecumenical co-operation wherever it is licit alongside equally enthusiastic and unashamed Catholic evangelization, for if the latter program is neglected, ecumenical action can degenerate into indifferentism—lowest common denominator

Christianity. Catholics, interested in ecumenism, may never duck Dr Ehrlich's sixty-four thousand dollar question: "What will we do with the Pope?" The answer must always be: "We have to keep him." But that never need be a reason for breaking spiritual ties with those who cannot accept him.

Our physical and social environment enabled us to enjoy effective communication with both Protestant and Catholic friends. Consequently we experienced the tension that must be experienced by all who engage in serious ecumenical encounter. On the one hand such people zealously live out their Christian vocation according to the fullness of the Faith of the Church to which they belong, and seek the perfection of that Church, while simultaneously they seek to foster spiritual communion with all others of good faith who are moved by the like aspiration. We were increasingly becoming aware of the paradox that the Mystical Body of Christ, whose membership can be known only to God, is substantially identical with the visible Church—a paradox that was to be expressed a few years later in the Vatican II document *Lumen Gentium*.

The situation in which we and many others found ourselves was, however, at times fraught with tension. The problem constantly arose of keeping spiritually in communion with other Christians who held different views from oneself, not so much on theological topics, but on moral issues. It was in this field that the Catholic view that the magisterium is of the essence of the Church became a factor in the creation of tension. Put in other terms, one could say that inter-Church relations were always complicated by the Catholic belief that individual conscience may be bound by the teaching of the Church. This problem has, of course, a theological application. Our own coming into the Catholic Church had resulted from our facing up to the theological aspect of this issue; but now we became more aware of the division that could be caused similarly in the sphere of morality. Several of our close friends and relations, whose good faith we would never doubt, disagreed with us on matters such as contraception and even abortion. I discussed these problems with Fr James Quinn, S.J., who remarked that in the end the big ecumenical problem would be conflict over moral teaching. And so our lives in Nile Grove in Morningside bubbled along in a kind of spiritual fermentation, and intellectual clarification of the Catholic Faith, always closely interwoven in the fabric of life.

A catastrophic and critical event was now not far off. Nicolas suffered his second onset of the symptoms of Hodgkin's disease, and again received radio-therapy, with all its agonizing side-effects. We were thus alerted to the approach of the end, for remission periods become successively shorter. Some months later the last phase came. At first Nicolas lived at home, visiting the Western General Hospital several times a week to receive radio-therapy. During this period Helen would sit with him until he fell asleep at night after receiving his medication; then I would rise between three and five in the morning to administer the dose of pain-killer and wait until he again fell asleep. For several months after he died I sometimes imagined I heard his bell ring in the night.

One day before we left for the hospital Fr James Rae came to visit him; and then on our way to hospital Nicolas said to me:

"You know, today I asked Fr Rae to anoint me."

"I'm glad," I said.

"Well," Nicolas went on, "now I haven't a care in the world."

His words gave me great comfort; but his next sentence filled me with wonder and with pride:

"When he anointed me I didn't pray for a miraculous cure, but that the medical scientists will find the cure for this disease, so that everybody who has it can be cured."

I was put in mind of a sentence in St Matthew's Gospel: "He cast out the spirits with a word and cured *all who were sick*" (Mt 8:16). We learned a lot about the sacrament of the Anointing of the Sick from the way Nicolas thought about it, and his thoughts had probably been formed mainly by his association with Lourdes. The Church's teaching about this sacrament had always been clear enough, but the recently published *Catechism of the Catholic Church* expresses that teaching admirably. In No. 1532 which is the conclusion of the brief summing up of the chapter on this sacrament we read:

> *The special grace of the sacrament of the Anointing of the Sick has as its effects:*
> - *the uniting of the sick person to the Passion of Christ, for his own good and that of the whole Church;*
> - *the strengthening, peace and courage to endure in a Christian manner the sufferings of illness or old age;*
> - *the forgiveness of sins, if the sick person was not able to obtain it through the sacrament of Penance;*
> - *the restoration of health, if it is conducive to the salvation of his soul;*
> - *the preparation for passing over to eternal life.*

Radio-therapy this time round was ineffective, and Nicolas had to remain in hospital to receive chemotherapy. During this spell in hospital his cousin Catriona visited him. She told me that she used to go, wondering how she could cheer him up:

"It was he who cheered me up," she said.

One day the consultant, who had done a superb job, asked Helen and me to meet him. It was obvious from his preamble that he wanted to tell us there was now no effective treatment, but I could see that he was uncertain how we would react. I anticipated what he might have said:

"It looks as if further treatment will be purely experimental and of no real help to Nicolas."

"Absolutely correct," he replied.

"Then why go on?" I asked.

"I'm so glad you see it this way," he answered, "so many people urge us to go on and on when it's pointless."

"We think that now he should be allowed to die in peace."

"That's it," he said, "can you arrange for him to be nursed and comforted?"

"The Blue Nuns at St Rafael's Hospital can take him," I explained.

"You couldn't do better."

That is what we did. Nicolas was taken to St Rafael's, where we had received our first Holy Communion, and which was so near our home, virtually in Morningside. When we visited Nicolas an hour after he got there he said:

"Mum, this is wonderful, it's so comfortable and they've stopped working on me and are letting me die in peace. Have you got a fag?"

For two weeks we were able to visit Nicolas and enjoy his company. One afternoon Fr Crampton, whom I knew slightly, paid us a visit. For a while Nicolas chatted with him and then said:

"Father, do you mind, I'll have to stop talking now, I'm dying this afternoon."

Fr Crampton blessed Nicolas and left. Soon after we began to say the Rosary. After one decade Nicolas said:

"We'll stop now."

A few minutes later we called in one of the Sisters, who told us that his pulse was gone.

Silently we drove home. In our living-room at the back of the house we sat down and prepared to drink tea, but for some reason switched on the radio—probably to hear the news, or merely for distraction—when a most extraordinary thing happened, the kind of thing one would expect to find only in fiction, but it really did happen in our home in the late afternoon of 16th July 1964. There came to us the strains of Papageno's song from *The Magic Flute*:

Tis love they say, love only,
that makes the world go round...

—the song I had sung to Helen a few hours after she gave birth to Nicolas twenty-two years before.

Joy shared increases in intensity; Helen and I knew this kind of sharing; but sorrow too increases with sharing. Helen and I now knew terrible sorrow, but each shared the other's sorrow, and this sharing of pain contributed greatly to our understanding of the union that is marriage.

20

After Nicolas' death we were to live on in Nile Grove in Morningside for another ten years, during which time much emotional energy was spent in coping with the progress of our two younger sons through teenage and the early twenties towards more or less settled adulthood. That experience need not be described, for it is a secret shared by all parents. Both sons, however, had to face up to the extraordinary trauma of their brother's death, which in the end they did admirably.

For some people extreme sorrow can disrupt marriage, for us it strengthened our union, and so in the years that followed our sorrow we became more and more aware of each other and of the mysterious depths of the unitive aspect of marriage. I still have a vivid recollection of how, while writing in a room overlooking the street, I would warm with delight on hearing the latch clicking on the garden gate, as Helen returned from shopping. All of our activities—and we were far from idle—converged on our being together; and yet this enduring mutual passion bore no trace of morbidity, but was liberating and energizing. Our home in Nile Grove became a port of call for countless friends and relations. My sons tell me that they owe much of their education to conversations at table with our friends.

The ecumenical dimension of our life continued to be important. As with the introduction of the Abbot of Nunraw to Presbyterian clergy, which led to the ecumenical meeting at Craiglockhart in 1961, so my brother-in-law the Rev Dr Roddie Smith played a key part in another liaison which, although private and unrecorded, had important consequences.

It was being planned that Dr Archie Craig, the current Moderator of the General Assembly of the Church of Scotland, should meet Pope John XXIII. The proposal was in danger of being dropped on account of problems connected with protocol. It was clear that the difficulty arose from ignorance of the structure of the Church of Scotland. The relationship of a Moderator of the General Assembly to the Church of Scotland is not analogous to the relationship of the Archbishop of Canterbury to the Church of England. The Moderator is not the leader of the Church of Scotland. There was a difficulty therefore over the way in which an invitation could be given, as there was over the competence of a Moderator to accept such an invitation. Some re-thinking of the system of protocol had to be undertaken.

Both Archbishop Gordon Joseph Gray and my brother-in-law Roddie Smith, who was Convener of the Inter-Church Relations Committee of the Church of Scotland, were determined that the current Moderator, Dr Archie Craig, meet Pope John XXIII. It fell to me and Helen to broker the negotiations, and the Archbishop and Roddie met in our sitting room in Nile Grove, when I was invited to sit in on the discussion as a kind of Chairman, for I was able to see the problem from both sides. I cannot recall the details of that discussion; what I do remember very clearly is that the Archbishop repeatedly applauded an oil painting on the wall, a still-life painted by Helen's cousin Catherine. That painting is now on the wall of my sitting-room in Portsoy. Ought I to have given it to Archbishop Gray since he admired it so much?

The Archbishop gathered all the relevant information, and as a result the technical hitch was overcome, and Dr Archie Craig did have an audience with the Pope. Dr Craig was accompanied on his Roman visit by Dr Stuart Louden, minister of the Greyfriars' Kirk in Edinburgh, who on his return gave a talk to one of our ecumenical groups, when he told us that his experience of negotiating Roman traffic had taught him how to walk by faith.

There was already some inter-Church communication in Morningside when we first went to live there, but the full impact of ecumenism was felt only after the Second Vatican Council, and in particular after the publication of the *Dogmatic Constitution on the Church* and the *Decree on Ecumenism* in November 1964. Those who are interested in the growth of the ecumenical movement in Scotland will not require any record written by me. They may, however, find the details of how things took off in Morningside interesting; a description of particular events tells us much more than a general survey. In relation to the purpose of this book, however, which is to provide an *Apologia* for my early acceptance of the Catholic Faith, and for my persevering in the same conviction, the account of the development of the ecumenical movement in Morningside is relevant, for through participation in that movement my view of the nature of the Church, and of faith, became more sharply focused.

The initiative towards the formation of a Christian Council in the district was taken by St Peter's, the Catholic parish, where the Vatican documents were already showing their influence. Among other things we had been stimulated by a parish mission, based on the main documents and given by Fr Charles Pridgeon, S.J. The parish council at St Peter's had appointed a sub-committee to consider ecumenical activity. This sub-committee composed a letter which was sent on 2 May 1970 to five other Christian denominations–comprising nine congregations. This letter, which fortunately I have kept in my files, is probably of historical importance, for it reveals the way the parish was thinking at that time, and so I quote it in full.

Dear Brethren,
In an attempt to develop the ecumenical understanding which has been growing in this part of Edinburgh during the past few years, the ecumenical sub-committee of the parish council of St Peter's R.C. Church in Falcon Avenue would like to invite you to send three representatives to an informal meeting in the parish room adjoining St Peter's on Sunday 24 May at 3 p.m. The purpose of this meeting would be very simple: to provide

*an opportunity for representatives of several different Christian
communities to get to know one another a little better. There
would be no formal agenda, but if anyone wished to do so he
might say a few words about how his Christian community
sees its mission and purpose in this district. In this way each
would gain some insight into the way others think. We could
describe this venture as an attempt at 'Christian Communication'. From this small-scale meeting some ideas might emerge
as to how ecumenical action in this district could be guided in
the future. This invitation is going to five denominations other
than our own. We do hope you will be able to accept it; but if
for any reason you feel unable in conscience to accept please do
not be afraid to say so, and we will fully respect your scruples.*

We are,
Yours fraternally in Christ, ...

There were thirty-one people present at the
meeting; all those invited had come. The tone of discussion
was most cordial, and pleasure was expressed that this
meeting had taken place. Tribute was paid to the local clergy
who for some time now had let it be seen that they knew
one another and co-operated with one another when that
was possible. Now it was time for congregations to follow
this lead. It was decided that those present should report
back to their congregations and that a second meeting be
arranged in the following month. On 26 June 1970 this
second meeting took place and was conducted in a very
business-like manner. Quite quickly it was declared that
we ought to form an organization that could direct action
along two main lines: one line was that of co-operation in
corporal works of mercy, the second was that of ecumenical
education. All of our activities should be carried out in the
awareness that our over-all objective must always be
evangelization.

In this way the Morningside Christian Council was
born. The name was proposed by the minister of the Baptist
Church and the aim was formulated by the Chairman of
St Peter's Parish Council : "To promote Christian friendship,

understanding, and activity where it is most needed at the local level." Each congregation was asked to nominate three representatives; the clergy would be members *ex officio*; all nominees were to come to a meeting on 8 November, and the first task of the Council would be to produce, by Christmas, a policy and a scheme of work.

A number of activities were carried on under the umbrella of the Morningside Christian Council, but the work in which I became deeply involved was that of ecumenical education, for I had been elected convener of the sub-committee responsible for devising programs. We started off early in 1971 by organizing five "At Homes" in succession in five different Churches. The host clergyman gave a twenty minute talk on "Christian Living in the Seventies," after which there was discussion lasting also about twenty minutes—people being seated round tables in groups—followed by tea and conversation. These "At Homes" proved a great success. The smallest number attending was 200, the largest 400. After attending several of these meetings, a parishioner of St Peter's remarked that now he began to identify those he saw on the street or in a shop as fellow Christians, not as just people.

The "At Home" format was maintained, but the programs became more defined and theologically more testing as time went on. An important milestone was reached in February 1972 when ex-Moderator Dr Archie Craig addressed an audience of about 400 in the Church Hill Theatre. He supplied us with a set of questions for study in our groups, which met in five centers on three occasions, after which we all assembled to listen to Dr Craig's summing up and commenting on the reports we had sent him of our discussions. An extraordinary amount of work and attention to detail went into the organization of the activities of the Morningside Christian Council.

The work of study went on, now sustained by several study groups rather than in the more relaxed atmosphere of the "At Homes," but still with enthusiasm. Before discussion there was a talk by one of the clergy or, when the subject required it, by two from different viewpoints. The titles of the subjects for December 1973 are interesting:

1. *Jesus Christ the Word of God*
2. *Scripture is the Primary Witness to Jesus Christ*
3. *The Continuing Witness*
4. *Creeds and Confessions*
5. *Implications*

The series for January–May 1974 is equally interesting:

1. *Pentecost*
2. *True Worship*
3. *The Eucharist*
4. *Gospel and Morality*
5. *What is Unity?*

Fully twenty years had passed since Helen and I left the Church of Scotland and were received into the Catholic Church. At first a sense of desolation, of being uprooted, was dominant; gradually we took root in the Catholic Church and became part of the human society in which the Church expressed itself; simultaneously, however, we were regaining contact with our friends of earlier times, and now, roughly at the time of the Second Vatican Council, we found ourselves immersed in a movement, the aim of which was not just to establish friendly relations between separated Christians, but to seek to resolve the causes of division and so promote organic unity amongst all who profess that Jesus Christ is Lord.

In the meantime, while the separate Christian communities are moving along in pursuit of this goal, the question remains, and must be answered: In what sense may all who believe in Christ and are yet visibly disunited be said to be members of the Mystical Body of Christ? In the last two or three months of my ministry in Logie-Easter

I already had a glimmer of the answer to this question—a tentative intuition—and it emerged from my awareness of the spirituality of men and women in my parish. They were incorporated into Christ by baptism, and they had turned towards him in faith. My experience is shared, I am certain, by many other Catholics; and it is a fact that finds expression in literature too. Only yesterday afternoon I listened on Radio 4 to the final episode in the *Chronicles of Barset* and was deeply moved by the last moments in the life of Mr Harding. In such a character—thanks to Trollope's genius—we are privileged to glimpse the depth of Christian spirituality which can exist outside the visible structure of the Catholic Church. The Mr Hardings of this world are most certainly "in Christ."

On 21 November 1964 the Church published *Lumen Gentium* which defined authoritatively the relationship between the Mystical Body of Christ and the Church we can see on earth. In n.8 that document speaks of "the visible society and the spiritual community," but it hastens to explain that these are not two entities but one complex reality. Moreover that complex reality "subsists in the Catholic Church, which is governed by the successors of Peter and by the bishops in communion with him." The next sentence states that "many elements of sanctification and truth are found outside its visible confines." The presence of these residual elements does not, however, add up to subsistence in separated communities of the complex reality that is the Church, but it generates a force that impels those who enjoy these elements towards Catholic unity. It is true also that the elements of sanctification and truth found disconnected from their living nucleus within the Catholic Church, may exist in great perfection.

In n.15 & n.16 *Lumen Gentium* describes the way in which individuals who are not fully incorporated into the Catholic Church are related to it. First the document speaks of those who share, in differing degrees of completeness, the fundamental beliefs of the Catholic Church; but it goes further than that: "Finally, those who have not yet received the Gospel are related to the People of God in various ways." First in line at this point the document places Jews and then Moslems, but the list does not end with these.

> *Nor is God remote from those who in shadows and images seek the unknown God, since he gives to all men life and breath and all things, and since the Savior wills all men to be saved. Those who, through no fault of their own, do not know the Gospel of Christ or his Church, but who nevertheless seek God with a sincere heart, and, moved by grace, try in their actions to do his will as they know it through the dictates of their conscience—these too may achieve eternal salvation. Nor shall divine providence deny the assistance necessary for salvation to those who, without any fault of theirs, have not yet arrived at an explicit knowledge of God, and who, not without grace, strive to lead a good life.*

The theology implicit in all of this seems to be that saving faith may indeed be the smallest of all mustard seeds, but it possesses an essentially moral quality. It lies in a fundamental disposition of the human soul, in a humble openness to truth. The extent to which it has grasped the truth is not the critical factor in determining salvation.

My own perception of the reality of the faith of individuals outside the visible unity of the Catholic Church, who did not enjoy the support of all of the means of salvation which that Church is able to supply, originated first in my own pre-Catholic experience, then in my acquaintance with people in my pastoral work, and it was deepened by the many contacts I made through the Morningside Christian Council; but however clear that perception was, it never lessened my certainty that the visible Church was an absolute necessity, for as the number of my non-Catholic friends grew, so did my awareness of the insecurity that existed in matters of doctrine. Even among devout Protestants, Gnostic ideas, deriving no doubt from biblical scholars like Bultmann, were already affecting the way people thought about the Gospel. Rejection of magisterial authority in the Church had left orthodoxy with rigid biblical literalism as its only bulwark against the attacks of humanism, and now that literalism had gone out of fashion there was no defense at all. It was becoming ever clearer that it is the meaning of scripture that matters, and unless the Church is there to interpret the scriptures, there will be a multitude of meanings on offer. There are now—and there were already in the sixties—devout Christians who denied the Virgin birth and also the Resurrection. The Christian Faith was on the way to becoming the Christian Myth. It may be true, as *Lumen Gentium* teaches, that the key factor in finding salvation is the inner disposition of the soul, but it is also true that the truth has been revealed and those who preach the truth must be totally faithful to that revelation; otherwise any genuine subjective disposition of faith will have no correlative object upon which to feed, and so no means of becoming "the perfect Man, fully mature with the fullness of Christ himself" (Eph 4:13).

Parallel with this insecurity in theological doctrine was uncertainty in moral matters. My own views were often sharply in conflict with those of my friends and relations, with whom I was now frequently engaged in ecumenical dialogue. One had to remain faithful to truths proclaimed by the Church, and believed to issue from the Word made flesh. These conflicts in the field of both theology and morals had to be reconciled with the realization of spiritual communion, on the basis of our common profession that Jesus Christ is Lord. How was this to be done?

The strain imposed by this produced the temptation to abandon the attempt to accomplish the first aim and avoid all ecumenical relations. This course had in fact been followed in Morningside by the Plymouth Brethren after their initial, courteous association with the Council; and one can understand the logic of their action. There was on the other hand the temptation to abandon or at least to soft-pedal the concept of the one visible Church and any dogmatic proclamation of the truths of faith and morals, and go for some kind of "Churchless Christianity," with a lowest common denominator belief. Our experience in the Morningside Christian Council, although very heartening in many ways, warned us to expect squalls on the future ecumenical voyage.

In the summer of 1968 there was an ecumenical Youth Conference in Edinburgh. I was invited to attend as a senior observer. The other observer was my old friend Fr James Quinn, S.J. He attended daily, but I was given a room on campus in the Pollock Halls, under the shadow of Arthur's Seat. In the midst of all these youngsters—plus or minus twenty years of age—I began to feel old, especially when I met one young woman student who turned out to be the daughter of a student I had met at the S.C.M. conference in Swanwick in 1939. It was a very hot summer, and every afternoon I walked a couple of miles home to report our ongoings to Helen, whom I would find weeding by hand in our garden—an occupation she loved.

There was plenty to talk about and much that provoked me to some vehemence. I found some of the senior members of the conference an irritation. There was one angry middle-aged man, whose name I forget, who urged the young people to take the law into their own hands and defy their elders, particularly in matters concerning Church order. I got a strong whiff of the spirit of Churchless Christianity that I had already detected in embryo in my earlier ecumenical encounters. Even more acute irritation was to come, not from the inter-Church arena, but from within the Catholic sector of the conference.

At this time everyone was waiting for Pope Paul VI to publish a definitive statement about birth control and about the contraceptive pill in particular. I had already become involved in discussion of this topic. A journalist, whom I knew well, had written in *The Sunday Times*, stating that the Pope would certainly adopt a much more liberal view on this subject than the Church had maintained in the past. There was no doubt in this journalist's mind that the Pill would be accepted as a legitimate means in the control of conception. The letter which I wrote contradicting this view was not published, but the editor replied to me, saying that he had sent my letter directly to the author of the article. In my letter I had said that I was quite certain that the Pope could not alter what was now the settled teaching of the Church on this subject, and that it was irresponsible for anyone to encourage people to think that he would do so. In my view the Church's teaching on the subject of contraception had been given with the full weight of the ordinary magisterium, and qualified to be classed as infallible in the terms of *Lumen Gentium* n.25.

While this Youth Conference was in session *Humanae Vitae* was published. I was relieved when I read at last what Pope Paul VI had to say; but the reaction of a large number of Catholic students attending the conference was quite different. In my innocence I had been unaware of the support there was in England for the views expressed by the commission which had proposed changes in the Church's teaching. That commission was composed of "experts"–experts in what? What appalled me most on this occasion, however, was that a priest from Liverpool Archdiocese, and who seemed to have some official position *vis à vis* the English Catholic contingent, organized a Mass on the morning after the publication of the encyclical, announcing that the intention of this Mass was that the Church would be able to retrieve herself from this catastrophe. I knew that there had been some resistance to the Church's traditional teaching, but never dreamed that it was so widespread and organized. One of the English students at the conference told me that in Liverpool for some time people had been encouraged to expect a change in teaching on this subject.

In the months following the publication of *Humanae Vitae* it became increasingly evident that there was considerable opposition to the teaching contained in the encyclical. The media delighted when prominent theologians joined the ranks of the dissidents. In Edinburgh we got a taste of this at an elevated level. Professor Hans Küng was invited to lecture in the Hume Tower at

Edinburgh University. I have no record of the date, but remember the occasion very clearly. There was a big audience, which included many prominent theologians and clergy of the Church of Scotland and other groups. As was to be expected, Hans Küng delivered a brilliant lecture. Near the end of his lecture he cited *Humanae Vitae* to illustrate what he had to say on the nature of authority in the Church. In fact he used it to prove a vital point, viz. that the view of the Church's magisterium commonly held by Catholics is false. He admitted that the teaching of this encyclical was indeed given with the full weight of the authority of the ordinary magisterium. He told us that he had researched the matter diligently in the hope of proving it to be otherwise, but had discovered that the teaching did satisfy the conditions, defined by Vatican II, to allow it to be classed as infallible. His conclusion, however, was not that the teaching should be accepted, but that because it was absurd, the Catholic notion of infallibility must be rejected. In his peroration he spoke quite fervently of the hope that must sustain the pilgrim Church as she journeys through a wilderness of error towards ultimate fulfillment. When he sat down he received thunderous applause. He had perfectly expressed the ecclesiology of his Reformed audience.

Hans Küng's lecture was most revealing, and yet the significance of his argument had not been appreciated. His fundamental premise was that on this particular moral issue he had formed a conclusion that differed from that of the magisterium. His private opinion was therefore the arbiter of the competence of the Church's magisterium. It was a simple case of private opinion versus the mind of the Church. The issue subsequently became a bit blurred by the introduction of the word "conscience" in place of "private opinion." The word "conscience," falsely understood, became the Trojan Horse within which rejection of the magisterium, indeed rejection of Catholic ecclesiology in general, was smuggled into the City of God. By the end of the sixties it seemed to me that the Church had got into a more perilous condition than it had been in at the time of the Reformation.

A sad feature of the whole story was the rather weak, sometimes ambiguous, response made by many episcopal conferences to the publication of *Humanae Vitae*, and by their leaving the way open to a misunderstanding of conscience. Certainly many of the clergy misled the faithful.

In 1968 *The Reformation in Germany* by Josef Lortz was published. I had translated the work and found it enlightening. In view of the turmoil that was growing in the Church I had noted in particular a short paragraph in which Lortz comments on the official handling of the crisis in Germany in the sixteenth century:

"Had there been about half a dozen theologians like Eck and Cochlaeus occupying German bishoprics from 1520 onwards, the course of the discussion, that was so decisive for the nation, would have been notably relieved of the lamentable burden of Catholic apathy" (Vol. II p. 213).

21

The perilous state into which the Church was moving, so soon after Vatican II, was made very clear to me by the events of that Youth Conference, and especially on the day when the priest from the Archdiocese of Liverpool offered Mass, praying that the Church would eventually find it possible to over-rule the declaration that Pope Paul VI had just made. On that day I walked through the leafy south side of Edinburgh, along Dick Place and down Canaan Lane, to take my afternoon break from the conference, still disturbed and angry over what had happened. I went quickly through our house to the longer garden at the back which, although on the north side of the terrace, was flooded from the west in afternoon sunshine. I saw a grey squirrel running jerkily along the high wall that separated the gardens of Nile Grove from those of Eden Lane. Helen on this occasion was not scrabbling in the herbaceous border, pulling out weeds, but lying spread out on a rug, worshipping the sun, or at least seeking maximum exposure to its rays. Sunbathing had always been one of her great delights.

"Go to the other side," she said, "your shadow's covering my legs."

I did as she asked and sat down on the rug beside her. Her presence was already making me feel much better, and my mood improved the more we talked about the events which had distressed me so much. Together we had struggled through, and finally solved the problems that faced us on our journey into the Catholic Church and through all of life's trials; now we were beginning to struggle with the problems caused by dissidence within the Catholic Church; and our unity of mind and heart was as firm as ever. In all of the problems that religion had created for us, our love, our amazing capacity to see eye to eye with each other, had been a source of strength. Put the other way round we could say that our attachment to the Faith and the things of faith, was the foundation of our union. At the very beginning it had been our common interest in the Student Christian Movement that brought us together, and it was our continuing pursuit of theological issues that had nourished our growing love. We shared a common attitude in these things, and also found it easy to communicate about them with each other. Helen had a theological mind—her favorite spiritual author was St Teresa of Avila—and I looked to her not just for support but often for direction in the hard thinking that was now demanded on the problems affecting the Church.

The underlying question now being asked was: Is the Church the same as it was before Vatican II, or has there been a fundamental change? I recall a Confirmation in St Peter's in the late sixties when Archbishop Gray preached, his theme being that no change had been brought about by Vatican II. I knew that this statement was correct, in the sense that the Church's dogmatic teaching had not changed, but at the same time it was obvious that some things had changed, so that many people had become confused, for not everyone is capable of distinguishing the essential and enduring from the accidental and transitory. Besides this there were people, some of them influential, who claimed that there had been a sea-change in theology and ecclesiology.

I was drawn into this argument by our relation, Rev Campbell MacLean, the minister of Cramond parish, who at that time hosted a religious chat-program on the BBC, and who asked me to be interviewed and questioned basically about the question: Has the Catholic Church changed? In the course of the interview I compared the essential structure and identity of the Church with the unchanging identity of a human being, in spite of development from embryo to old age, and change in clothing and so on, unaware of the fact that this simile had been used centuries ago by Vincent of Lerins. On the following week Campbell MacLean put Hans Küng in the same seat in the studio in Queen Street and was able to elicit from him a response that more or less contradicted what I had said. There could be no doubt that the Church was in trouble. Helen and I were both deeply disturbed by these things, and constantly discussed them.

It was the incipient attack on the Church's magisterium that disturbed us, not the external changes that came about after the Council. On the whole we welcomed the liturgical revival that was taking place. The replacement of Latin texts in the Liturgy of the Word by vernacular texts seemed eminently rational, and the removal of accretions to the Mass helped one to concentrate on the Mass itself. I had never been one to advocate the change over to the vernacular in the Canon of the Mass, for although I did not understand Latin, having been educated in a modern and very scientific school, I had become accustomed to following the eucharistic prayer in English in my Missal, and so felt no deprivation. On the first occasion, however, when I heard the Canon of the Mass recited in English in our parish church, it struck me immediately that now I had no need to perform the customary feat of mental gymnastics in order to follow the Mass intelligently. On the matter of the quality of the English translation I was not competent to judge. The revisions being made to the liturgy did not seem to me to constitute a change in the doctrine of the Eucharist.

Our parish priest set about another bit of liturgical reconstruction which did arouse some argument in the parish. He decided to provide a Blessed Sacrament chapel in one of the side aisles of the church. The reasoning behind this, as conciliar documents explain, is that the altar should be regarded as the place where the sacrifice of the eucharist takes place rather than as the place where the Blessed Sacrament is reserved. Some objections to the establishment of this chapel were voiced in a parish council meeting. I supported the scheme, although as time passed I noticed that when people visited the church, they did not pay much attention to the chapel, but knelt in the main church. There was now an architectural or psychological disunity in the building. I wondered if we had indulged in precious, purist theorizing, and had made an unnecessary, possibly damaging, distinction between the place of action and the place of reservation.

Sometimes I would reflect on the function I fulfilled in the Church. There was of course the work I did for the Converts' Aid Society, but there were so many other things too, sometimes as a result of the contacts I made through my work, for I traveled all over Scotland, and would be invited to talk, often on an ecumenical topic, sometimes on a wider theological theme, in parishes throughout the country, and occasionally at meetings of clergy. Only the other day—that is thirty years later than the events recorded here—an elderly lady told me that when she was a student I had spoken in her parish in Lanarkshire. Neither she nor I could recall what the subject of the talk had been.

After the National Ecumenical Commission was formed in 1968 I found a more formalized channel for my interest in inter-Church relations and in theology in general, for I became a lay representative for the Archdiocese of St Andrew's and Edinburgh on that Commission. There was one particular operation arising from my membership of this Commission which gave me great satisfaction, and a sense of being useful to the Church—something that is very important for a convert clergyman. I was friendly with the late Bishop Joseph McGee of Galloway, whose brother Denis lived in our parish, and whose nephews and nieces were friends of our sons. The Bishop came to lunch with us one day in order to discuss some ecumenical matters about which he thought I might have direct knowledge. The outcome of this meeting was that I visited the Galloway Diocese in order to talk on an ecumenical topic to the clergy and other interested people, and try to answer questions. On this occasion it was the questions I provoked that were important. I carefully noted all of these questions. Not long after, the National Ecumenical Commission, having published its *Presentation of the Ecumenical Directory, Part I,* set about the composition of *Guide-Lines for Ecumenical Activity,* and at one stage in the operation entrusted a working group–Fr James Quinn, S.J., Fr Henry Doherty, and me–with the job of preparing a draft for these Guide-Lines. The three of us sat round our kitchen table in Nile Grove and worked out this draft, for the most part simply addressing the questions that had come from the Diocese of Galloway, as a result of the inspired practicality of Bishop Joseph McGee.

My free-lance theological activities took me very occasionally over the Border. I remember a long, wearisome expedition in very cold weather with Helen to Cheltenham where I gave a lecture to the Newman Association on *The Bishops' Report.* I have no idea why they were interested in the argument going on in the Church of Scotland about the possibility of blending episcopacy with presbyterianism. Our bedroom in Cheltenham was furnished with twin beds, to which we were unaccustomed; we were nearly frozen to death.

A more interesting and profitable adventure, which took place probably in the early sixties, was the result of a plan conceived by Fr James Christie, S.J., then superior at the Sacred Heart Church in Edinburgh, who wanted the Jesuits to consider some form of devolution for Scotland, possibly even the establishment of a Scottish Province.

"Would you consider going down to Heythrop," he asked me, "and put Scotland on the map so to speak?"

He explained more fully what he had in mind and I responded:

"It would be a kind of P.R. stunt really? You want me to go down among the Sassenachs and do a kind of theological Harry Lauder act."

"Exactly," he said.

And so Helen and I set off during a spell of beautiful weather by car for Chipping Norton, where we stayed in a hotel for two nights. Country hotels are quaint places, and quaint people visit them. All I remember of that hotel was a middle-aged couple eating at the next table to ours. Although the husband was by no means invalid or senile, his wife—we could not help observing—cut his food up for him so that he could convey it to his mouth using only a fork.

At Heythrop we were received very politely and kindly by Fr Diamond, the superior, who seemed however, to be a bit in the dark as to the purpose of our visit. Soon we were passed on to the care of Phil Leonard, whom I already knew, for during my spell of teacher-training in 1949 I had been assigned to his class in St Ninian's primary school where I learned much from him, for he was a gifted and imaginative teacher. I learned also to admire him for his great courage and faith. At that time his wife was very ill, and he would come into work in the morning, having spent all night nursing her. After his wife's death Phil entered the Society of Jesus. It was a great loss to the Church when, still young and not long after his ordination to the priesthood, Phil himself died. When we visited Heythrop he was full of life and very amusing. He told many anecdotes of life at Heythrop, and we judged that he was quite a thorn in the flesh of the authorities. His Scots sense of humor and mischievousness must have confused others. He continued to show us round until quite late, so that we became concerned in case he would miss his supper.

"Don't worry about me," he said, "I've got my own secret outfit in the basement, including a radio transmitter; I won't starve."

In the talk I gave I described the ecclesiastical and theological scene in Scotland, mentioning the difference in ethos between Scots and English Protestantism, and trying to erase some of the caricatures of Scots life and religion that are current in England. The thing I stressed most, believing that it would arouse the right kind of interest, was that the faculty of divinity at New College was the place where English-speaking students, notably the Americans, who were not renowned as linguists, and hesitated therefore to study in Germany or Switzerland, came to listen to Karl Barth through the mouth of his prophet Tom Torrance. I gave New College, for which I had great affection, a very big write up as a school of European theology, and even if I may have exaggerated a little, my conscience did not trouble me in the least, for I was after all on a public relations assignment. I embroidered my talk with reminiscences and anecdotes of my own years spent at New College, and was astonished at the hilarity I aroused. Phil Leonard explained afterwards that several of my portraits of professors at New College had neatly matched with members of the staff at Heythrop.

Reflecting on the kind of work we were doing, Helen and I thought that it might well be classified as "prophecy" in the sense that word has in the Acts of the Apostles. This function was akin to teaching in that it had to do with the application of the truth of the Gospel to life's situations. A footnote to Acts 11:27 in *The Jerusalem Bible* states:

> *Their (the prophets') chief work was evidently to explain the oracles of the scriptures under the guidance of the Holy Spirit, especially those of the OT prophets, 1 P 1:10-12, and thus expound the 'mystery' of the divine plan,...*

To be a prophet in this New Testament sense, one had to live by the Spirit, and through the power of the Spirit become able to apply one's natural gifts to the work of evangelization. Every believer therefore is called upon to be a prophet; distinctions between different people are only in respect of the mode in which the function is exercised. For Helen and me, in accordance with our gifts and education and temperament, the mode of functioning was in theological and moral discernment. Above all we believed that our marriage was our chief prophetic proclamation. We enjoyed a full life, with many activities, but in the end we lived for each other. Marriage was the fundamental act of worship, the ultimate manifestation of the Spirit in our life. The unicity of our marriage was a sacramental declaration that "the Lord our God is One

God," and so we loved each other "with all our heart and with all our soul and with all our strength."

For my part, I suppose that the work of theological and moral discernment was supremely important. All through the sixties I was kept theologically active partly though my work in the ecumenical field and partly through the work of translating German theology. There was, however, another influence on my theological and spiritual development, the importance of which I did not appreciate at the time. I had bought a copy of *The Interim Breviary*, which I used regularly. In that Breviary there was an indication of the scripture passages for the Office of Readings, although the excerpts from spiritual writers were not given. Every day I would read the scripture passage noted and in addition read carefully every footnote and cross-reference supplied by *The Jerusalem Bible*. This practice provided me with a thorough course in biblical theology.

Towards the end of 1970 there came a lull in translating work, and I seized the opportunity to do what I had long wanted to do: I began work on a set of biblical meditations on the mysteries of the Rosary. Ever since our reception into the Church I had found private meditation on the Rosary a most satisfying form of prayer. The little book I planned to write would therefore encourage people to dwell upon the incidents recounted in the mysteries, to enter the biblical scene held in their imagination, and so draw near to the sacred humanity of our Lord, listening to his words and observing his actions. According to St Teresa of Avila this is the only safe method of contemplative prayer. I wanted to show also that behind each mystery lies a wealth of holy scripture.

The book of meditations was published in the USA in 1972 and entitled, *The Glory of Israel*, but was written during Lent 1971. The creation of the book was much more than an intellectual exercise. It was an act of continuous meditation; and a curious thing happened: throughout the whole time I was at work on the book, Helen and I, without having mentioned the subject or made any conscious resolution, found ourselves following the suggestion St Paul made in 1 Corinthians 7:5: "Do not refuse each other except by mutual consent, and then only for an agreed time, to leave yourselves free for prayer; then come together again..."

It was at about this period in our lives that I was suddenly overtaken by a brief, morbid fantasy. There must have been some mention in the media of the relation between smoking and cancer. When Nicolas was at home during the final stage of his illness, Helen used occasionally to have a cigarette along with him. After his death she continued the habit–not very seriously, but it must have caused me to think of the dangers mentioned in the press. The question suddenly erupted in my mind: If Helen became ill and were to be taken from me, what would I do? The answer came immediately: I would have to follow some mode of contemplative life. This answer, as I analyzed much later, was implied in the way Helen and I regarded marriage. Marriage is a form of contemplation of God, through the great icon of divinity that is the human person. If that icon is removed, there can be no compensation except to move beyond the icon and draw closer to the reality of which it is an icon. To me its uniqueness was of the essence of the icon, so that there could be no replacement of the icon. This morbid thought was past in a flash, but its meaning remained stamped upon my consciousness.

Our expedition to Heythrop may have helped to advance Fr James Christie's scheme; for whatever reason, in the seventies the Society of Jesus moved its novitiate to Woodhall House at Colinton, close to the Pentland Hills, in the suburbs Edinburgh. I had several very good friends among the Jesuits at the Sacred Heart in Edinburgh, and now my association with the Society became closer, for Fr John Hughes, S.J., who was Master of Studies at the novitiate in its new abode at Woodhall House asked me to help by conducting a class for the novices in writing, that is in literary composition.

I performed this task for a year, during which I learned a great deal myself about the art of writing. Learning a subject is advanced by nothing so much as the necessity to teach it. This fact had already struck me when helping to run Bible-study in St Peter's parish. One of the principles I inculcated was that the writer should keep his eye on the subject—just as a painter must concentrate on the model. A good exercise in writing is therefore to describe physical objects, in this way learning how to match words with things. At one lesson in the spring when a colony of rooks were setting up house in the grounds I asked the class to describe a crow's nest. One student allowed piety to over-rule my advice. He wrote about how St Francis Xavier used to escape on board ship up to the crow's nest where he engaged in solitary prayer. I was not impressed; but I was impressed by the work of another who, describing a tree in winter, painted a word-picture, not of a perfectly bare tree, but of a tree with a solitary leaf still clinging to a high branch. How this one leaf accentuated the bareness!

During the following year I was asked to teach a second class in doctrine. Fr Hughes believed that regularly, throughout training, students should rehearse the Faith in its wholeness in order to counterbalance dangers inherent in detailed academic analysis. He thought it necessary also to discover what knowledge of the Faith the novices had on coming up from secondary school. The material that emerged from these seminars I used later in a series of doctrinal lectures for the Poor Clare Nuns at Liberton, and it ended up as an unpublished book which I called *The Pillar of Truth.* Mowbray's, an Anglican publisher, told me that they would have published it had they not been forced by the economic climate to start cutting back.

Almost every year since 1965 we had taken a holiday during the first fortnight of August at Trochrague Guest House near Girvan. This was a small hotel run by the Sisters of St Joseph of Cluny. The hotel was competently run under the vigilant eye of Mother Stanislaus, an exheadmistress–for the Cluny Sisters were an educational congregation, renowned for the modernity of their teaching methods; and it was very comfortable and quite inexpensive–excellent for families. Our friends the Shannons introduced us to the place, and when we got there we discovered that during the first fortnight in August a group of regulars, coming from different parts of Scotland and England, more or less took the place over. The same group–the unchanging nucleus comprised about eight families–went there year after year, and had become like an extended family. There was plenty of scope for the amusement of younger children around the house and in the woods, and the beach was only two miles distant. One of the Girvan fisherman organized long sea expeditions, and from time to time one or two of us would come home with an enormous quantity of mackerel. The preoccupation of most guests was with golf, Girvan possessing an excellent little course, one in the chain of golf-courses that makes up such a large proportion of the Scottish coast-line.

Two fervent worshippers at the shrine of golf were Canon Bernard Mullan and Fr Forshaw, both priests from Liverpool, who had been visiting Trochrague in August for many years, and who had become assimilated into the family. In August 1973 Canon Mullan told me about a meeting of the National Priests' Council of England at which the proposal had been made and accepted, that convert clergymen ought to be eligible for ordination to the Catholic priesthood. One of the reasons for this proposal was that convert clergymen often find it very hard to find work for which they are fitted by education and experience, whereas their past experience could be a preparation for pastoral work in the priesthood.

"What do you think about that," he asked, "do you feel that you have been cheated out of twenty-five years you might have given to the Church in the ordained ministry?"

"The thought of becoming a priest has never entered my head since I became a Catholic," I replied.

"The last thing I ever want to do is to dilute my devotion to Helen, by giving to other people the devotion they have a right to expect from a priest. Marriage and the priesthood are both sacraments, earthed in the same matter: the man's maleness. I certainly could never give myself totally, as I do to Helen, twice over."

"Listen," he said, "you've got to write about this, because you can write from direct experience."

I did write about it, and at the end of the year *The Furrow* published my article in which I argued that celibacy is the appropriate, perhaps the necessary, state of life for one ordained to the priesthood. As well as appealing to my experience I took as the scriptural basis of my argument St Paul's assertion in 1 Cor 7:32: "I would like to see you free from all worry. An unmarried man can devote himself to the Lord's affairs, all he need worry about is pleasing the Lord; but a married man has to bother about the world's affairs and devote himself to pleasing his wife: he is torn two ways." I was still able to recall that sense of being torn two ways when I had been a parish minister.

An important feature of the article was that I approached the subject not from the point of view of the priest, as was the common procedure, but from the point of view of the married man, asking not: May priests be married? but: Should a married man be permitted to become a priest? All of the arguments in favor of married priests are flawed mainly—in my opinion—because they implicitly put marriage in second place. The inherent sublimity of marriage is the obstacle in the way of ordination.

Canon Mullan's question suggested also that I may have felt that for twenty-five years I had not been usefully employed. I did not think this at all, for I believed the work I had been doing for twenty-five years had been work of the lay apostolate, and the lay apostolate is vital. Moreover, it has to be seen as genuinely lay, not as a kind of semi-sacerdotal ministry, although the teaching element in a lay ministry, especially of the prophetic kind which illumines the meaning of the Gospel, sometimes causes people to think of such ministry as sacerdotal. The lay apostolate, which every layman and woman exercises in a particular way, flows from the common priesthood of all believers but is not part of the ordained ministry.

When Canon Mullan told me of the proposal made by the National Priests' Council of England and Wales that all convert clergy–married as well as single–ought to be eligible for ordination, it struck me that the readiness with which such a proposal could be taken up was a sign not only of blindness to the status of marriage, but also of a deeply entrenched clericalism that still persists in the Church. Would it not have been better to try to solve the problems which undoubtedly arise for convert clergy–as I so well knew–by using these men primarily in lay apostolates, particularly in varieties related to teaching? That of course would have required radical thinking and planning and, possibly, funds.

At this time, influenced no doubt by my experience at the Jesuit Novitiate and by the writing and translating of theology in which I had been intermittently engaged, I began to look for an opportunity to teach in a more formal way. Ideally I would have liked to find work at the teachers' training college at Craiglockhart. I had the academic qualifications to conduct courses at least in biblical studies. I discussed my ideas with our parish priest, Fr Walter Glancy, who had connections with the educational system. There was no opening exactly in the direction I had in mind, but he urged me to apply for the post of principal teacher of religious education, which was to be created in August in Holy Rood, one of the Catholic secondary schools in Edinburgh.

Winter was slowly loosening its grip when I drove through the King's Park, past Duddingston Loch where there were still traces of ice, to pay a visit to Holy Rood secondary school. It had been arranged for me to teach there on one day each week for the remainder of the spring term and then throughout the summer, after which I was to decide whether or not to apply for the post of principal teacher of religious education.

Twenty years had passed since I last taught in school, and so on this occasion I entered the class-room with some trepidation. The youngsters were not unruly or troublesome; what struck me was the apathy of most pupils. I could not tell whether this was directed towards education in general or just towards religious education. In one of the brighter classes I found about five pupils, sitting near the front, who showed some interest, but the rest were half asleep, making no attempt even to feign interest. The atmosphere was quite different from what I had known in Dalkeith twenty years earlier. It began to dawn on me: the problem lay not in the school but in society, in the Church in fact. When I had been teaching in Dalkeith about ten per cent of the pupils in a class could be reckoned to come from lapsed families; now it looked as if only ten per cent were not lapsed. The school was no longer a place for the formation of the families of the Catholic faithful, but a mission field.

Even more distressing was my interview with the head teacher. I asked about the syllabus used and about the general policy in the school. There was some kind of catechetical program in process of being written for the Archdiocese. I judged it to be rather amateurish and D.I.Y. in style, and its printing and presentation were unprofessional. I raised the subject of moral teaching, and the head teacher said that one had to assess the consensus of opinion among parents. I said that I thought it necessary to have a normative catechism, even if only as a symbol that there is such a thing as the Catholic Faith, and he remarked that such a catechism would have to be composed by the children themselves.

Quite soon I saw two facts clearly. First I had been too long out of school, out of practice in class management; and second, even more important, if I took up this post I would find myself caught up in conflicts, for I could not accept the ethos that had developed in the Catholic educational system. I decided to go no further with the plan to apply for the post, and withdrew immediately from the trial scheme. I felt great relief on making this decision, and yet I did feel a scruple. Was I running away from a challenge? Might I not have a part to play in helping to provide genuine Catholic catechesis? I came upon a passage in *The Ascent of Mount Carmel* by St John of the Cross in which he describes the tendency in people to avoid what is God's will for them as they would avoid death. This worried me. Was I avoiding the unpleasant situation I could foresee when in fact it was my duty to deal with it? On the other hand I thought of the parable of the king who, before setting out on a campaign, weighed up whether or not he had the resources to do so successfully. Our Lord's parable outweighed in my mind the comments of St John of the Cross. Calmly I decided that it would be imprudent to burn my boats and go back into school-teaching.

As winter gave way to early spring Helen and I continued to reflect on how we could best carry out the lay apostolate that was our lot. For me it seemed that I should carry on work as before, but with the hope of expanding the literary side of my work—I was planning a second series of biblical meditations on the Rosary. We also spoke of the possibility of returning to the country, for we had always looked back to the few years spent in Easter Ross as a golden age, but we decided that we should wait until we knew where our sons, who were now married, would finally settle. During the early spring of 1974 we were content with the direction our life and work were taking.

One morning at 3 a.m. I awoke and found myself thinking about marriage, about our marriage, I suppose. Love to begin with, it seems, is self-centered; both partners in love desire each other, being instinctively impelled towards the pleasure, the delight, the comfort that they find in the other. Soon nature teaches them that love reaches out into self-giving—to each other and also to the children. But, I reflected, is love, married love in particular, always characterized by self-love? In a sense, yes; but it must be possible, I thought, for such love to attain a perfection in which there is no self-seeking at all, for in the Christian view, marriage reflects, is a sacrament of, the love between the Creator and mankind, and the Creator's love contains no trace of self-interested desire. Likewise, the response of man or woman to God's love, while it contains an element of gratitude for gifts received, to be perfect, must contain nothing but appreciation of the One loved. We thank God for his gifts: we adore him for what he is. Marriage too, the sacrament of divine love, should be able to acquire this pure form that is a form of adoration. I thought of the way I loved Helen. It was true that I had loved her mainly in the sense of enjoying the comfort she gave me. Could I not from now on learn more and more to love her simply for who she was? Ought I not to try to be her servant? I resolved that I would indeed try to discover what she wanted, what she wanted to do, where she would like to live, what she wanted me to do. I felt that if I could reach the height of perfectly non-selfish love, our lives would become fully purposeful. These reflections led me on to consider that already we had achieved such close union in our marriage that we could not be brought any closer through the kindly comfort that mother nature's impulses provided. We had been blessed with a glimpse into the kingdom where there is no giving in marriage, but where perfect love remains. Just as sleep was returning, without any shock or amazement, the thought came to me: I don't think that Helen and I will sleep with each other again.

Fr Michael Bell was a good friend; his home was in our parish, and when he visited his mother, as he did regularly, he came to see us too. He had invited us to his parish of Strathblane to help him with some ploy he had in hand, and so we went over on Friday 10 May 1974, meaning to stay for the weekend, and while there to attend a meeting in Glasgow on Sunday at which the Apostolic Delegate was to be present. On Sunday afternoon Helen felt unwell, but was unable to explain what was wrong.

She went to bed, complaining of a dull ache in the lower chest and abdomen. I was disturbed, however, more by her expression. She was a little distraught and unwilling to talk. It was clear that she could not go to the meeting. After about two hours she said:

"I feel a little better now, but let's go home."

We went home and Helen's debility was gone. That evening the Radio News carried the report that during the afternoon the Apostolic Delegate had announced the name of the new Archbishop of Glasgow. It was to be Thomas Winning.

On Tuesday at about 10.30 a.m. we set off for Aberdeen in order to call on parishes there, in particular to visit Fr Charles McGregor, administrator of the Cathedral, and afterwards to travel on to Hopeman to spend a few days with a step-cousin of Helen's whose husband was a housemaster at Gordonstoun. We had been talking about the events of the past month or two, and as we were crossing the Forth Bridge Helen said:

"You know, I don't think you need look for a new job; our life-style's fine—we enjoy it, and month by month things seem to open out for both of us."

"I'm glad to hear you say that," I answered, "I sometimes worried I was wrong to turn down that teaching job."

"No," she said, "that wasn't for you; you're an individualist; keep on as you've been doing for the past twenty-five years—see how many interesting things have happened."

"That's true," I said, "and I'm really satisfied with the way things are working out; but at the same time I feel we need some kind of spiritual break-through."

We decided to leave the motorway at the junction after Milnathort and continue via Cupar and over the Tay Bridge through Dundee. We were discussing whether to stop for our picnic lunch just before or just after Dundee, when I read the signs "Tay Bridge" and "St Andrews," and pulled over into the exit road. The next thing of which I was conscious was a searing and most peculiar pain in my groin and hip and hearing Helen whimpering:

"Are you alive?"

"Yes," I gasped, "but I'm afraid I've dislocated my hip."

I raised my eyes and saw, right in front, the underside of a van.

22

Helen, although distressed, seemed unharmed. As for me, as well as damage to the pelvis, I had struck my head against the protruding edge of the small triangular window, open on my side. Concussion from this blow had blotted out all memory of the accident. Later Helen described what had happened. A baker's van had approached the old main road onto which we had emerged from the slip-road, but instead of halting at the dotted line, had proceeded straight ahead onto the main road. I had braked violently—the pedal went right through the floor and never returned—but could not avoid colliding with the van, which was overturned, although my speed—as the police told me—was estimated at only 45 mph.

Once more the world around faded out, and when I regained consciousness I saw a doctor beside the car and heard his colorful expressions of impatience as he awaited the arrival of an ambulance. We were both taken into the ambulance, and for me the journey of about half an hour to Bridge of Earn hospital was endured partly in, and partly out of, consciousness. I was taken immediately to the orthopedic department where, X-rays having been taken, the dislocated hip was put back into place—for the time being. The consultant was on vacation, and his assistant told me that he would prefer to wait for the consultant's return before they tried to retrieve the bits and pieces of acetabulum, which had become lodged some inches away from the pelvis, and fit everything together again. Helen was taken to the surgical side of the hospital, some distance away. Quite soon I was informed that she was in good enough shape—some broken ribs and bruising on the chest from the seat-belt. Although Bridge of Earn hospital was only a collection of one-story huts—an improvisation dating from the Second World War—it was most efficiently staffed and well equipped. The consultant, Ian Sutherland, a Caithness man and a cousin of one of my Morningside minister-friends, returned within a few days and performed a most expert job on my damaged acetabulum. I was then trussed up in plaster, with weights hanging from my foot, and began a vigil of about eleven weeks.

Before I had received the final repairs, on the morning after the accident, a deeper drama was already beginning to unfold. Quite early I saw the matron enter our ward and hold a whispered consultation with the ward sister; then she walked over towards me and at once I felt an acid sensation in my stomach.

"Good morning," she began.

"Good morning, Matron," I replied, innocent of my political incorrectness, for even as early as the seventies a matron was known as a Number Seven.

"I've got not very good news for you," she said, "during the night your wife's blood pressure fell—she was hemorrhaging from internal injuries—compression from the seat-belt. The surgeon had to operate and remove a kidney, the spleen and part of the liver."

I could say nothing. She went on.

"I can't pretend it's not serious, but she's very tough. We'll wait and see how things go, but at the moment she's unconscious."

"Can I see her?"

"As soon as she regains consciousness, they'll get you onto a trolley and bring you over."

Number Seven departed and our delightful ward-sister, who like the consultant was a native of Caithness, came over and sat down for a while with me to make sure I was all right.

Both of our sons had come up on the evening of our accident, and they returned during the next day as soon as they heard the bad news. The hospital staff were both efficient and hospitable: they provided an overnight room for the family, who later found a bed and breakfast place near the hospital. I have no clear memory of the time-scale at this point. What I do remember very clearly is that during the hours after the news had been broken to me, it struck me that I only now realized how much I loved Helen. I thought that I knew how much I did, but now that the prospect of losing her was so real, I knew it with blazing certainty.

It was one or perhaps two days after Number Seven brought me the bad news, in the afternoon I think, that Christopher came into my ward, very excited, and almost shouted:

"Mum's regained consciousness!"

The maneuver required to shift me onto a trolley–along with the gear to which I was already attached–was quite complicated, but the staff did it with a right goodwill and wheeled me over to Helen's ward which was about a quarter of a mile away. Helen's niece Catriona, who was very fond of her, was already in the room, and it was she who spoke first:

"She's put her face on for you–she didn't want to look like an invalid; and by golly isn't she glad to see you!"

"Not half as glad as I am to see her!"

Helen's first words were:

"I was so worried. I thought you had died and they were keeping it from me."

We chatted for some time and Helen told me what had happened on the road. The evening meal was brought for both of us, but after that they had to take me back to my ward. On the days that followed it was not possible for me to be taken back to visit Helen, but I wrote to her every day and she replied, the notes being delivered by the hand of a helpful nurse.

Helen had always written in a very bold and distinctive hand, and her hand-writing continued to have this quality in these notes written in hospital, until one day, about a week after I had been taken across to visit her, its character changed. It disturbed me to see that it had become shaky, spidery. I was not left long wondering over this for early the next morning Number Seven was back and heading for my bed. This time I really did become agitated.

"I'm afraid your wife has had a rough night," she began, "her blood-pressure's been dropping during the night. I think I'll arrange for them to take you over to see her."

They did take me, and I stayed with her most of the day. Helen smiled and talked a little, but she was very weak. At night I was wheeled back to my ward and brought back again early on the following morning. Helen had held her own during the night, but I could see that she was now weaker than ever. I spent the whole day with her; our sons and their wives came and spent several short spells with us. Fr James Rae came too and anointed Helen. Shortly after this she asked Fr Rae to give her some water and said:

"It's strange, isn't it; we come into this world in water, we are born into eternal life through water, and when we are about to move on from this life the only thing we want is water."

Then she pointed towards me and, with an amused smile, said to Fr Rae:

"Darby and Joan—he's my very, very best friend."

Helen lived on through another night, but when I was brought back in the morning it was evident that she had very little strength, and was barely conscious. I asked her:

"Do you know who I am?"

"Of course," she whispered, "you're Ronnie, my darling husband."

These, words, I consider to be the definition of who I am. Shortly afterwards, our two sons and their wives having joined us, she whispered almost inaudibly:

"I love you all."

She died at about noon on Tuesday 28 May 1974.

After a short but decent interval I was moved into another room where Number Seven took charge of me and began to insist that I eat a proper dinner.

"May I," I requested, "have some of my favorite food?"

"Certainly," she said, apparently relieved.

"Well, all I want at the moment is some white bread and real butter."

"All right, then," she capitulated, "I'll not argue."

She was really a very nice Number Seven, and wisely left me alone for a while until the food was brought.

On the day of Helen's funeral the ward-sister let me occupy an empty single room, where I followed the funeral mass and the burial liturgy, at the hour when these liturgies were being celebrated. The Mass was celebrated in St Peter's, Falcon Avenue, and in the evening Fr Glancy came to visit me and give a report on all that had happened. He had never seen such an enormous crowd anywhere at a parish funeral. After the Mass it took almost an hour to clear the cars from Falcon Avenue and the adjoining streets. I was delighted to learn that he had asked Duncan MacDiarmid to take part in the Prayers of the Faithful. Our neighbors the Doigs had been present and Anne Doig told me later that it had all been very sad to start with, but quite suddenly towards the end of the great prayer the mood changed completely, and she had never experienced such a sense of joy. Helen had brought much joy into the world, and she bequeathed it to us when she left. After the funeral our sons and their wives entertained guests hospitably and with great dignity at our home in Nile Grove. So several of our friends told me, saying that I could be very proud of our boys.

For me the problem of deciding what to do immediately after bereavement did not arise. There was nothing I could do, for I was immobilized, confined in a hospital bed, and with no prospect of getting out of it for a long time; but I was determined to get well and persevered diligently with physiotherapy and whatever else was required to ensure that I did. I could not at first read much but persevered in reading the Psalter at more or less the appropriate hours. When the first severe shock began to lessen, slowly I found myself considering how my life ought to proceed once I did get back on my feet. I was in no hurry to make decisions, and my thinking was guided mostly by images that came into my mind. I had day-dreams in which I imagined I was in a little cottage at Cullicudden on the Black Isle, gazing out over the Cromarty Firth and meditating. I recalled how once I had asked myself what I would do if Helen were ever taken from me. The meditative mood that possessed my mind now in hospital connected with the answer I had given then, that I would have to pursue a contemplative life. Quite soon during the time of convalescence I began to understand why this was so. The uniqueness of our marriage had been so absolute that I could not imagine the possibility of creating such a unique relationship more than once. And yet life had to progress, otherwise it would become trapped in nostalgia and attempts at compensation for what had been lost. Now for me life would have to progress into a new dimension, and that was the dimension of the contemplative life. I did not, however, think of a monastic life like the Cistercians, but saw myself more as a kind of free-lance Carthusian.

One day quite unexpectedly when I was about three weeks into convalescence, I had a visit from Alex Gillanders, a West Highlander, born and brought up in Applecross where Helen's father had been minister, and a close friend of Helen's family. It was very thoughtful of him to visit me. He was a retired doctor and a man of liberal education. In respect of religion he was a lapsed Free Presbyterian. On the rare occasions I had met him in the past he had shown an interest in us because we were Catholics. His biblical fundamentalist background had left him deeply interested in religion, although he maintained no connection with the Church of his youth. On this surprise visit he paid me in Bridge of Earn, almost his first sentence was:

"I expect now you will become a priest."

"Why on earth do you say that?"

"Well, you work for a Church organization, you translate theology and you have a good biblical education, and you were once a minister. It seems a sensible thing to do."

"It's a great mistake," I said, "to think that the Church can be served only by the ordained clergy. I'm interested in a prophetic ministry, and I'm already qualified for that–I think. It would be wrong of me to jump to the conclusion that now I ought to become a priest."

My response led to a bit of discussion in the course of which it became plain to me–although I had already been aware of the fact–that in general, Presbyterians of all shades saw service to the Church confined within a very clerical framework. Any lay apostolate there was in Presbyterian Churches assumed a clerical aura. There were lay-preachers and lay-missionaries, but all were in a sense quasi ministers of the word. I saw things in a different light, and I hoped that the encouragement of lay ministries in the Catholic Church would not lead to the same mistake being made. My own life, I believed, was now pointing in the direction of a prophetic and contemplative ministry, neither of which required that I become an ordained priest. Nonetheless my conversation with Alex Gillanders made me admit that the ordained priesthood was one option.

This option gained stronger advocacy when, a week or two later, my old friend Fr James Quinn, S.J., came to see me. I told him of the conversation I had with Alex Gillanders and he said:

"I think the priesthood may be the right place for you now, but I wouldn't try to persuade you one way or the other; it's something you will have to decide entirely on your own."

"The reason I would argue against my asking to be ordained," I replied, "is because I see the need for the prophetic ministry, and I think I have already been exercising such a ministry."

"That's true," he said, "but it's not an *either–or* question. Being a priest does not prevent a man exercising a prophetic ministry. Being a priest may provide him with greater opportunity to exercise it."

"True," I thought.

"We'll leave the discussion there," he went on, "for it's better to let you work it out entirely on your own. But there's one thing I would say. If you were to decide on the priesthood, you'd have to think very carefully about the question of incardination."

"What's that exactly," I asked.

"A priest has to be incardinated into a diocese, and in the case of a late vocation, and particularly in your case, for you must be free to use your specific gifts, it is important to find the right set up. In some dioceses the man could be destroyed by the machinery. You could be destroyed."

"You're a realist," I remarked, "and a bit of a cynic too."

He gave one of his belly-laughs.

These thoughts simmered on in my mind, but I knew that I had plenty of time to think things out carefully, but while still in hospital I received another significant mental stimulus. A priest came to visit me one day, bringing with him a copy of the current issue of *The Osservatore Romano*.

"Look at this," he said, and showed me, prominently presented, my article on "Celibacy and the Priesthood," which had been published in *The Furrow* the previous December.

"But they've got something wrong," he continued, "the editor can't have read it himself, otherwise he would have known that it was written by a married man, who was a former Presbyterian minister. They've attributed the article to the Very Rev. Canon Roland Walls, and he's an Anglican canon and a celibate member of the religious community at Roslin."

I never bothered to find out how this error had come about. What struck me immediately was that my article had been published in *The Osservatore Romano* at the very time of Helen's death. The thought that now came into my mind was: everything I ever could have done, including the exercise of a prophetic or contemplative ministry, would have been done better with Helen beside me—all except the work of the ordained priest. Was I to see the publication of this article at this precise moment as a hint that I ought in some way to demonstrate in life what I argued in theory? Was I now to show that I could fulfill the function of ordained priest with the single-mindedness that was possible—as I had argued—only for a celibate? The coincidence of Helen's death and the publication of the article could not be the decisive factor in settling the argument I was conducting with myself, but I certainly paid heed to it. And there was another factor, perhaps the weightiest one of all, that inclined me towards the option of the ordained priesthood. One morning when I was still scarcely awake a memory came to me suddenly, although it must have emerged out of the processes that were going on in my mind.

In a semi-dream I was back in the time just before I met Helen, when I was quite sure that I was called to the ministry of the word. With fellow students I had been discussing the question of celibacy, and had concluded that it was immaterial whether a Presbyterian minister were married or celibate, and I thought that I could have lived as a celibate, if that were the way things turned out. And then I met Helen, and although I accepted the tradition of the Church of Scotland concerning a married clergy, it was not long before I began to feel that there was a tone of idolatry about our love that stood in the way of the proper fulfillment of the ministry of the word. In retrospect I came to know that what I feared was idolatry was not idolatry at all, but the first acute awareness of the sublimity of marriage. Thirty-four years later I was lying in a hospital bed, convalescing from a fractured pelvis and from the shock of Helen's death and now recalling that long past phase of our life; but the most significant part of the recollection was of the momentary thought that had struck me one night as I walked home after leaving Helen, that I would be able to give true devotion to the ministry if Helen were not there—if she died. I had dismissed this morbid fantasy immediately, and completely forgotten about it. I had chosen Helen, and eventually it was the ministry that died for me, and I had no regrets. But now Helen was gone, and I remembered that my impulse towards a ministry of the word in the Church had come to me before I knew Helen. We had both regarded our marriage as a vocation and one that demanded our total devotion. The work of that vocation had been completed. Was I now being nudged towards what had been my original vocation? Not so long ago with all sincerity I had secretly resolved that from now on I would try to live the style of life that Helen wanted; I would be her servant. Perhaps she wanted me now to follow my original vocation. To do so would be an ultimate act of love for her, for according to what we both believed, for me to follow the vocation of priest required our separation. Had she willingly accepted death so that this could be? If she had, I would dishonor her did I fail to follow the one course that necessitated her sacrifice.

The weeks in hospital rolled on slowly. I worked hard at the prescribed exercises. There had never been acute pain, but often I was demented by the itch beneath the plaster, which of course I could not scratch. One fine day the team came to me and removed the plaster. Mr Sutherland, the consultant, arrived, took hold of my leg and began gently to bend the knee and flex the hip. His face beamed, not with pride, but delight, and he said:

"We do our best, but there's always an element of luck."

It wasn't long before I was moving about on crutches. While on my back I had used my arms and hands a lot, pulling myself up by the grip dangling above my head. Now I discovered how valuable that exercise had been, for the trick with crutches is to have a strong grip. The last hurdle to be surmounted was the climb up a few steps and down the other side, using crutches. It was Friday and Miss Welsh, the elderly physiotherapist before whom everyone trembled, agreed that if I could cope with the steps I would get home next Tuesday. I passed the test and David picked me up, and at last I was back in Nile Grove. I declined all invitations to stay with the family, for after all that had happened I only wanted to be back in my own home, even though I was to be alone; but I did not feel alone, and have never felt alone since. Someone came in to clean on two forenoons a week, and I was able to cook for myself, having all the gear within easy reach near the table; and the shops being so near it was easy to get provisions, which I used to collect in a little bag that I hung round my neck. I had got back home just in time to get over for part of the first fortnight in August to Trochrague, where I found the comfort and support of so many good friends. After that I settled down to spend autumn and winter at home, where I was able to do some work by letter and telephone; but much of my time was spent writing a second series on the biblical background to the mysteries of the Rosary.

It was at this time of restricted horizons that I began to take notice a pair of corbies, regular visitors in the garden, whom I tried to tame by putting out scraps of raw dog's mince, but they would come no closer than the middle of the back-garden where Helen used to sunbathe. I became very attached to these birds, and wherever I have traveled since I have always been on the look-out for their kin. On visiting the Holy Land in 1976 I had the pleasure of greeting a pair, who cawed to me from the top of a tree outside the Shepherd's Field at Bethlehem; and near every house in which I have lived since I left Nile Grove, I have found a pair of nesting corbies. I wonder if the Lord sent corbies to me as he sent their larger cousins, the ravens, to Elijah at the Wadi Cherith as he prepared for his mission; and did Elijah speak to his ravens as I speak to my corbies? By the end of autumn my subconscious had had a chance to sort out my thoughts. I decided that I would set Easter as the deadline for a firm decision, but meantime, because I now saw the priesthood as a reasonable possibility, I would discuss the matter with a bishop, so that if I did go in that direction there would be time to arrange for my training. I had another collogue with Fr Quinn, telling him that I would now systematically examine the question: do I seek to enter the ordained priesthood? and before Easter make some kind of retreat before coming to a decision.

"I've thought over what you said about incardination," I told him, "and have decided to approach Bishop Foylan of Aberdeen. You see, in Aberdeen Diocese almost every priest has to live quite on his own. Some men, especially if they're young, would find that difficult, but I relish the idea; and when you're my age, you have to work at your own speed."

"That may well be the answer," he replied, "I'd never thought of Aberdeen."

Bishop Foylan invited me to meet him in Aberdeen and told me that he would accept me as a candidate for the priesthood. I explained that I wanted to leave the matter open until Easter, but that at Easter I would give him a firm answer. He agreed and said that he would book a place for me in the *Collegio Beda* in Rome, for if I did decide to proceed towards the priesthood it might be too late by Easter to get a place.

At Easter I had made up my mind that the best course for me was to seek ordination to the priesthood. I now appreciated better Fr Quinn's view that the contemplative and prophetic vocations, for which I felt I was fitted and could have fulfilled as a layman, need not be over-ridden by receiving ordination. There was, moreover, a great need for priests in Scotland at this time. I wonder, however, if my decision was not influenced most of all by Helen's intercession; and I kept remembering her tranquil almost smiling death. I wrote to Bishop Foylan telling him of my decision, and he got me a place at the *Beda* for the following October. I asked my sons if they would be unhappy if I disappeared for a few years to study abroad.

"What on earth are you up to," they asked.

"Well," I said, "I'm booked in at the *Beda* in Rome—
you know the Geriatric Seminary—to begin studies for the
priesthood."

"That's great, Pa!" they exclaimed, "I bet Mum's
pleased."

The Vice-Rector of the *Beda* at that time was
Monsignor Molyneaux. During the summer vacation I
visited him in Lancaster. After scrutinizing my *curriculum
vitae* he judged that I would not need to take the courses in
biblical studies or Church history, and he devised a course
consisting mainly of moral theology and canon law, a
course that could be completed in two years. I knew that
this would please Bishop Foylan, for it meant I could return
to the Diocese and start work all the sooner; and it pleased
me, for I wanted to get down to work before I was too old.

In October 1975 I set off on what I suspected was
the beginning of the ultimate phase of my life. I felt
excitement such as is felt in anticipation of a holiday abroad;
at the same time I was apprehensive as I joined the bus in
London, along with the motley crew who were to be my
companions during the next two years, for I had never
before, apart from eleven weeks in hospital, lived in an
institution. For a spell at least I was about to enter a new
and unknown world. The bus took us to Luton. Our flight—
which cost only £25—was uneventful, but inconvenient,
for we arrived on the hot tarmac of Campoccino in heavy
rain and in the middle of the night. A bus deposited us at
the securely locked gate of the *Collegio Beda* in the *Viale di
San Paolo*, opposite the basilica of St Paul-without-the-walls.
Glad to have come to this journey's end, but not in
noticeably high spirits, for it was now past four in the
morning, we made our several ways as best we could to
the rooms assigned to us, and went to sleep. At the age of
fifty-five I had gone back to school.

Epilogue

After two years profitably and enjoyably spent in the *Collegio Beda*, my subjective call to the priesthood was confirmed by the Church when on 30 June 1977, Mario Conti, Bishop of Aberdeen, ordained me priest in St Peter's, Falcon Avenue, Edinburgh, the church where for many years Helen and I and the family had worshipped, and where after leaving Logie Easter in October 1948, we had attended our first Sunday Mass.

In the *Prologue* to this book I said I would bring my autobiography up to date. No autobiography, unless it is a continuous journal, can extend to the very end of a life, so that one has to decide at which point it is appropriate to bring the story to an end. The quotation marks which enclose the story of my life, insofar as it is relevant to my purpose in recording it, begin at four-thirty in the morning of the day I faced the prospect of going to school in Corstorphine and end at the same time in the morning when I arrived at the *Beda* in Rome to prepare for a new life, for by that time I had experienced all that could influence my view that the Catholic Church was still substantially the same as it had always been, and the reason for my writing the story, as I declared in the *Prologue*, was to prove this point. My work as a priest in Banchory/ Aboyne, Thurso/Wick and in St Joseph's, Aberdeen and during three years in retirement when I have gained a wider knowledge of the Diocese of Aberdeen through work as a supply priest, has not changed my view but confirmed it. It is true that within the Church there is much dissent, but it is also true that the Church precisely in this age of dissent and threatened schism has produced a classic statement of the Catholic Faith in the *Catechism of the Catholic Church*, demonstrating that the substance of the Faith is still intact, and the magisterium alive and effective.

I will not therefore labor this thesis further nor attempt to recount anecdotes of parish life but will round off this *Epilogue* with the reminiscence of a delightful holiday I spent in September 1988, in the South Tyrol when I had an opportunity to see the Church from a fresh perspective and muse a little on the pattern of my past life.

It is not easy, especially in the Diocese of Aberdeen, for a priest to find another who can replace him and enable him to go off on a carefree holiday. I found it difficult also to make up my mind about what kind of holiday would be most beneficial but, in the autumn of 1988, while priest in the most northerly parish in mainland Scotland, I had been able to get a supply and make up my mind where to go on holiday. It so happened that I had recently read the *Ratzinger Report* which mentioned that Cardinal Ratzinger sometimes took a vacation in Brixen (Bressanone) in the South Tyrol where board and lodging could be had during the summer recess at the seminary in that town. If Cardinal Ratzinger could go there why couldn't I? I wrote to the seminary and received a most welcoming letter from the administrator, Dr Aloys Troy.

I set off by plane to Frankfurt, continued by train to Augsburg where I stayed overnight and next day enjoyed a wonderful jaunt via Munich and Innsbruck through the Brenner Pass down into the South Tyrol, most of the way in the company of a group of cheerful old-age-pensioners who had been given a reserved carriage to which the guard directed me thinking I would feel at home there, which I did. By mid-afternoon we reached Brixen where I was met by Dr Troy who drove me to the seminary. I discovered that Dr Troy was not a priest but an economist and business manager.

The seminary, formerly a Jesuit house, was a large and very beautiful Baroque building. The interior had been thoroughly modernized and everything was smoothly organized. There were one or two groups on holiday, and these used the large refectory. I was given a room in the staff quarters and ate with the few members of staff who were in residence. Some of the cathedral canons also had meals there. The company was excellent and often amusing. Some of the older men who were cared for in the house spoke a dialect which I found a little difficult to follow. As well as enjoying the hospitality of the house I had the privilege of concelebrating Mass every morning at 6.45 with several priests in the cathedral.

I was befriended specially by Dr Mayr, a historian and former Rector of the seminary, now a canon of the cathedral who took me with him to a reception in the school in nearby Kaltern to launch the publication of his biography of Anton Sepp, S.J., a native of Kaltern who had taken part in the Paraguayan Reductions at the end of the 17th century. My visit to Brixen proved to be one of the most refreshing events of my life.

Having spent so many years in the Catholic diaspora, latterly on the north coast of Scotland, this visit to Brixen restored historical perspective. In the South Tyrol I saw the contemporary Catholic Church more sharply defined than I could see it at home. In this picturesque little corner of Europe where Austria and Italy marry, one finds more than a vestige of Christian civilization and culture. The past is no mere museum-piece put on show for the tourist, but lives on in the houses adorned outside with mural paintings, usually of Christian subjects, in the wayside shrines and Stations of the Cross lining the mountain tracks, and in the smiling greeting one receives on the streets— *"Grüss Gott."*

The continuation of the Catholic past—I should say rather a manifestation of the continuous Catholic present— I perceived most clearly, however, in the relaxed formality of Sunday Mass at 9:00 am in the cathedral. Very beautiful German hymns were sung with gusto by the congregation, the Ordinary of the Mass was sung in Latin by a large and professionally trained choir, the eucharistic prayer was said in Latin, the readings and other texts were all in German. It happened to be the anniversary of the dedication of the cathedral church, and in the homily we were treated to a very tidy exposition of the history of salvation, with emphasis on the presence of God among his people, first in the tabernacle of the wilderness, then in the successive temples in Jerusalem, and finally in our Lord, God's living Temple on earth whose presence continues for ever both in his people and in the mystery of the Real Presence in the eucharistic tabernacle.

A day or two after I arrived in Brixen I set off in the late afternoon to explore the town and find the way to the foothills. I crossed the fast-flowing, greenish river and entered–so a decorated sign indicated–the *Fürsttum von Stufel.* My street plan guided me along the *Untereschutzen-gelgasse,* that is the Lower-guardian-angel-gate. I followed this narrow street to the end where on the left I noticed an open door. Curiosity led me through this door which entered into a diminutive church dedicated to the guardian angels. It was a typical Baroque building Above the altar hung a huge painting that depicted the archangel Raphael leading the young Tobias by the hand; Tobias was clad not in the garb of an 8th century BC Israelite exile, but in that of a late Renaissance gentleman. In spite of anachronism the message was clear, that God's providence acts through the mediation of the pure spirits we call angels.

I was moved by the atmosphere of this little chapel and knelt for a while praying and reflecting on how I could see in retrospect that my life had followed a developing pattern. The good fortune which I had so often enjoyed even in trivial incidents usually connected with journeys, was not just haphazard luck but the working of providence which had overseen my way, guiding my intellectual and emotional development and the details of material and social life, to bring me at last to serve God in the ministry of Word and sacrament within the unity of his one visible Church on earth. The full-blooded Baroque painting of Tobias with his hand in the hand of the archangel meant a lot to me, and it was on that evening after I had visited the chapel of the guardian angels that I first thought seriously about the need to write an account of my life.

On leaving Brixen I traveled north to Regensburg in Bavaria, partner city to Aberdeen, where I spent four days with Bishop Conti, acting as interpreter. Thereafter we both went to Erfurt to attend a European ecumenical conference, which took place in the convent where Martin Luther had been a monk. Erfurt was at that time behind the Iron Curtain, and there were moments, especially at the frontier, when we felt that we had got into a Le Carré novel.

Back home in Caithness at the end of autumn I realized that the pressure of parish work would prevent my carrying out the intention to expand and complete my autobiography. Even after my chance meeting with Charlie Smith in Cockburn Street in Edinburgh the following year, by which time I was serving a busy city parish in Aberdeen, the stimulus and encouragement he gave me to write had meantime to be ignored. The semi-retirement which has now made the writing of this book possible is a fresh witness to the mysterious workings of providence, for my retirement was made necessary by the long-term effects of the road accident which took Helen from me and turned the direction of my life towards the priesthood.